*An Introduction to*

# ECCLESIOLOGY

## Ecumenical, Historical & Global Perspectives

## Veli-Matti Kärkkäinen

IVP Academic

An imprint of InterVarsity Press
Downers Grove, Illinois

*InterVarsity Press*
*P.O. Box 1400, Downers Grove, IL 60515-1426*
*World Wide Web: www.ivpress.com*
*E-mail: email@ivpress.com*

*InterVarsity Press® is the book-publishing division of InterVarsity Christian Fellowship/USA®, a student movement active on campus at hundreds of universities, colleges and schools of nursing in the United States of America, and a member movement of the International Fellowship of Evangelical Students. For information about local and regional activities, write Public Relations Dept., InterVarsity Christian Fellowship/USA, 6400 Schroeder Rd., P.O. Box 7895, Madison, WI 53707-7895, or visit the IVCF website at <www.intervarsity.org>.*

*Scripture quotations, unless otherwise noted, are from the* New Revised Standard Version of the Bible, *copyright 1989 by the Division of Christian Education of the National Council of the Churches of Christ in the USA. Used by permission. All rights reserved.*

*Cover illustration: Roberta Polfus*

*ISBN-10: 0-8308-2688-2*
*ISBN-13: 978-0-8308-2688-9*

*Printed in the United States of America* ∞

**Library of Congress Cataloging-in-Publication Data**

*Kärkkäinen, Veli-Matti.*
  *Introduction to ecclesiology/Veli-Matti Kärkkäinen.*
    *p. cm.*
*Includes bibliographical references and index.*
  *ISBN 0-8308-2688-2 (pbk.: alk. paper)*
  *1. Church. I. Title.*
  *BV600.3 .K37 2002*
  *262—dc21*

2002007486

| **P** | 23 | 22 | 21 | 20 | 19 | 18 | 17 | 16 | 15 | 14 | 13 |
| **Y** | 22 | 21 | 20 | 19 | 18 | 17 | 16 | 15 | 14 | 13 | |

# Contents

Introduction: *The Role of Ecclesiology in (Systematic) Theology* . . . . . . . . 7

## PART ONE: ECCLESIOLOGICAL TRADITIONS

1  The Church as an Icon of the Trinity:
   *Eastern Orthodox Ecclesiology* . . . . . . . . . . . . . . . . . . . . . 17

2  The Church as the People of God: *Roman Catholic Ecclesiology* . . . . 26

3  The Church as Just and Sinful: *Lutheran Ecclesiology* . . . . . . . . . . 39

4  The Church as Covenant: *Reformed Ecclesiology* . . . . . . . . . . . . 50

5  The Church as the Fellowship of Believers:
   *Free Church Ecclesiologies* . . . . . . . . . . . . . . . . . . . . . . . 59

6  The Church in the Power of the Spirit:
   *Pentecostal/Charismatic Ecclesiologies* . . . . . . . . . . . . . . . . . 68

7  The Church as One: *The Ecumenical Movement Ecclesiologies* . . . . . . 79

## PART TWO: LEADING CONTEMPORARY ECCLESIOLOGISTS

8  John Zizioulas: *Communion Ecclesiology* . . . . . . . . . . . . . . . . . 95

9  Hans Küng: *Charismatic Ecclesiology* . . . . . . . . . . . . . . . . . . . 103

10  Wolfhart Pannenberg: *Universal Ecclesiology* . . . . . . . . . . . . . . 113

11  Jürgen Moltmann: *Messianic Ecclesiology* . . . . . . . . . . . . . . . . 126

12  Miroslav Volf: *Participatory Ecclesiology* . . . . . . . . . . . . . . . . 134

13  James McClendon Jr.: *Baptist Ecclesiology* . . . . . . . . . . . . . . . . 142

14  Lesslie Newbigin: *Missionary Ecclesiology* . . . . . . . . . . . . . . . . 151

Concluding Reflections on Leading Ecclesiologists . . . . . . . . . . . . 160

**PART THREE: CONTEXTUAL ECCLESIOLOGIES**

15  The Non-Church Movement in Asia . . . . . . . . . . . . . . . . . 167

16  Base Ecclesial Communities in Latin America . . . . . . . . . . . 175

17  The Feminist Church . . . . . . . . . . . . . . . . . . . . . . . . . 184

18  African Independent Churches' Ecclesiology . . . . . . . . . . . . 194

19  The Shepherding Movement's Renewal Ecclesiology . . . . . . . . 202

20  "A World Church" . . . . . . . . . . . . . . . . . . . . . . . . . . 211

21  The Post-Christian Church as "Another City" . . . . . . . . . . . . 221

Epilogue: *Ecclesiological Challenges for the Third Millennium* . . . . . . . . 231

Names Index . . . . . . . . . . . . . . . . . . . . . . . . . . . . . . . 234

Subject Index . . . . . . . . . . . . . . . . . . . . . . . . . . . . . . . 237

# Introduction

## THE ROLE OF ECCLESIOLOGY IN (SYSTEMATIC) THEOLOGY

E ven though contemporary systematic theology, as any other academic discipline, offers such a variety of approaches and areas of interest that it easily defies any generalizations, it can be said with full legitimacy that two areas have especially caught the attention of many theologians, namely pneumatology and ecclesiology. Significantly enough, these two loci happen to share a number of mutual connections between them. If it is true that we are living amidst a pneumatological renaissance, there is no denying the fact that the last two decades or so have also seen the appearance of surprisingly many full-scale treatments of ecclesiology.

### Ecclesiological Renaissance

What might be the potential reasons for such a revived interested in the church? One could also counterattack the claim for the resurgence of the doctrine of the church simply by referring to the prevalent individualism of the Western world and its growing influence on the rest of our world. In an individualistic, postmodern cacophony of differing voices and pluralism, it does not sound appealing to begin talking about a collective called the church, especially since the term *church* for better or worse reasons has been loaded with so many unfortunate connotations from authoritarianism to coercion to antiquarianism.

In my opinion, the main catalyst for the rapidly growing ecclesiological interest has been the ecumenical movement. No other movement in the history of the Christian church, perhaps with the exception of Reformation, has shaped the thinking and practice of Christendom as much as the modern movement for Christian unity. Now, it is true that the history of *formal* ecumenism in terms of the formation of the World Council of Churches (WCC) in 1948 is quite brief—less than half a century—but its roots go back at least to the end of the nineteenth century. Any talk about the unity of the church presupposes some tentative understanding of what the church is. One cannot unite entities without knowing what kind of organisms one is trying to put together. The ecumenical movement has also helped open up a fruitful dialogue about the church and related issues. The older controversial approach has given room for mutual learning and appreciation. The Second Vatican Council of the Roman Catholic Church (1962-1965), without doubt the most significant council of the modern Christian church, completely changed the horizons of the largest church of the world with regard to efforts for unity. Also, at the same time, the Eastern Orthodox churches, with the leadership of the Russian churches, joined the WCC and broadened significantly the membership basis. Eastern tradition is theologically pregnant both in ecclesiology and pneumatology.

Two other developments in Christendom, partly interrelated but also independent to some extent, have challenged theology considerably, especially thinking about the church: the rapid growth of Christianity outside the West, so much so that currently the majority of Christians are in the Two-Thirds World,[1] and the rise of nontraditional forms of the church both in the West and elsewhere. The latter development is in general connected to what are nowadays known as "Free churches." The expression *Free churches* involves two primary meanings. It designates first those churches with a congregationalist church constitution, and second those churches affirming a consistent separation of church and state.[2] New congregational models are emerging especially in the Two-Thirds World but also in the West, and many specialists are of the opinion that the Free church congregational model will be the major paradigm in the third millennium. Even the current prefect of the Congregation for the Doctrine of the Faith in Rome, who has expressed severe criticism of congregational ecclesiologies, has admitted that this is the direction in which Christian *oikumene* is heading.[3]

---

[1]Statistics are revised annually in the January issue of *International Bulletin of Missionary Research*, with detailed calculations from David Barrett and Todd Johnson.

[2]Miroslav Volf, *After Our Likeness: The Church as the Image of the Trinity* (Grand Rapids, Mich.: Eerdmans, 1998), p. 9 n. 2.

[3]Joseph Cardinal Ratzinger, *The Ratzinger Report: An Exclusive Interview on the State of the Church, Joseph Cardinal Ratzinger with Vittorio Messori* (San Francisco: Ignatius, 1985), pp. 45-47.

If one is not ready simply to discount the ecclesiality of Free churches and other nontraditional church forms, it poses the question of the conditions for being a church. Of course, the approach of traditional theology has too often been to impose its own often quite-limited definition of churchhood on its younger counterparts. Naturally, those churches that define what ecclesiality means usually themselves fulfill the requirements of their own definitions! But ecumenically, it does not further the discussion. For older churches, just to discard the enormous potential and force of nontraditional churches by classifying them as something less than a church is both dangerous and useless. Younger churches have shown their vitality in their lives, and now it is left to theology to catch up with these developments. This has always been the main task of theology: to reflect on and make sense of what is happening in Christian life and churches.

The expansive growth of Christian churches outside the traditional "Christian" West has also posed another challenging question to theology, namely, how to account culturally for the existence of churches in various contexts. What does it require to be a church amidst an animistic culture in Africa or highly spiritualistic Asian cultures? What from the mainly Western heritage is transferable to the rest of the world, and what has to be revised and corrected? Furthermore, there are other contextual challenges: what would the church look like if it were to make women and other minorities feel at home and find their potential? Or, what does it mean for a church to be a church for those who struggle for freedom and equality?

There is no denying the value of ecclesiological traditions in classical theology. It simply is the fact that most ecclesiological thinking and even experimenting has taken place within the confines of classical Christendom up until the expansion of the modern missionary movement. And even then, almost until our day, theologies were still Western. Even though today in any meaningful teaching and study of theology full hearing has to be given to voices from outside the West, it is only naïve and harmful to imagine that two thousand years of theological tradition could be easily disregarded.

## The Emergence of Ecclesiology as a Separate Locus in Theology

It might come as a surprise to many students of theology that ecclesiology, the doctrine of the church, did not gain its own established standing in systematic theology until the time of the Reformation, and even then many crucial topics, as they are discussed nowadays in systematic treatments of the church, received hardly any attention. Ecclesiology was not a separate locus either in the early church or in the Middle Ages.[4] The systematic outline included topics such as the trinitarian God, creation, reconciliation in Christ and the sacraments; it is noteworthy that sacraments as such were considered to be so crucial a topic that it required its own locus, even without direct reference to the church.[5] The first separate treatments on the church go back to the fifteenth century.

Of course, the church fathers had many things to say about the church. The church, in its confession of faith, is said to be connected with the Holy Spirit. The church is named in the creeds[6] in the clause after the Holy Spirit.[7] According to the *Traditio apostolica* of Hippolytus, the third baptismal question runs, "Do you believe in the Holy Spirit in the Church?"[8] The patristic author Faustus of Riez of the fifth century commented on the fact that the last clauses in the Nicene-Constantinopolitan Creed were connected with the Holy Spirit:

> Whatever in the Creed follows the words "the Holy Ghost" should be understood without reference to the preposition "in," so that our belief about the Holy Church, the communion of saints, etc., is said as part of our appeal to God. This means we believe that these things have been ordered by God and derive their existence from him.[9]

This ecclesial conviction about the integral relationship between the Spirit and the church was expressed clearly by Irenaeus: "For where the Church is, there is also the Spirit of God. And where the Spirit of God is, there is also the Church and all grace; for the Spirit is the Truth."[10]

Also, the description of the church as one, holy, catholic and apostolic became a theme in the Catechetical Lectures of Cyril of Jerusalem in the fourth century.[11]

---

[4]A detailed brief outline of the emergence and history of ecclesiology can be found in Wolfhart Pannenberg, *Systematic Theology* (Grand Rapids, Mich.: Eerdmans, 1997), 3:21-27.

[5]It is indicative that, e.g., in the Catechetical Oration (chap. 33) of Gregory of Nyssa and in *De fide orthodoxa* of John of Damascus (4.9) the discussion moves directly from Christology to a discussion of baptism. See further Pannenberg, *Systematic Theology*, 3:21.

[6]E.g., the Creed of Constantinople and the (Western) Apostles' Creed.

[7]Michael Garijo-Guembe, *Communion of the Saints: Foundation, Nature, and Structure of the Church*, trans. Patrick Madigan (Collegeville, Minn.: Liturgical Press, 1994), p. 2. See also Thomas Aquinas *Summa Theologicae: A Concise Translation*, ed. Timothy McDermott (London: Eyre and Spottiswoode, 1989), 2.1.1-2.1.9, question 5.

[8]Hippolytus, cited in Garijo-Guembe, *Communion of Saints*, p. 1.

[9]*De Spiritu Sancto* 1.2.; *Corpus Scriptorum Ecclesiasticorum Latinorum* 21:103ff.; see further Garijo-Guembe, *Communion of the Saints*, p. 1.

[10]Irenaeus *Adversus Haereses* 3.24.1 (ed. J.-P. Migne, *Patrologia Graeca* [Paris: J.-P. Migne, 1844-1902], 7:966).

[11]See further Adolf von Harnack, *History of Dogma* (London: Williams & Norgate, 1897), 3:233-39.

Famous is the judgment of the church historian Adolf von Harnack, according to which the treatment of the church in the fathers was so underdeveloped that it did not even connect to the doctrine of redemption.[12] To be true, this observation applies even to those rare works of the fathers that really did focus more on the church; for example, the celebrated work of Cyprian on church unity is more in the nature of a polemic than a constructive proposal. Even Augustine failed to offer any kind of separate treatment of the church, even though he has contributed significantly to our understanding of the church.[13]

Even the great work of Peter Lombard, *Sentences*, one of the first comprehensive *summas* of Christian doctrine, surprisingly did not have a separate locus on ecclesiology, and what it does say about the church is included under the heading of Christology. The first separate ecclesiologies were *Tractatus de Ecclesia* (1433/1435) of Johann of Ragusa and *Summa de Ecclesia* of John of Torquemada, of the same period.

With regard to the Reformation era when the more comprehensive treatments were written, it is instructive to see how slowly the consciousness of a need for a separate discussion of the church emerged. The first edition of the *Loci* (1521) of Melanchthon, Martin Luther's Reformation colleague and the drafter of many of the Lutheran Confessional texts, did not yet include ecclesiology. Only in the later edition in 1535 did Melanchthon insert a section *De Ecclesia* which elucidates the statements of the Augsburg Confession about the church. "It has been rightly said that here for the first time, on the basis of the new reformation beginning, Melanchthon tried to project and develop a theology of the church as a whole."[14] Interestingly enough, the very same principle applies to John Calvin's *Institutes*. The first edition (1536) lacks ecclesiology, but the 1539 revision added an expanded section on the concept of the church, and the last edition (1559) has an even more developed discussion.

## Salvation: Individualistic or Communal?

One of the most famous statements of Friedrich Schleiermacher, the father of modern theology, is that what distinguishes Protestantism from Roman Catholicism is that the former makes the relation of individuals to the church dependent on their relation to Christ, whereas the latter, conversely, makes the relation

---

[12]Ibid., 3:236.

[13]See further J. N. D. Kelly, *Early Christian Doctrines,* 2nd ed. (New York: Harper & Row, 1960), pp. 412-17.

[14]Pannenberg, *Systematic Theology,* 3:22.

of individuals to Christ dependent on their relation to the church (§ 24 Thesis).[15] Paradoxical as this statement is, it is also both an overstatement and historically inaccurate. Both Protestant and Catholic theologies traditionally have discussed the means of salvation, including the sacraments, prior to the topic of the church, the implication being that salvation is received individually and then the faith received is nurtured by the church community. Even the Catholic dogmatic manuals up until our day followed the same route.[16] With few exceptions, this is the rule even in most contemporary systematic theologies.

Wolfhart Pannenberg's *Systematic Theology* first discusses the foundational theological issues concerning the church and then launches into the topic of faith and salvation.[17] By doing so, it challenges the established canons of systematic theologies. Pannenberg contends that if we ignore the disciples, "the fellowship of individuals with Jesus is always mediated by the church, by its proclamation and its administration of the sacraments."[18] The same order is followed in the recent massive Catholic doctrinal manual, *Mysterium Salutis*,[19] which offers a salvation-historical approach to theology.

It is another thing to acknowledge the fact that even though faith is ecclesially mediated, it is still addressed to individuals for personal appropriation. It was typical of Jesus' proclamation that he addressed individuals directly, and did not, like other Jewish movements of the time, attempt to achieve a gathered eschatological community or any other form or historical manifestation of the true people of God.[20]

## Approaches to Ecclesiology

In order to orient the reader, it might be helpful to chart the waters of ecclesiology and provide an orientation for navigation, especially since the area, as already mentioned, is developing quickly in contemporary theology. The following gives an outline of various approaches to ecclesiology studied in the present book. In the introduction to each major part of the book, a more detailed explanation is offered as to why these particular movements and per-

---

[15]F. E. D. Schleiermacher, *Christian Faith* (New York: Harper & Row, 1963).

[16]See, for example, L. Ott, *Fundamentals of Catholic Dogma* (St. Louis: Herder, 1957).

[17]For the necessary ecclesial mediation of faith, see also Miroslav Volf, *After Our Likeness: The Church as the Image of the Trinity* (Grand Rapids, Mich.: Eerdmans, 1998).

[18]Pannenberg, *Systematic Theology*, 3:24.

[19]J. Feiner and M. Löhrer, eds., *Mysterium Salutis: Grundriss heilsgeschichtlicher Dogmatik*, vols. 4/1-2 (1972) and 5 (1976).

[20]See further Pannenberg, *Systematic Theology*, 3:27.

sons have been selected for discussion.

First, there are several more or less established traditional approaches that are related to specific denominations, such as Eastern Orthodox, Roman Catholic, Lutheran and Reformed. Each of them approaches the church from a distinctive perspective, based on its overall theological program. To these traditional approaches have to be added some others that in the contemporary world have become significant, namely Free church ecclesiologies, which mostly go back to Baptist views and even further to Anabaptism from the time of Reformation. Also, some newer and statistically overwhelmingly important ones are the ecclesiologies of Pentecostalism and later Charismatic movements. In fact, numerically, with the exception of the Roman Catholic Church, Pentecostals almost equal the number of all other Christians. However, even the most recent theology textbooks usually either totally ignore these two latter traditions or just offer some passing comments. Since the present textbook wants to be ecumenically sensitive, the first major part of the book concludes with a detailed discussion of the role and views concerning the church in the theologies of the ecumenical movement.

Second, the doctrine of the church has surfaced in the systematic theologies of some of the most noteworthy contemporary theologians, such as the Orthodox John Zizioulas; the Catholic Hans Küng; the Lutheran Wolfhart Pannenberg; the Reformed Jürgen Moltmann; the ecumenical Miroslav Volf, who has roots in both the Pentecostal and Reformed traditions; the Baptist James McClendon Jr.; and the Anglican Lesslie Newbigin. All of them bring to the understanding of ecclesiology their specific voices. On the one hand, they represent all the major theological traditions (with the exception of Pentecostalism, for which there are simply no full-scale ecclesiologies available yet). On the other hand, all of them are also ecumenically very sensitive, and they transcend their own specific denominational boundaries. For example, even though Pannenberg certainly takes notice of the best of Lutheran heritage, by no means can he be considered an exclusively Lutheran theologian.

Third, contextual ecclesiologies will be treated in the final major part of the book. The ones chosen for a closer look are feminist ecclesiologies, liberationist ecclesiology, Catholic base communities in Latin America, the non-church movement begun in Japan and extended to Asia, and the ecclesiologies of African Independent Churches. Also, the ecclesiologies of the Charismatic Shepherding movement, the novel idea of the "world church" and the vision of the "church as another city" will receive our attention. Many other contextual or intercultural ecclesiologies could be added, but with the limitations of space not everything can be said, and no one theologian is equipped to do so.

There is a specific focus to the discussion of ecclesiology in the present book. It might be helpful to take a parallel from Christology. Traditionally, Christology has been divided into two parts, namely the person and the work of Christ: the former part deals with foundational issues, in other words, who Christ is, while the latter looks at the derivative topics, such as atonement and faith. While ecclesiology does not fall that easily into discernible parts, it is possible to apply that same kind of division to the discussion of the church. "Ecclesiology proper," the main interest of this book, focuses on the question of the ecclesiality of the church, that is, what makes the church church, or what are the conditions for being a church. The second part of ecclesiology, then, deals with questions such as the ministry, the structure and the sacraments of the church. Those issues receive only secondary treatment in this book, not because they are not important, but simply for the fact that in order to meaningfully survey such a broad territory as is our intention here, there have to be limitations.

The present book attempts what is sometimes called "comparative ecclesiology," which has became popular especially in ecumenical circles. According to the widely used textbook *Models of the Church* by one of the leading Catholic ecclesiologists, Avery Dulles, S.J., the term *comparative ecclesiology* "signifies a systematic reflection on the points of similarity and difference in the ecclesiologies of different denominations."[21] Dulles's preferred term for this enterprise is *model*. By this he wishes to indicate his conviction that the church, like other theological realities, is a mystery. "Mysteries are realities of which we cannot speak directly. If we wish to talk about them at all we must draw on analogies afforded by our experience of the world."[22] Comparative ecclesiology usually draws from two kinds of sources: more or less official denominational confessional writings, and texts of representative theologians. In principle, our approach is no different from that. However, the present book goes beyond the traditional comparative ecclesiology in that the last part of the book also focuses on what may conveniently be called "contextual" (sometimes also "global") ecclesiologies.

---

[21] Avery Dulles, *Models of the Church* (Garden City, N.Y.: Doubleday, 1974), p. 7.
[22] Ibid.

# Ecclesiological Traditions

A natural way to begin a survey of ecclesiologies is to introduce major theological and confessional traditions that have emerged during church history. This is the task of the first part of the book. With regard to major confessional traditions such as Eastern Orthodoxy, Roman Catholicism, Lutheranism and the Reformed family, the task ahead of us is quite straightforward. Each of these traditions has established doctrines and views of the church, though it has to be noted that especially during the last century a proliferation of ideas in each of these established traditions has occurred. Roman Catholic theology is a case in point: while there is an official, normative Catholic doctrine concerning the church, a plethora of (more or less) legitimate varieties have also arisen. Furthermore, both major Protestant traditions are often less accurately defined by their theologies because they do not have an official magisterium, that is, teaching office of the church, even though they do have confessional statements. These traditions naturally leave more room for the views of individual theologians.

Concerning more recent ecclesiological traditions—those stemming from the Protestant Reformation but going beyond it and expressing quite a lot of disagreement with their forebears—the task of introducing ecclesiological views is more complicated. The complication comes from two interrelated questions. First of all, which traditions to choose for presentation? Should one try to discuss all the varieties of, say, what has come to be known as "Free churches," or should one lump them together and try to discern common features? Second, once the decision is made as to which recent views to present, should one search only for a *theology* of the church, or is it legitimate to try to derive the ecclesiological views by looking at how the movement lives out its ecclesiality. The fact is that many of those newer Christian traditions have not yet produced much *theology* of the church, even if in their everyday life they do, of course, live out their "churchliness."

The approach of the present book is to divide the more recent traditions into two categories: Free churches and Pentecostal/Charismatic churches. The term "Free churches" here denotes the heritage of the Radical Reformation, such as Anabaptists, Quakers and Baptists. Even though each of these Free churches also displays distinctive features, they share enough common foundations to treat them together. For more fine-tuned discussion, the reader is referred to specific sources in the text. With regard to Pentecostal/Charismatic traditions, one could also place them in the Free church category. The reason for not doing so in the present study is twofold. First, currently the Pentecostal/Charismatic family of churches represents the biggest Protestant constituency, so that on the basis of numbers alone it would be unfair to lump it together with the rest of the Free churches. Second, even though this newest Christian tradition has not yet produced much theology of the church, a closer look at its church life and related doctrines strongly indicates that a distinctive kind of ecclesiology is emerging—one based on the Charismatic spirituality of the movement.

The last chapter of part one may seem strange at first glance: the ecumenical movement ecclesiologies. What this section attempts to accomplish is to take stock of the emerging ecumenical thinking about the church, primarily as it has taken place among the World Council of Churches constituencies and related ecumenical venues such as the Faith and Order movement. Here there is even more variety than within any individual Christian tradition; but there are also trends and orientations that seem to point toward a growing consensus, even if under the much-used label "unity-in-diversity." The name of the section itself, "the ecumenical movement ecclesiologies" may not be the most appropriate one, since the ecumenical movement, a heterogeneous body of various organizations itself, is not a theological tradition similar to, for example, Roman Catholicism; however, in want of a better name, that term will have to suffice.

# 1

# The Church as an Icon of the Trinity

## EASTERN ORTHODOX ECCLESIOLOGY

### The Patristic Roots of the Eastern "Spirit-Sensitive" Theology

Eastern Orthodox theology draws heavily from the early sources, namely the church fathers of the East. Therefore, any inquiry into the distinctives of Eastern thought should bear in mind the experiences and theological developments of the early centuries. A fine introduction to modern appropriations of those ancient patristic thoughts is offered by C. N. Tsirpanlis in his *Introduction to Eastern Patristic Thought and Orthodox Theology.*[1]

Generally speaking, it can be said that Eastern theology has been more "Spirit-sensitive"[2] than its Western counterparts. Eastern Orthodox theology is heavily imbued by pneumatology; Western theology in the main is built on christological concepts rather than on pneumatological. This pneumatological orientation does not, however mean neglecting either Christ[3] or the Trinity[4] in Orthodox theologizing. One thing that guards Eastern thought from a one-sided concentration on the Spirit is its focus on the primacy of the Father in the doctrine of the Trinity. Tsirpanlis's words are illustrative of the Eastern mindset:

> Those who speak of an Orthodox "Pneumatocentrism" opposed to the so-called Christocentrism of the Roman Church, may express their own personal theology, but they speak a language alien to the Fathers and to the saints of the Eastern Or-

---

[1]C. N. Tsirpanlis, *Introduction to Eastern Patristic Thought and Orthodox Theology* (Collegeville, Minn.: Liturgical Press, 1991).

[2]The phrase is taken from Robert Imbelli in his recommendations of Y. Congar's book, *I Believe in the Holy Spirit*, three volumes in one (New York: Herder, 1997).

[3]See, e.g., Nikos A. Nissiotis, "Pneumatological Christology as a Presupposition of Ecclesiology," in *Oecumenica: An Annual Symposium of Ecumenical Research* (Minneapolis: Augsburg, 1967), pp. 235-52.

[4]See, e.g., Vladimir Lossky, *In the Image and Likeness of God*, ed. John H. Erickson and Thomas E. Bird (New York: St. Vladimir's Seminary Press, 1985), chap. 4.

thodox Church. The three Persons, in the Holy Trinity, share in activity of each of
them. The Father and the Son are included in every action of the Spirit.[5]

There is a genuine trinitarian outlook in the Eastern view: "The Father does all
things by the Word in the Holy Spirit."[6]

The mystical theology of the Eastern wing of the church is often more expe-
rience-based and concrete than Latin theology. This comes to focus even in
their pneumatology: "As he who grasps one end of a chain pulls along with it
the other end to himself, so he who draws the Spirit draws both the Son and
the Father along with it."[7]

The doctrine of the church can never be isolated from other theological loci;
ecclesiology is kind of a *summa* of any given theological tradition. What gives
special flavor to the Eastern view of the church is that its doctrine of salvation
is not focused on guilt concepts and sin—as in the West—but focuses rather on
a gradual growth in sanctification culminating in deification, becoming like
God. This orientation shapes the doctrine of the church in a profound way. According to Eastern theology, Latin traditions have been dominated by legal, juridical and forensic categories. Eastern theology, on the contrary, understands
the need for salvation in terms of deliverance from mortality and corruption
for life everlasting. Union with God is the goal of the Christian life, even becoming "in-godded." The underlying anthropology[8] is not necessarily more
positive but, instead of operating mainly in guilt concepts, it looks upward, so
to speak, to the image of God to be fulfilled in mortal human beings.[9] The idea
of divine-human cooperation in salvation is not only accepted but enthusiastically championed, although it is not understood as nullifying the role of
grace. Prayer, asceticism, meditation, humble service and similar exercises are
recommended for the attainment of this noble goal. The notion of merit,
though, is foreign to the Eastern tradition. Redemption has as its immediate
aim our salvation from sin, but salvation will have its ultimate realization in
the age to come in our union with God, the deification of the created beings
whom Christ ransomed. In general, their attitude toward grace and free will is
less reserved than their Western counterparts. In the East, the question of free
will has never had the urgency which it assumed in the West from the time of

---

[5]Tsirpanlis, *Introduction to Eastern Patristic Thought*, p. 85.
[6]Athanasius, *A Serap.* 1.31.
[7]Basil *Letter* 38, 4.
[8]See John Meyendorff, *Byzantine Theology: Historical Trends and Doctrinal Themes* (New York: Fordham University Press, 1974), chap. 11.
[9]See, e.g., ibid., pp. 161-63.

Augustine onward. The Eastern tradition never separates grace and human freedom. Therefore, the charge of Pelagianism (that grace is a reward for the merit of the human will) is not fair. It is not a question of merit, but of cooperation, of a synergy of the two wills, divine and human. Grace is a presence of God within us that demands constant effort on our part.[10]

## Church: A Lived Experience

According to Bishop Kallistos, Eastern Orthodox theology has not yet redeemed its promise of creating a full-scale theology of the church, even though many observers would say that the doctrine of the church is one of the distinctive strengths of that tradition. This lack of a systematic treatment of the church has been acknowledged by such great theologians of the East as P. Evdokimov, who contended that the church is simply assumed, since it is a lived experience, and V. Florovsky, to whom ecclesiology is still a chapter in Christology.[11]

Even though strict definitions are still lacking—one may even ask if those will ever appear in a theology that is characterized by the principle of apopathicism[12]—several characteristics of Eastern ecclesiology can be mentioned: First, the church is seen as the image of the Trinity.[13] Just as each person is made according to the image of the Trinity, so the church as a whole is an icon of the Trinity, "reproducing on earth the mystery of unity in diversity."[14] Not only is the church as such the image of the Trinity, but in Eastern thinking even other social institutions may be as well: the family, the school, the workshop, the parish, the church universal.[15]

The church as the image of the Trinity represents the principle of identity and mutuality simultaneously:

---

[10]See, for example, Vladimir Lossky, *Mystical Theology of the Eastern Church* (Crestwood, N.Y.: St. Vladimir's Seminary Press, 1976), pp. 196-97. For a recent discussion, see Grigorios Larentzakis, "Die Teilnahme am trinitarischen Leben: Die Bedeutung der Pneumatologie für die Ökumene heute," in *Der Heilige Geist: Ökumenische und reformatorische Untersuchungen* (Veröffentlichungen der Luther-Akademie Ratzeburg; Erlangen: Martin Luther Verlag, 1995), pp. 225-44.

[11]Bishop Kallistos, "Incarnation and the Church," unpublished lecture, International Charismatic Consultation on World Evangelization (ICCOWE), Prague, Czech Republic, August 23-27, 2000.

[12]The term *apopathic* means doing theology in a way that does not necessarily have the explicit purpose of defining its objects positively but rather comes to a preliminary understanding by negation. The opposite term is *katapathic,* the general orientation of much of Western theology.

[13]See further Lossky, *Mystical Theology,* pp. 176-77.

[14]Kallistos Ware, *The Orthodox Church,* rev. ed. (London: Penguin, 1993), p. 240.

[15]Kallistos Ware, *The Orthodox Way* (New York: St Vladimir's Seminary Press, 1999), p. 39.

In the Trinity the three are one God, yet each is fully personal; in the Church a multitude of human persons is united in one, yet each preserves her or his personal diversity unimpaired. The mutual indwelling of the persons of the Trinity is paralleled by the coinherence of the members of the Church.[16]

This principle of "unity in diversity" means that just as each person of the Trinity is autonomous, so the church is made up of a number of independent, yet related autocephalous churches. On the other hand, just as in the Trinity the persons are equal, so in the church no one bishop can claim to wield absolute power over all the rest.

There is also a vivid consciousness of community: "We know that when any of us falls, he falls alone; but no one is saved alone. He is saved in the Church, as a member of it and in union with all its other members."[17] The "spiritual way," as the journey of the Christian is often called, presupposes that individuals come together and join in community. The journey is undertaken in fellowship with others, not in isolation. The Orthodox tradition is intensely conscious of the ecclesial character of all true Christians.[18]

At the very core of Orthodox theology in general and ecclesiology in particular is the relation of humanity to creation as whole, the cosmos. The church is described in cosmological terms. In this understanding the church is the center of the universe, the sphere in which its destinies are determined. Eschatologically, at a given moment when the church has attained to the fullness of growth determined by the will of God, the external world, having used up its vital resources, will perish. The church is also necessary since all the conditions required for us to attain union with God (*theosis*, divinization, deification) are given in the church. It is in the church that human beings are restored to their original role as cocreators with God.[19]

## Eucharistic Ecclesiology

At the heart of Eastern Orthodox ecclesiology stands the Eucharist. The Eucharist both represents the general principle of sacramentalism, common also to the Western Catholic traditions, and is the sacrament of primacy. Sacramentalism here means that God's grace is both mediated and experienced by and through the sacraments of the church. It does not downplay the meaning of

---

[16]Ware, *Orthodox Church*, p. 240.
[17]This clause is attributed to G. Khomiakov in Ware, *Orthodox Church*, p. 239.
[18]See further Ware, *Orthodox Way*, pp. 107-8.
[19]Lossky, *Mystical Theology*, p. 178.

faith, as is often depicted in Protestant caricatures of sacramentalism, but rather brings faith into focus. It is through faith that sacraments are received, even though the sacraments also give birth to faith.

In the church and through the sacraments human nature enters into union with the divine nature. Human nature becomes consubstantial with the deified humanity, united with the person of Christ in the power of the Holy Spirit. This union is fulfilled in the sacramental life.[20]

One may ask, "What is the church for?" The biblical answer is to be found, for example, in 1 Corinthians 10:16-17, which speaks of the partaking of the bread and wine at the Eucharist and implies that the church is to bear witness to salvation in Christ—not only "telling" but also "doing" in remembrance of Christ. This is the function of the Eucharist. Therefore, the basic ecclesiological rule that goes back to the fathers says, wherever the Eucharist is, there is the church. Or, the church makes the Eucharist, and the Eucharist makes the church. Eastern theologians point to the fact that in Paul talk about the Eucharist is not only analogical but causal ("therefore" denotes causality).[21]

Several implications follow: *ekklēsia*, the church, is not just any kind of assembly but God's people gathered for Eucharist. The bishop is one who watches over rather than simply administers the celebration. This kind of Eucharist gathering can only be a local gathering, and therefore in every celebration the whole Christ is present. The important ecclesiastical corollary overall is that every local church is a true church.

Local churches are then on the one hand independent of each other, but on the other hand united in terms of their identity. Some recent Orthodox ecclesiologists, just as John Zizioulas, have drawn attention to the fact that the older Eucharistic ecclesiology may easily turn into an overemphasis on the local church, and thus compromise the equally important principle of collegiality and communion. Bishop Kallistos reminds us that we should not isolate the Eucharist from the context of unity.[22]

The Eucharist also stands at the center of Eastern Orthodox liturgy and worship. In a sense, church life is "liturgy after liturgy," even in its mission. The earthly liturgy is a foretaste and icon of the heavenly worship when the

---

[20]Ibid., pp. 181-82.
[21]Kallistos Ware, "Incarnation and Church," paper presented at ICCOWE, Prague, August 23-27, 2000.
[22]Ibid.

church has finished its course and the members have reached the fulfillment of the earthly sojourn, that is, have become deified.[23]

## Sobornost

One of the catchwords in the Eastern Orthodox ecclesiology, deriving from Russia, is *soborny*, which has the double meaning of "catholic" and "conciliar." Its theological usage goes back to Alexis Khomiakov[24] but is nowadays widely used by many. The term has several facets.[25] It refers to the organic unity of the church, not by negating individuals but by employing them. Each member contributes to the common activity of the church, and each member does his or her work with the help of others. So individuality is preserved not extinguished. Even though Orthodox ecclesiology is hierarchical in the sense that the bishop is representative of and appointed by God to guide the church,[26] there is also the equality of all members; all members are equal in honor.

The principle of *sobornost* also denotes the idea that church institutions are expressions of unity. The Spirit creates the structures of the church and they can never be independent of the Spirit. Consequently, all believers are interrelated, and all believers are needed to guarantee unity.

Orthodox ecclesiology holds a firm belief that the church is one. "Its unity follows from the unity of God."[27] According to Bishop Kallistos, if we take seriously the bond between God and his church, then we must inevitably think of the church as one, even as God is one. Since Orthodox theology refrains from separating the "invisible" and "visible" church, oneness is not relegated to something unseen. The church of God on earth is one. It is a bold claim, but still legitimate from the Orthodox point of view, the view that it believes itself to be that one visible church.[28]

## Pneumatological Ecclesiology

The general pneumatological orientation of the Eastern tradition carries over

---

[23]See further Ware, *Orthodox Church*, chaps. 13 and 14.

[24]See, for example, "The Church Is One," in *Russia and the English Church*, ed. W. J. Birkbeck (London: SPCK, 1895).

[25]I am indebted to Miroslav Volf, "ST503 Systematic Theology III: Ecclesiology and Eschatology," unpublished class notes (Pasadena, Calif.: Fuller Theological Seminary, summer 1988).

[26]For an exposition of what *hierarchical* means in Orthodox ecclesiology, see, e.g., Ware, *Orthodox Church*, pp. 248-49.

[27]Khomiakov, "The Church Is One," section 1.

[28]Ware, *Orthodox Church*, p. 246.

to the doctrine of the church. For instance, the Eastern fathers attribute to the Spirit all the multiplicity of names that can be attributed to grace,[29] as is evident, for example, in Gregory Nazianzen and Basil. They freely speak about the Holy Spirit as effecting deification, perfection, adoption and sanctification.[30] Therefore, as the Spirit inspires and empowers the process of deification, the role of the Spirit in the church comes into focus.

Ecclesiologies have been traditionally built on either of the two classical rules, that of Ignatius of Antioch or of Irenaeus. Ignatius suggested the ecclesiality of the church could be secured by reference to Christ's presence: "Wherever Jesus Christ is, there is the universal church."[31] According to Irenaeus, what is decisive is the presence of the Spirit of God: "Wherever the Spirit of God is, there is the church, and all grace."[32] It is understandable that very soon, especially in the East, the question arose as to the role of the Spirit in the building of the church. The answer was obvious: Christology and pneumatology must be seen as simultaneous rather than exclusive. And it is noteworthy that this finding was not so much due to sophisticated theological analysis—in fact, as is well known, the fathers did not have ecclesiology as a separate theological *locus* (topic)[33]—but rather it came through their lived experience in the church. Irenaeus, Athanasius and others were pastors and bishops in the church. They realized that God works in the world using "both of his hands," as Irenaeus put it.[34]

Consequently, in the Eastern Orthodox understanding, the church is founded on a twofold divine economy: the work of Christ and the work of the Holy Spirit.[35] Eastern theologians speak about the church as the body of Christ and the fullness of the Holy Spirit.[36] Significantly enough, Basil contended that "Christ comes, the Spirit goes before. He is present in the flesh, and the Spirit is inseparable from him."[37] This is a noteworthy theological statement since it

---

[29]For a careful analysis of the relation between grace and the Holy Spirit in Latin theology, see Wolfhart Pannenberg, *Systematic Theology* (Grand Rapids, Mich.: Eerdmans, 1997), 3:197-200.

[30]For a sample of representative texts, see Lossky, *Mystical Theology,* 163-66.

[31]Ignatius *Letter to the Smyrneans* 8:2.

[32]Irenaeus *Adversus Haereses* 3.24.1.

[33]For details, see Pannenberg, *Systematic Theology,* 3:21-26.

[34]Irenaeus *Adversus Haereses* 4.4; for a detailed discussion, see Hans Urs von Balthasar, *Theologik,* vol. 3, *Der Geist der Wahrheit* (Basel: Johannes Verlag, 1987), p. 151.

[35]Vladimir Lossky, "Concerning the Third Mark of the Church: Catholicity," in *The Image and Likeness of God,* ed. John H. Erickson (Crestwood, N.Y.: St. Vladimir's Seminary Press, 1985), pp. 177-78.

[36]Lossky, *Mystical Theology,* pp. 157, 174.

[37]*De Spiritu Sancto,* pp. 19, 49.

anchors the work of Christ in the church in the economy of the Spirit. Not only that, but, as already mentioned, there is also a trinitarian outlook. The Eastern Church teaches that that which is common to the Father and the Son is the divinity that the Holy Spirit communicates to humans within the church, making them partakers of the divine nature.[38] So deification means participation in the life of the triune God.

The mutual relation between the Son and Spirit is manifested in that just as the Son comes down to earth and accomplishes his work through the Spirit, so also the Spirit comes into the world, being sent by the Son (Jn 15:26). The work of the Spirit is not subordinate to the work of the Son, nor is Pentecost a continuation of the Incarnation, but rather its sequel, its result.[39]

As a result of the mutual work of the Son and the Spirit, catholicity[40] of the church means two things: the unity of the church (as a result of its being the body of Christ) and the diversity of the church (as a result of its being the fullness of the Spirit).[41] The Holy Spirit who rests upon Christ, the "Anointed One," communicates himself to each member of this body, creating, so to speak, many christs, the anointed ones.[42]

The christological aspect creates the objective and unchangeable features of the church, while as a result of the pneumatological aspect there is a subjective side of the church. In other words, the christological aspect guarantees stability while its pneumatological aspect gives the church a dynamic character.[43]

Eastern pneumatological ecclesiology, ideally, balances hierarchy and charisms:

> But the Church is not only hierarchical, it is Charismatic and Pentecostal. "Quench not the Spirit. Despise not prophesying" (1 Thessalonians 5, 19-20). The Holy Spirit is poured out upon all God's people. . . . In the Apostolic Church, besides the institutional ministry conferred by the laying on of hands, there were

---

[38]Lossky, *Mystical Theology*, p. 162.

[39]Ibid., pp. 158-59.

[40]For the understanding of catholicity in the Eastern tradition, see Lossky, "Third Mark of the Church," pp. 169-80.

[41]Ibid., pp. 178-79; Meyendorff, *Byzantine Theology*, pp. 174-75; Lossky, *Mystical Theology*, p. 176. "This is the unfathomable mystery of the Church, the work of Christ and of the Holy Spirit; one in Christ, multiple through the Spirit, *a single human nature* in the hypostasis of Christ, *many human hypostases* in the grace of the Holy Spirit" (Lossky, *Mystical Theology*, p. 183, emphases in the text). The classical biblical locus of this twofold nature of the church according to Eastern theology is Eph 1:23: "the church, which is his body, the fullness of him who fills everything in every way."

[42]Lossky, *Mystical Theology*, p. 174; see also p. 166.

[43]Ibid., pp. 190-92.

other *charismata* or gifts conferred directly by the Spirit: Paul mentions "gifts of healing," the working of miracles, "speaking with tongues, and the like" (1 Corinthians 12, 28-30). In the Church of later days, these Charismatic ministries have been less in evidence, but they have never been wholly extinguished.[44]

---

[44]Ware, *Orthodox Church*, pp. 249-50; see also pp. 240, 243.

# 2

# The Church as the People of God
## ROMAN CATHOLIC ECCLESIOLOGY

### The Church as the "Continued Incarnation"

The Roman Catholic Church is currently the world's largest Christian body, claiming the membership of about half of all Christians. Catholic theology represents, together with the Eastern Orthodox Church, the growth of tradition over two millennia. Therefore, whatever general characterizations can be made concerning Catholic theology in general and ecclesiology in particular, they are no more than generalizations. Furthermore, one has to take into account the enormous changes brought about as a result of the Second Vatican Council, one of the most decisive councils ever. That Catholic theology builds on tradition does not mean a repetition of something already said but rather a Spirit-guided reappropriation and often critical reshaping of ancient dogmas. All these factors, and the fact that this church literally extends to all corners of the earth with innumerable contextual varieties of church life, should make one cautious about attempting to discern the leading developments in Catholic ecclesiology.

The immediate roots of current Catholic ecclesiology go back to the nineteenth century with definitions of Vatican I and an oscillation between placing emphasis on either Christ or the Spirit as the point of departure for the doctrine of the church. One of the Catholic theologians of the past, Jean Rigal, defined the church as oppressive, dogmatic, pyramidal, lifeless and remote from modern realities. Often in the past, the Catholic Church did not welcome its critics: Antonio Rosmini wrote in 1832 (and published in 1846) his *The Five Wounds of the Church*; his work was placed on the Index of Forbidden Books in 1849. Vatican I (1871) championed a predominantly hierarchical view of the church. The council became famous especially for the way it defined papal infallibility. The pope is infallible in relation to morality and religion when he teaches *ex cathedra* (literally: from the chair), in other words, with the intent to give a definite doctrinal or moral pronouncement meant for the whole church. The power of the pope is universal, *ordinaria* ("ordinary," it exists by virtue of the office) and immediate, in that it can be used without any other media.

J. Adams Möhler is known as the originator of the influential view of the church as the continuation of the incarnation of Christ. Möhler, however, first wrote an ecclesiology, *Unity in the Church or the Principle of Catholicism* (1825), which clearly opted for a Spirit-centered ecclesiology.

In that work, he argued for the importance of the Spirit as the guiding principle of the doctrine of the church. Soon, however, with the rest of the Catholic ecclesiologists of that time, he came to view the church as the continued incarnation. According to B. E. Hinze, the "twentieth-century renewal of pneumatology in Catholic ecclesiology could be constructed in part as an attempt to reaffirm Möhler's early Spirit-centered approach and to reintegrate it with his later incarnational ecclesiology within a fully developed trinitarian framework."

A little later, M. J. Scheeben (d. 1888) wanted to develop Möhler's neglected pneumatological dimension in the church and spoke about the church as a "kind of incarnation of the Holy Spirit." Even though the intention of this endeavor has to be welcomed, the approach is a problematic way of describing the Spirit: it is totally foreign to the New Testament and its content is unclear. In the New Testament, the church is never called the "body of the Spirit," but rather the body of Christ.

Characteristic of the earlier Catholic ecclesiology is the papal encyclical *Divinum illud munus* by Leo XIII (1897), according to which Christ is the head and the Holy Spirit is the soul of the church. The problem with this approach is that it makes the church and its structures absolute, divine in its origin, while the only task of the Spirit is to "animate" the already existing ecclesiastical apparatus. Not much better ecclesiologically was the message of another encyclical, *Mystici Corporis*, in 1943. It essentially reaffirmed the basic teaching of its predecessor, but it still contains one of the most significant theologies of the Spirit for the twentieth-century Catholic Church. Yves Congar criticizes it for still viewing the church in institutional terms.[1] Congar also argues that the Catholic theology created several sorts of "substitutes" for the Holy Spirit, such as the Eucharist, the pope and Mary.[2]

Several noted theologians, such as Hans Küng, Heribert Mühlen and Karl

---

[1]Congar, *I Believe in the Holy Spirit* (New York: Crossroad Herder, 1997), 1:154.
[2]Ibid., 1:160-64.

Rahner, played a crucial role in initiating a fuller recovery of the early patristic roots of the Catholic doctrine of the church on the eve of Vatican II and afterward. For example, Mühlen,[3] while criticizing the view of the church as a continued Incarnation, argued that the church should be seen as a continuation of Jesus' anointing with the Holy Spirit in his baptism. In Mühlen's estimation attention to the identity of the Holy Spirit in the anointing of Jesus and of Christians helps to avoid hierarchical (in Mühlen's terminology, "naturalistic") and mystical tendencies, both represented in precouncil ecclesiologies.

## The Ecclesiology of Lumen Gentium

One of the most significant ecclesiological documents in ecclesiology is *Lumen Gentium* of Vatican II. Its creative, often tension-filled approach to the ancient doctrine of the church marks a watershed not only in Catholic theology but also in ecumenical theology of the church.

Perhaps the most important development of Vatican II was the replacement of the old *societas perfecta*, institutional-hierarchic ecclesiology, with the dynamic "people of God" notion in which the church is seen first of all as a pilgrim people on the way to the heavenly city. The view of the church as a perfect society had enjoyed widespread support from the time of the Counter Reformation through the first half of the twentieth century.[4]

Even the structure of the document gives clues to its purpose: rather than beginning with a chapter on hierarchy, which was the outline of the draft, the final version placed the chapter on the People of God at the beginning of the document, just after the opening chapter, "The Mystery of the Church," to be followed by the treatment of hierarchy and laity. Then there is a call to holiness to the whole church, not only to the religious. The document ends with a profound vision of the "Pilgrim church." Finally, a chapter on Mary, "Our Lady," was attached to the document on the doctrine of the church, since that is the proper context for honoring the First Lady of the Church.

Instead of beginning with a description of the church as the perfect society, the first chapter of *Lumen Gentium* notes the reflection of the inner life of the

---

[3]Mühlen's pneumatological ecclesiology is developed in his two earlier works: *Una Mystica Persona: Die Kirche als das Mysterium der Heilsgeshichtlichen Identität des heiligen Geistes in Christus und den Christen: Eine Person in Vielen Personen,* 3rd ed. (Munich: Ferdinand Schöningh, 1968), and *Der Heilige Geist as Person: In der Trinität bei der Inkarnation und Im Gnadenbund: Ich-Du-Wir,* 3rd ed. (Munich: Verlag Aschendorff, 1969).

[4]*Lumen Gentium* 4. Note that the reference numbers following Vatican II documents refer to paragraph numbers.

triune God within the church itself. Borrowing a phrase from Saint Cyprian of Carthage (d. 258), the council states, "Hence the universal church is seen to be a 'people brought into unity from the unity of the Father, the Son and the Holy Spirit.'" Along with this trinitarian approach to the doctrine of the church, the Second Vatican Council came to speak of the church as a "mystery" and sacrament. The opening section of *Lumen Gentium* states, "The Church in Christ, is in the nature of sacrament—a sign and instrument, that is, of communion with God and of unity among all human beings."[5] This notion is far removed from the older views of the church, which tended to understand it first of all as a hierarchical institution. This understanding of the church as sacrament has also enlarged the notion of (traditional) sacraments, and consequently opened the way for less polemical and ecumenically more fruitful thinking about sacramental celebration and sacramental theology.[6]

Whereas in *Vehementer Nos* by Pius X (1906) the church was described as "an unequal society" composed of two categories of persons, "the pastors and the flock" (and the flock having "no other duty but to allow itself to be led and to follow its pastors as a docile flock"), *Lumen Gentium* rehabilitates the whole people of God as the church. Every local gathering of the church, under the bishops and pastors, is a legitimate church. There is a lot of ecumenical potential in the way a recent Roman Catholic theology textbook invests the local church with the fullness of meaning, based on the ancient formula "one, holy, catholic, apostolic" church:

> The church is one because of the indwelling of the one Holy Spirit in all the baptized; it is holy because it is set apart by God's graciousness for the reception of a mysterious love of predilection; it is catholic in the original sense of the word, meaning that it is whole and entire, possessing all the parts needed to make it integral; and it is apostolic because it remains in continuity in essentials with the original witnessing of the first-century apostles. . . . Catholics are often inclined to apply these descriptive characteristics only to the worldwide, universal church, yet they are beginning to learn from the eastern Orthodox churches and others that these characteristic are meant to apply just as truly to the local church.[7]

---

[5]*Lumen Gentium* 1.

[6]R. A. Duffy, "Sacraments in General," in *Systematic Theology: Roman Catholic Perspectives*, ed. F. S. Fiorenza and J. P. Galvin (Minneapolis: Fortress, 1991), pp. 203-7.

[7]Michael Fahey, "Church," in *Systematic Theology: Roman Catholic Perspectives*, ed. F. S. Fiorenza and J. P. Galvin (Minneapolis: Fortress, 1991), p. 43.

## The Church as Communion

According to Avery Dulles one of the models of the church is the church as "mystical communion."[8] Taking his point of departure from both sociological theory and Protestant ecclesiologies such as Dietrich Bonhoeffer's *The Communion of Saints,* which describes the essence of community as "the complete self-forgetfulness of love,"[9] and Emil Brunner's *The Misunderstanding of the Church,* which describes the church as "a pure communion of persons,"[10] Dulles argues that the Catholic ecclesiology of communion goes back to the New Testament witness and was never abandoned, even though at times other models towered over it.

Communion language goes back to the early church in Acts 2: "So, if one is true to the dynamics of Acts, one would add immediately after the imparting of the Spirit, *koinonia*/communion, i.e., community formation together with its Eucharistic expression. The language of Luke is communion language."[11] In its basic meaning, the term *koinonia*/*communion* denotes "a sharing in one reality held in common."[12] Synonyms for *koinonia* are sharing, participation, community, communion. Early patristic development incorporated other biblical communion texts in order to lay bare the inner source of the church's life. These display a pronounced trinitarian dimension: "The grace of the Lord Jesus Christ and the love of God and the fellowship *[koinonia]* of the Spirit be with you" (2 Cor 13:13; see Phil 2:1). The basic communion themes, especially the Eucharistic one, constituted the ecclesiological supposition "for most, if not all, of the earliest councils,"[13] and remained a force as an ecclesiological model for about the first thousand years.[14] *Lumen Gentium* defines the essence of communion ecclesiology neatly when it states that God "has, however, willed to make men holy and save them, not as individuals without any bond or link between them, but rather to make them into a people who might acknowledge him and serve him in holiness."[15]

The communion in the church is based on the communion among the mem-

---

[8]Avery Dulles, *Models of the Church* (Garden City, N.Y.: Doubleday, 1974), chap. 3.

[9]Dietrich Bonhoeffer, *The Communion of Saints* (New York: Harper & Row, 1963), p. 123.

[10]Emil Brunner, *The Misunderstanding of the Church* (London: Lutterworth, 1952), p. 17.

[11]Kilian McDonnell, "Communion Ecclesiology and Baptism in the Spirit: Tertullian and the Early Church," *Theological Studies* 49 (1988): 674.

[12]McDonnell, "Communion Ecclesiology," p. 674.

[13]John Zizioulas, *Being as Communion: Studies in Church and Personhood* (New York: St. Vladimir's Seminary Press, 1985), p. 156.

[14]McDonnell, "Communion Ecclesiology," p. 676.

[15]*Lumen Gentium* 9.

bers of the Trinity. The trinitarian communion of the persons of the Trinity is the highest expression of unity for Christians, the "deepest meaning of *koinonia*": "This is the sacred mystery of the unity of the Church, in Christ and through Christ with the Holy Spirit, energizing its various functions. The highest example and source of this mystery is the unity, in the Trinity of Persons, of one God, the Father and the Son in the Holy Spirit."[16]

Catholic theology in general and ecclesiology in particular are sacramental, not unlike Orthodox. Therefore, the communion is sacramental in nature. For Roman Catholics, primary in the "sharing in holy things," *communio in sanctis*, are baptism, confirmation and Eucharist, as constitutive of the church. For Catholics there is a double relationship between the sacraments and the communion of the church. On the one hand, the sacraments mediate the communion of life with God, and thus they are constitutive of the church. On the other hand, the sacraments are acts of the church inasmuch as it is a communion. The sacraments are at the starting point of the church as a communion.[17] Since baptism and the Eucharist have a foundational role in building up the church as a communion, they simultaneously provide a structural form for the church. Baptism is the sacrament that introduces the faithful into the *koinonia* (1 Cor 12:13). Thus baptism gives to the church its body. Confirmation, in conjunction with baptism (the two cannot be theologically separated), also contributes to the foundation of church order. Moreover, baptism, which already unites the body of Christ, only reaches its full aim by common participation in the Eucharist, through which the unity of the church becomes effective (1 Cor 12:27). Legrand argues that the oldest reference to the Eucharist, 1 Corinthians 10:16-17, clearly expresses the causal subordination of the church's ecclesial body to its eucharistic body.[18] "The assertion that *before* making the eucharist the Church is made by the eucharist is of capital importance in Catholic theology."[19] Furthermore, Catholic theology also sees ordination as in the service of church communion, although ordination is not put on the same level as baptism and the Eucharist. Legrand summarizes the Catholic view of the relationship between *koinonia* and the sacraments: "According to Catholic ecclesiology

---

[16]*Unitatis Redintegratio* 2; see also the opening paragraphs of *Lumen Gentium* with its trinitarian structure.

[17]Harvey Legrand, "Koinonia, Church and Sacraments," The Catholic Position Paper for the International Dialogue Between the Roman Catholic Church and Pentecostal Churches, Venice, Italy, August 1-7, 1987 (unpublished), pp. 6-14.

[18]Ibid., p. 8.

[19]Ibid., p. 9 (emphasis his).

one can and one must say that the sacraments make the church inasmuch as they are operated by Christ, celebrated in faith and in the communion of the Holy Spirit."[20]

## The Spirit and the Structures of the Church

On the eve of Vatican II, Karl Rahner, one of the main architects of the council, wrote a passionate appeal for the openness to the Spirit, titled "Do Not Stifle the Spirit,"[21] in which he spoke about the great potentialities and challenges facing the church. He issued a serious warning: the Spirit who blows everywhere "can never find adequate expression simply in the forms of what we call the Church's official life, her principles, sacramental system and teaching."[22] He was very concerned about the Charismatic element of the church:

> It is a situation by a spirit which has been rather too hasty and too uncompromising in taking the dogmatic definition of the primacy of the pope in the Church as the bond of unity and the guarantee of truth, this attitude objectifying itself in a not inconsiderable degree of centralization of government in an ecclesiastical bureaucracy at Rome.[23]

A couple of years later, while the Council was still going on, he published another appeal for the Charismatic in the church, *The Dynamic Element in the Church*.[24] Rahner issued a powerful call for the Charismatic structure of the church by reminding us that the Holy Spirit is promised and given first and foremost to ecclesiastical ministry, not to suppress the free flow of the Spirit but to make room for it.[25] The church should be until the end the "Church of the abiding Spirit."[26]

Rahner suggested that one must learn to perceive charismata when they first appear.[27] Rather than canonize Charismatic persons after their death,

> it is almost of greater importance to perceive such gifts of the Spirit on their first appearance, so that they may be furthered and not choked by the incomprehension and intellectual laziness, if not ill-will and hatred, of those around them, ecclesiastics included. . . . But the Charismatic is essentially new and always

---

[20]Ibid.

[21]Karl Rahner, "Do Not Stifle the Spirit," in *Theological Investigations VII* (New York: Herder, 1971), pp. 72-87.

[22]Ibid., p. 75.

[23]Ibid., p. 76.

[24]Karl Rahner, *The Dynamic Element in the Church* (New York: Herder & Herder, 1964).

[25]Ibid., pp. 42, 44-45.

[26]Ibid., pp. 47-48.

[27]Ibid., pp. 82-83.

surprising. To be sure it also stands in inner though hidden continuity with what came earlier in the Church. . . . Yet it is new and incalculable, and it is not immediately evident at first sight that everything is as it was in the enduring totality of the Church. . . . And so the Charismatic feature, when it is new, and one might almost say it is only Charismatic if it is so, has something shocking about it.[28]

According to Rahner, the Spirit is constitutive of the church in a way more basic than its institutional structure.[29] Where there is one-sided emphasis on Christology, church structures tend to become dominating (this has also been the result of the older Catholic view of church as continued incarnation). The Charismatic element "does not merely stand in a dialectical relationship to the institutional factor as its opposite pole, existing on the same plane. Rather it is the first and the most ultimate among the formal characteristics inherent in the very nature of the Church as such."[30] Rahner also says that the church is primarily the "historical concretization of the Charismatic as brought about by the Spirit of Christ."[31] And it is clear that in Rahner's view the term *Charismatic* does not refer to any specific group in the church but to the life and ministry of all believers. If the church is founded in the sovereign action of the Spirit, then the church has to be understood as an "open system."[32] It means that the church cannot be understood or defined from a point within the church itself but rather from outside, from the Spirit of God.[33]

The practical results of Rahner's view of the Charismatic structure of the church are obvious. First, there is an openness to the promptings of the Spirit: "Do Not Stifle the Spirit." Second, the Spirit has primacy over the structures and offices of the church, even if the structures in themselves are expressive of the Spirit (Rahner never champions individualism). Third, legitimate plurality results from the sovereign action of the Spirit.[34]

## Charisms in the Service of the Church

Vatican II was instrumental in the new Catholic theological and ecclesiological

---

[28]Ibid., pp. 82-83.

[29]Rahner, "Observations of the Factor of the Charismatic in the Church," in *Theological Investigations XII* (New York: Seabury, 1974), p. 97.

[30]Ibid., p. 97.

[31]Ibid., p. 86.

[32]Ibid., p. 88.

[33]See John R. Sachs, "'Do Not Stifle the Spirit': Karl Rahner, the Legacy of Vatican II, and Its Urgency for Theology Today," in *Catholic Theological Society Proceedings* 51 (1996): 30.

[34]See Rahner, "Heresies in the Church Today?" in *Theological Investigations XII* (New York: Seabury, 1974), pp. 117-41.

renaissance. Vatican II, more so than any previous council, also paid attention to the role of the Spirit in the church.[35] Pope John XXIII, when formally announcing the Council, wrote, "This getting together of all the bishops of the Church should be like a new Pentecost."[36] This council could be called the "Council of the Holy Spirit" for, as Pope Paul VI pointed out, there are 258 references to the Holy Spirit in the pages of the Council documents.[37] And since the Council, the popes have urged theologians and lay people alike to revive their interest in the Spirit.[38]

As already mentioned, *Lumen Gentium* opens up with a trinitarian outlook in which pneumatology has its own secure place in ecclesiology. This approach widens the earlier christological concentration of traditional doctrines of the church. The church is the work of the Spirit, who makes believers one in the unity of the triune God.[39] The document insists that the Holy Spirit sanctifies and leads the people of God not only through the sacraments and church ministries, but also through special charisms bestowed freely on all the faithful in a variety of ways. Believers have "the right and duty to use them in the Church and in the world for the good of humankind and for the upbuilding of the Church."[40]

The explicit emphasis upon the pneumatic nature of the church, including the gifts and graces of the Holy Spirit, was secured in the Council by Leon Joseph Cardinal Suenens, who played such a critical role in assuring the college of bishops of the importance of the Holy Spirit and of spiritual gifts to the future of the Roman Church.[41] The Catholic systematician Michael A. Fahey states that "another way that the church is described in the perspective of the Second Vatican Council is as a community of charisms."[42] In this understanding the church is seen as the Body of Christ "created, ordered, and sustained

---

[35]Two basic sources that summarize neatly the pneumatological perspectives of Vatican II are Hans Urs von Balthasar, *Creator Spirit: Explorations in Theology*, vol. 3 (San Francisco: Ignatius Press, 1993): 245-67; and Congar, *I Believe in the Holy Spirit*, pp. 167-73.

[36]Germain Marc'hadour, "The Holy Spirit over the New World: II," *The Clergy Review* 59, no. 4 (1974): 247.

[37]Marc'hadour, "The Holy Spirit," p. 248. See also E. E. O'Connor, *The Pentecostal Movement in the Catholic Church* (Notre Dame: Ave Maria, 1971), p. 184.

[38]For papal documents and evaluations of their significance, see Kilian McDonnell, *Open the Windows: The Popes and Charismatic Renewal* (South Bend, Ind.: Greenlawn Press, 1989).

[39]*Lumen Gentium* 4; see also Sachs, "Do Not Stifle the Spirit," pp. 17-18.

[40]*Apostolicam Actuositatem* 3.

[41]Jerry L. Sandidge, *Roman Catholic-Pentecostal Dialogue (1977-1982): A Study in Developing Ecumenism*, vol. 1, Studien zur interkulturellen Geschichte des Christentums 44 (Frankfurt: Peter Lang, 1978), p. 25.

[42]Michael Fahey, "Church," in *Systematic Theology: Roman Catholic Perspectives*, vol. 2, ed. F. S. Fiorenza and J. P. Galvin (Minneapolis: Fortress, 1991), p. 39.

by the Charismatic inspirations of the Breath of the risen Jesus."[43] Since the Holy Spirit pervades the church and accomplishes a profound communion among the believers, every member of the church is meant to be permeated with Christ.[44] "Not only clergy but also lay people are urged to live every dimension of their existence, including married and family life, their daily tasks and recreation in the anointing and power of the Holy Spirit."[45] Vatican II also presents a firm faith that the "body of the faithful as a whole, anointed as they are by the Holy One, cannot err in matters of belief."[46]

Several Vatican II documents (especially *Lumen Gentium* but also others)[47] establish the existence and contribution of charisms under the supervision of the shepherds of the church. Vatican II emphasized repeatedly the Spirit's sovereign freedom in dispensing the charisms.[48] The council insisted on the universal availability of the charisms: the Spirit calls all Christians, ordained and lay alike, to some form of Charismatic ministry.[49] *Lumen Gentium* freely accepts both kinds of gifts, ordinary and extraordinary, but adds a helpful corrective:

> Whether these charisms be very remarkable or more simple and widely diffused, they are to be received with thanksgiving and consolation since they are fitting and useful for the needs of the Church. Extraordinary gifts are not to be rashly desired, nor is it from them that the fruits of apostolic labors are to be presumptuously expected.[50]

Along with ecclesiological rethinking, a reassessment of sacramental theology has also taken a pneumatological course with the idea of the church as the sacrament of the Spirit and sacraments consequently integrated with *epiclesis*, the prayer for the Spirit. The Constitution on the Sacred Liturgy *(Ad Gentes Divinum)* in a special way emphasizes the role of the Spirit. Since the liturgy is the "summit" and source of the church's life, believers can grow most deeply in the life of the Spirit precisely through sacramental celebrations.[51]

---

[43]Donald L. Gelpi, "The Theological Challenge of Charismatic Spirituality," *Pneuma: The Journal for the Society for Pentecostal Studies* 14, no. 2 (1992): 187. He refers to the following Vatican II documents: *Lumen Gentium* 6, 32, 48, 50; *Unitatis Redintegratio* 3; *Apostolicam Actuositatem* 3.

[44]*Lumen Gentium* 12; See also Mary Ann Fatula, *The Holy Spirit: Unbounded Gift of Joy* (Collegeville, Minn.: Liturgical Press, 1998), p. 89.

[45]*Lumen Gentium* 34; Fatula, *Holy Spirit*, pp. 89-90.

[46]*Lumen Gentium* 12.

[47]*Lumen Gentium* 12, 30; *Apostolicam Actuositatem* 3; *Presbyterorium Ordinis* 9.

[48]*Apostolicam Actuositatem* 3; *Ad Gentes Divinum* 23; *Lumen Gentium* 7.

[49]*Apostolicam Actuositatem* 3, 28, 30; *Lumen Gentium* 4.

[50]*Lumen Gentium* 12.

[51]*Sacrosanctum Concilium*, p. 10.

By means of the invocation of the Spirit on the sacramental elements, earthly realities such as water and oil, bread and wine are transformed to mediate the Holy
Spirit's presence and power. But the renewed liturgical rites stress, too, that the
Holy Spirit is invoked also upon the Church community celebrating the sacraments, so that our own hearts and lives may be transformed as well.[52]

The Jesuit theologian Donald Gelpi, though, criticizes his own church for
not taking seriously the Charismatic and pneumatological teaching of the
Second Vatican Council. He thinks that the responsibility to renew the
church does not belong to the so-called Catholic Charismatic Movement, but
it is precisely the burden of the whole church with its theologians and teach-
ers to implement what was rediscovered in the Council.[53] He argues that the
charisms play an indispensable role in the life of the church and they therefore cannot be confined to the first generation of Christians, as most Catholics before Vatican II were taught to believe.[54] Kilian McDonnell, OSB, said
that "the charisms of the Spirit play an indispensable role in the life of the
Church because they create the shared faith consciousness of the Christian
community."[55]

## Ut Unum Sint: The Catholic Vision of Christian Unity

Ecumenically, a radically new perspective was launched with Vatican II, which
brought a new appreciation of other churches and their contribution to the
Christian testimony. It was admitted that the other churches carry with them
saving function—although less full than that of Rome—and are transmitters of
the gifts of the Holy Spirit.[56] The old dogma *extra ecclesiam nulla salus* ("outside
the church there is no salvation") no longer applied exclusively to the Roman
Church; the new openness toward other churches came to be expressed by the
slogan *Una sancta ecclesia subsistit in* ("One holy church subsists in [the Roman
Church]").[57] *Lumen Gentium* stresses that the Catholic Church "recognizes that
in many ways she is linked" with other Christian communities by a true union

---

[52]Fatula, *Holy Spirit*, p. 90.

[53]Gelpi, "Theological Challenge," pp. 188-89

[54]See Donald J. Gelpi, *Charism and Sacrament* (New York: Paulist, 1976), pp. 97-110 especially;
*The Divine Mother: A Trinitarian Theology of the Holy Spirit* (Lanham, Md.: University Press of
America, 1984), pp. 103-5.

[55]Kilian McDonnell, "Communion Ecclesiology and Baptism in the Spirit: Tertullian and the
Early Church," *Theological Studies* 49 (1988): 671.

[56]*Lumen Gentium* 15 describes in detail "the elements of sanctification and truth" that are
present in other churches.

[57]*Lumen Gentium* 8.

in the Holy Spirit.[58] Rahner expresses this beautifully, saying that in the Spirit "all of us 'know' something more simple, more true and more real than we can know or express at the level of our theological concepts."[59]

The most recent papal encyclical on ecumenism, *Ut unum sint* ("That They May Be One"),[60] leaves no doubt about the firm commitment to further Christian unity. John Paul II confesses, besides the doctrinal differences, the burden of long-standing misgivings inherited from the past, and of mutual misunderstandings and prejudices,[61] as well as the weaknesses of his church in all of this.[62] Speaking about the "inseparable sacrament of unity,"[63] he calls all Christians to do their utmost, not just for the unity of the church but also for the "unity of all divided humanity."[64] He includes in this endeavor of realizing unity all "those who invoke the triune God and confess Jesus as Lord and Savior."[65] Referring to the positive elements found in other churches that *Lumen Gentium* affirms, the pope writes that the Western and Eastern fathers have always believed that "in the Pentecost Event God has already manifested the Church in her eschatological reality." This reality is something already given.[66] "Ecumenism is directed precisely to making the partial communion existing between Christians grow toward full communion in truth and charity."[67] Each church has to ask itself honestly whether it is faithful to the apostolic tradition, that is, "whether they truly express in an adequate way all that the Holy Spirit has transmitted through the Apostles."[68] In accordance with *Unitatis Redintegratio*, the pope reaffirms the primacy of "spiritual ecumenism" in terms of prayer and other forms of spirituality,[69] at the same time acknowledging that it does not do away with the importance of doctrine.[70] To demonstrate the de-

---

[58]*Lumen Gentium* 15.

[59]Rahner, "Some Problems in Contemporary Ecumenism," in *Theological Investigations XIV* (London: Darton, Longman & Todd, 1976), pp. 245-53 (quote on p. 251); see also his "Church, Churches, and Religions," *Theological Investigations X* (New York: Herder, 1973), p. 42.

[60]John Paul II, *Ut Unum Sint* (1995). See also his speech at the Roman Coliseum on Good Friday 1994 with the Ecumenical Patriarch of Constantinople, 1995, p. 88.

[61]John Paul II, *Ut Unum Sint* 5.

[62]Ibid., 6.

[63]Ibid., 9.

[64]Ibid., 10.

[65]Ibid., 11, 13.

[66]Ibid., 18.

[67]Ibid., 14.

[68]Ibid., 16.

[69]*Unitatis Redintegratio* 8.

[70]John Paul II, *Ut Unum Sint* 23-27; cf. *Unitatis Redintegratio* 6.

termined commitment of the Roman Catholic Church to ecumenism, John Paul II argues that the movement promoting Christian unity *"is not just some sort of 'appendix'"* added to the church's life, but rather, "ecumenism is an organic part of her life and work, and consequently must pervade all that she is and does."[71] The Holy Spirit, who gives growth to the church down the centuries, is leading the church toward greater unity.[72] However, for Pope John Paul II, as for his predecessors, there is no unity without the primacy of the bishop of Rome. This is clearly attested in the encyclical *Ut Unum Sint.*[73]

---

[71]John Paul II, *Ut Unum Sint* 20, emphasis in original.
[72]Ibid., 7.
[73]Ibid., 88-97.

# 3

# The Church as Just and Sinful

## LUTHERAN ECCLESIOLOGY

### The Communion of Saints

> Thank God, a seven-year-old child knows what the church is, namely, holy be-
> lievers and sheep who hear the voice of their Shepherd (John 10:3). So children
> pray, "I believe in one holy Christian church." Its holiness does not consist of sur-
> plices, tonsures, albs, or other ceremonies of theirs [the papists] which they have
> invented over and above the Holy Scriptures, but consists of the Word of God
> and true faith.[1]

Even though Luther's understanding of the church according to this delightful passage may appear simple and naive, it emerged out of a severe conflict and it displays marked tensions.[2] To understand Luther's view of the
church—and Luther's theology in general—one has to take note of the fact
that he had to fight on two fronts: on the one hand, against the Catholic position that, according to Luther's interpretation, regarded the church/hierarchy
as absolute; on the other hand, against the Enthusiasts who appealed to the
Spirit in their claim that they were the true Reformers.[3]

Luther stressed the noninstitutional character of the church; he disliked
the word *Kirche* and preferred terms such as *Sammlung* (assembly) and *Gemeinde* (congregation). For him the church was in the first place a communion of saints, a gathering of believers. Luther maintained that the church as
the "communion of saints," in accordance with the Apostles' Creed, is

---

[1]Schmalcald Articles 3.12:2-3. All the Lutheran confessional writings can be found in *The Book
of Concord*, trans. and ed. Theodore G. Tappert (Philadelphia: Fortress, 1959).
[2]Fittingly, Eric W. Gritsch and Robert W. Jenson title their chapter on ecclesiology "Church-
Body in Conflict" in *Lutheranism: The Theological Movement and Its Confessional Writings* (Philadelphia: Fortress, 1976), p. 124.
[3]For Luther's harsh judgment against the Enthusiasts (*Schwärmerei*), see further Yves Congar,
*I Believe in the Holy Spirit* (New York: Crossroad Herder, 1997), 1:139-40.

"called together by the Holy Spirit."[4] In fact, his most famous definition of the church simply says that the church is "the gathering of all believers, in which the gospel is purely preached and the holy sacraments are administered in accord with the gospel."[5] Consequently the church is not an institution for the supply of blessings as conceived in much of ecclesiological thinking of that time and especially of medieval times. In other words, the Lutheran Reformation had from the start an actualist understanding of the church: "the church is something *going on* in the world."[6]

As such the church is both a hidden community and a visible fellowship. It is hidden since faith is "the conviction of the things not seen" (Heb 11:1) and visible because of the preaching of the gospel and the administration of the sacraments. Luther wanted to retain this dialectic, since on the one hand, "God does not want the world to know when he sleeps with his bride" (the hidden), and on the other, "the assembly of the church is visible for the sake of the confession of faith" (the visible).

## The Marks of the True Church

Luther's shorthand for distinguishing the true church from a false one is the excerpt from the Augsburg Confession cited above: the church is "the gathering of all believers, in which the gospel is purely preached and the holy sacraments are administered in accord with the gospel."[7] There are two formative elements, the Word and the sacraments. Luther's theology is always centered on the gospel of Christ: "Where the word is, there is faith; and where faith is, there is the true church."[8] Significantly, Luther sometimes called the church "mouth house." Not only was the gospel to be read but also preached. But the gospel does not work alone, it is associated with the sacraments. Together they point to and draw from Christ and his salvation.

Ecumenically, it is highly significant that the Word and sacraments are the only necessary marks of the church. Everything else—the structures, minis-

---

[4]Martin Luther *Weimarer Ausgabe* 7.219; 30.190. *Weimarer Ausgabe* is the standard collection of the German/Latin original of Luther's works. For the convenience of English readers, where available, I give references to the standard American edition of *Luther's Works*, ed. Jaroslav Pelikan (St. Louis: Concordia, 1955-1986). See further Paul Althaus, *The Theology of Martin Luther*, trans. Robert C. Schultz (Philadelphia: Fortress, 1966), pp. 294-323.

[5]*Augsburg Confession* 7:1.

[6]Gritsch and Jenson, *Lutheranism*, pp. 130-31 (quote on p. 131).

[7]*Augsburg Confession* 7:1.

[8]*Luther's Works* 39.xii.

try patterns, liturgy and so on—could vary from church to church, even within the Lutheran family, as it in fact does. For example, Scandinavian and many other European Lutheran churches are episcopal (they have a bishop), whereas most American ones have not had bishops.[9] The unity of the church is given in the gospel event itself rather than in ecclesiastical uniformity: "It is sufficient for the true unity of the Christian church that the Gospel be preached in conformity with a pure understanding of it and that the sacraments be administered in accordance with the divine Word." Lutheran confessions make a careful and significant distinction between the "gospel" and "ceremonies"; the "church usages" are not necessary for salvation or for the ecclesiality of the church.

Since the church is not a human invention but a creation of the Word, it will remain, whatever may happen. One of the Luther's most famous ecclesiological maxims states, "One holy Christian church must be and must remain forever."[10]

## The Community of Saints and Sinners

Luther's soteriological maxim, the believer as *simul justus et peccator,* just and sinful simultaneously, also shapes his doctrine of the church. In fact, even the church is just and sinful at the same time. Sometimes the marks of the church—the "pure" preaching of the Word and the "right" administration of the sacraments—is interpreted in a sectarian way, as if Luther would make a distinction between the true and false church based on how the members or the leaders pass this test. Luther's understanding is much more realistic; he takes it for granted that this church of Christ, the communion of saints, is also always a communion of sinners, until the Lord of the church will return. In other words, ecclesiastical purity is not a moral but a functional phenomenon (even though the first is not a matter of indifference either); as long as the church is guided by the Holy Spirit, mediated by the Word and sacrament, it will remain pure:

> Creation is past and redemption is accomplished, but the Holy Spirit carries on his work unceasingly until the last day. For this purpose he has appointed a community on earth, through which he speaks and does all his work. For he has not yet gathered together all his Christian people, nor has he completed the granting of forgiveness. Therefore we believe in him who daily brings us into his commu-

---

[9] As a result of Lutheran-Episcopalian dialogue, the Evangelical Lutheran Church of America appointed a bishop to each of its synods in the late 1990s.

[10] *Augsburg Confession* 7:1.

nity through the Word, and imparts, increases, and strengthens faith through the same Word and the forgiveness of sins.[11]

On earth, the church is incomplete, a "mixed body": "In this life many false Christians, hypocrites, and even open sinners are mixed in among the godly."[12] Luther rejects the idea of a "pure church" as Donatism. Consequently, "Sacraments are efficacious even if the priests who administer them are wicked men."[13] Therefore, there is no way for humans to distinguish between the true followers of Christ and the wicked in the church:

> If the church, which is truly the kingdom of Christ, is distinguished from the kingdom of the devil, it necessarily follows that since the wicked belong to the kingdom of the devil, they are not the church. In this life, nevertheless, because the kingdom of Christ has not yet been revealed, they are mingled with the church and hold office in the church.[14]

## The Priesthood of All Believers

In addition to his doctrine of justification, Luther is best known for the rehabilitation of the idea of the priesthood of all believers. His view, built on the theology of the early church and the Middle Ages, about the sharing of all the baptized in the priestly and kingly office of Jesus Christ,[15] appealed especially to 1 Peter 2:9. According to Luther, sharing in Jesus Christ on the basis of baptism includes also sharing in his priesthood.[16] His entire understanding of the church as the community of saints can be described by the priesthood as the law of the church's life. When Christ bears our burdens and intercedes for us with his righteousness, he does the work of a priest; mutual bearing of burdens and the taking of the other's place in the church is also priestly activity. The inner life of the church is the priesthood of Christians for each other. The priesthood of Christians flows from the priesthood of Christ.[17]

---

[11]*Large Catechism*, in *The Book of Concord*, trans. and ed. Theodore G. Tappert (Philadelphia: Fortress, 1959), 2:61-62.

[12]*Augsburg Confession* 8:1.

[13]Ibid.

[14]*Apology of the Augsburg Confession* 7:1-8:17.

[15]For details, see Wolfhart Pannenberg, *Systematic Theology* (Grand Rapids, Mich.: Eerdmans, 1997), 3:373.

[16]Martin Luther *Weimarer Ausgabe* 7.56-57.

[17]See, for example, Martin Luther *Weimarer Ausgabe* 6.407, 564; 10.309; 17.6. See also Althaus, *Theology of Martin Luther*, pp. 313-18.
See also Pannenberg, *Systematic Theology* 3:373.

Sharing in Christ's priesthood gives the right to come before God in prayer and teaching for others.[18] The priesthood of all believers means for Luther primarily the right to preach the Word and administer absolution and discipline.[19] The right to preach does not contradict the limitation of public preaching to those who have been called through the community.[20] The whole church is also authorized to proclaim the forgiveness of sins,[21] the task that is in fact the community's glory.[22]

According to Paul Althaus, Luther follows two lines of argumentation concerning the foundation of the office: one "from below" and one "from above."[23] On the one hand, all Christians are called to minister in Word and sacrament. But in order to avoid confusion, the community entrusts the public service to ordained people, who carry out this duty in the name of the church.[24] In this case, the difference between the one who occupies the office and the other members of the community lies purely on the level of service.[25]

On the other hand, the fullness of the authority of the office is grounded in its institution by Christ, that is, the office derives directly from its institution by Christ without reference to the universal priesthood.[26] It has to be noted, though, that not even the latter nullifies the general priesthood of all believers.[27] The apparent contradiction between these two forms of ministry is solved by deriving the special (ordained) office from the universal. Luther distinguished the necessary exercise of the priestly office "between brother and brother" from the public administration of the ministry of the Word for the entire congregation.[28] The special office is necessary for the sake of order (1 Cor 14:40).[29] "Thus the only distinction between the ecclesiastical office of

---

[18]Martin Luther *Weimarer Ausgabe* 7.25-26.

[19]Ibid., 7.57; 11.412.

[20]Ibid., 6.408; 11.412.

[21]Ibid., 2.722.

[22]Ibid., 2.723. It is noteworthy how close Hans Küng comes to Luther's view in his *The Church* (New York: Doubleday, 1976), pp. 361-480.

[23]Althaus, *Theology of Martin Luther*, pp. 323-29; Miguel M. Garijo-Guembe (*Communion of the Saints: Nature and Structure of the Church*, trans. Patrick Madigan [Collegeville, Minn.: Liturgical Press, 1994], p. 141) follows Althaus.

[24]Martin Luther *Weimarer Ausgabe* 12.189; 50.633.

[25]Ibid., 6.657.

[26]Ibid., 50.647.

[27]Althaus, *Theology of Martin Luther*, pp. 324, 325.

[28]Martin Luther *Weimarer Ausgabe* 12.189. I follow here the interpretation of Althaus (*Theology of Martin Luther*, pp. 324-25). The issue is debated among Lutheran experts; for the discussion, see Pannenberg, *Systematic Theology* 3:375-77.

[29]Martin Luther *Weimarer Ausgabe* 12.189.

the ministry and the universal priesthood is the public character of the official ministry of the Word and sacrament to the entire community."[30] It is easy
to see Luther's main targets here: the Catholic idea of a special "priesthood"
of ordained persons, and the special status by virtue of ordination of ordained persons. Both of these are denied by Luther.

The lasting contributions of the Protestant principle of the priesthood of
all believers are obvious. First, it rehabilitates the New Testament usage of
the term "priest"[31] as referring not to individual ordained persons (as in the
earlier Catholic understanding) but to the whole people of God as they fulfill the Christ-given mandate. Second, it abolishes the difference between
ordained and nonordained in the sense of these two groups differing from
each other ontologically (even if the difference of ministerial status still remains). Third, the Protestant view sought to legitimize the use of ordained
ministry in a way that should not—at least in principle—lessen the importance of the rest of the people of God. In other words, the task of the ordained in the church was to help do what the rest of the church members
were doing.

## The Spirit, Word and Sacraments

In Luther's view, the Spirit works in the church and in the believer's life
through the preached Word and the sacraments. This is perhaps the most
characteristic of Luther's ideas of the work of the Holy Spirit. The Spirit is
indispensable for preparation for faith: "I believe that I cannot believe in
Jesus Christ my Lord, or come to him, of my own reason or power but the
Holy Spirit has called me by the gospel, enlightened me with his gifts, sanc-
tified and upheld me in true faith."[32]

Two seemingly opposing tendencies are present in Luther's understanding
of the relationship between the Word, the Spirit and church. On the one hand,
there is total dependence on the ministry of the Spirit, as the quote above clearly shows. On the other hand, the ministry of the Spirit is tied to the Word and
the sacraments; the Spirit never works apart from these:

---

[30]Althaus, *Theology of Martin Luther*, p. 327.
[31]I am well aware of the fact that the term *priest* in the New Testament occupies various nu-
ances and the trajectory is quite complex. A general exegetical and theological consensus
nowadays is that, in distinction to the Old Testament usage, the New Testament does not
coincide with the (patristic and Medieval) understanding of "priest" as a sacramentally des-
ignated person in the church.
[32]Martin Luther *Weimarer Ausgabe* 30.1367-68.

Neither you nor I could ever know anything of Christ, or believe in him and take him as our Lord, unless these were first offered to us and bestowed on our hearts through the preaching of the Gospel by the Holy Spirit. . . . For where Christ is not preached, there is no Holy Spirit to create, call, and gather the Christian church, and outside it not one can come to the Lord Christ.[33]

In other words, the Word and Spirit belong together: the church is not an invisible Platonic reality of *Schwärmerei* (Luther's pejorative term for the Enthusiasts of his time), nor an infallible unchanging institution of the pope. The Holy Spirit, mediated through the Word and sacrament, sanctifies and makes holy the believers.[34]

In his insistence on the integral relation between the Spirit and the Word, Luther limits the phenomena of Pentecost (tongues, fire, wind) to the apostolic era: they refer to proper instruments of the Holy Spirit given to the church, namely the Word and sacraments, that is, the visible Word. The wind and fire symbolize the encouragement and zeal given to the apostles, and speaking in tongues symbolizes the gospel itself, preached in every tongue.[35]

In other words, the work of the Holy Spirit is "clothed" in the Word and sacraments. This was Luther's insistence against the spiritualists, who in his view sought for an immediate access to grace apart from the Word and sacraments. According to Luther, this is the order set up by God himself with regard to the work of the Spirit. Against the "Heavenly Prophets" he differentiates two ways God approaches us: (1) the "outer" way, through preached Word and sacraments; and (2) the "inner" way, through the Holy Spirit and his gifts. Both ways are needed, but the outer is primary; the inner is a function of the outer, not vice versa. God does not give his Spirit apart from the preparing work of the Word and sacraments.

Luther argues that in the Bible nobody is given the Spirit without mediation. In this sense, the outer Word for him has a sacramental nature. However, this does not mean domesticating the work of the Spirit exclusively to the outer Word, insofar as the Spirit has already come to live inside the person. As an example, he mentions a special kind of prayer wrought by the Spirit that causes human words to cease. Furthermore, some spiritual gifts, such as healing, were a normal part of spiritual life in Luther's time.

---

[33]*Large Catechism* 2:38, 45.

[34]See further Gritsch and Jenson, *Lutheranism*, p. 125.

[35]Here one should note the decisive role Luther played in the translation of the Bible to make it available to every Christian in his or her own language.

## The Christian as Christ to the Neighbor

All works except for faith have to be directed to the neighbor. For God does not require of us any works with regard to himself, only faith through Christ. That is more than enough for him; that is the right way to give honor to God as God, who is gracious, merciful, wise and truthful. Thereafter, think nothing else than that you do to your neighbor as Christ has done to you. Let all your work and all your life be turned to your neighbor. Seek the poor, sick, and all kinds of wretched people; render your help to those; surrender your life in various kinds of exercises. Let those who really need you enjoy you, insofar that is possible with regard to your body, possessions, and honor.[36]

Martin Luther is usually looked upon as the theologian of justification by *faith*, the doctrine that settles our relationship to God; that he was also a theologian of *love*, both divine and human, is often neglected. His distinctive understanding of the nature of God's love and the power of the love poured out into the believer's heart as a result of Christ's real presence in the Christian offers an exciting perspective on human relationships and neighbor love.[37] It also shapes radically his view of the church. The church becomes a place where Christians are given a chance to exercise God-like love, inspired by the Christ living in the heart of the believer through the Holy Spirit.

To gain a perspective on the importance of neighbor love in Luther's theology in general and in his view of the church in particular, we should note his distinctive understanding of two kinds of love, namely human love and God's love. Human love is oriented toward objects that are inherently good— self-love defines the content and the object of the love. Men and women love something that they believe they can enjoy.[38] God loves in a way opposite to human love: "The love of God does not find, but creates, that which is pleasing

---

[36]Martin Luther *Weimarer Ausgabe* 10:1.2, 168 (*Advent Postil*, 1522; my translation).

[37]Research on ecumenical implications of Luther's theology conducted by the scholars at the Department of Systematic Theology of the University of Helsinki under the mentorship of Professor Tuomo Mannermaa since about the mid-1970s has opened up a new perspective on Luther's theology. A major study on Luther's understanding of neighborly love is Antti Raunio, *Die Summe des christilichen Lebens: Die 'Goldene Regel' als Gesetz der Liebe in der Theologie Martin Luthers von 1510 bis 1527*, Systemaattisen teologian laitoksen julkaisuja 13 (Helsinki: Yliopistopaino, 1993); the book will be published in German by Veröffentlichungen des Instituts für Europäische Geschicte, Mainz. A brief summary in English can be found in Mannermaa, "Why is Luther so Fascinating? Modern Finnish Luther Research," in *Union with Christ: The New Finnish Interpretation of Luther*, ed. Carl E. Braaten and Robert W. Jenson (Grand Rapids, Mich.: Eerdmans, 1998), pp. 1-20.

[38]See further Alister E. McGrath, *Luther's Theology of the Cross: Martin Luther's Theological Breakthrough* (New York: Oxford University Press, 1985), pp. 77-83.

to it. . . . Rather than seeking its own good, the love of God flows forth and bestows good."[39] Luther sometimes calls God's love *amor crucis*: "This is the love
of the cross, born of the cross, which turns in the direction where it does not
find good which it may enjoy, but where it may confer good upon the bad and
needy person."[40]

We can certainly do nothing for our salvation, but our neighbors need our
work, that is, our love: "Every man is created and born for the sake of others."[41]

> For if I do not use everything that I have to serve my neighbor, I rob him of what
> I owe him according to God's will. A Christian, then, becomes a 'work of Christ,'
> and even more a 'Christ' to the neighbor; the Christian does what Christ does.
> The Christian identifies with the suffering of his/her neighbor.[42]

Christ is the subject of good works, since Christ lives in the believer and
makes the believer to do the works Christ did. Justification for Luther means
primarily participation in God through the indwelling of Christ in the heart
through the Spirit. It is not only forgiveness of sins, but a real participation in
God, in God's characteristics such as goodness, wisdom and truthfulness.
Luther even expresses this truth by saying that God in fact becomes truthful,
good and just in the person when God himself makes the person truthful,
good and just. Never is there reason to boast, however, since even the presence
of Christ and its consequences are always hidden in the Christian.

Out of this emphasis on neighborly love grows Luther's understanding of
the church as "hospital to the sick."

## The Church as a Hospital for the Incurably Sick

Since Christians are living in the world, they are involved with people who are
both sinful and less than perfect; therefore, the church of Christ in the world
cannot be anything else except a hospital for the incurably sick.[43] The *summa*
of the Christian life is to bear the burden of one's neighbor. Consequently, the
task of the bishops and pastors is to act as if each diocese were a hospital and
church members were sick and in need of medical treatment:

---

[39]*Luther's Works* 31.57.
[40]*Luther's Works* 31.57.
[41]Martin Luther *Weimarer Ausgabe* 21.346.
[42]*Luther's Works* 31.55-56.
[43]This section is heavily indebted to Tuomo Mannermaa, *Kaksi rakkautta: Johdatus Lutherin
uskonmaailmaan*, 2 painos, Suomalaisen Teologisen Kirjallisuusseuran Julkaisuja 194 (Helsinki: STKJ, 1995), pp. 97-100.

> This is the *summa* of the Gospel: The kingdom of Christ is a kingdom of mercy
> and grace. It is nothing else than the continuous bearing of [each other's] bur-
> dens. Christ bears our wretchedness and sicknesses. Our sins he will take upon
> himself and he is patient when we are going astray. Even now and forever he car-
> ries us on his shoulders and never tires of carrying us. . . . The task of the preach-
> ers in this kingdom is to console consciences, associate in a friendly spirit with
> the people, feed them with the nourishment of the Gospel, carry the weak, heal
> the sick and take care of everybody according to their need. That is also the
> proper ministry for every bishop and pastor.[44]

The theological basis for this kind of caring attitude is Luther's idea of the
church members as Christs to each other. This comes to focus in the celebration
of the Lord's Supper. As Christ has given himself to Christians in the bread
and wine, so also do Christians form one bread and one drink as they participate in the Eucharist. The Christian is bread to feed the hungry neighbor and
drink to quench their thirst: "Also with us it happens so that we all become one
cake and we eat each other," Luther explains.[45] He compares the eucharistic
eating to the baking of bread in which the ingredients get completely mixed
and are indistinguishable from each other, or the preparation of wine in which
the grapes are mashed together.

Luther employs the beautiful ancient symbol of the church as mother. In
fact, he compares the church with the physical womb of the mother to deliver
a baby. The task of the church is noble: "The church namely teaches, cherish-
es us warmly, carries us in her womb and lap and arms, shapes us and makes
us perfect according to the form of Christ until we grow to become perfect
men."[46]

Luther also knows the most interesting dialectic between the Christian as
"Lord" and "servant" at the same time. On the one hand, as a result of the
presence of Christ, the Christian is "above all" and on the other hand "under all." Through faith the spirit of the Christian is taken into the heights of
God, but at the same time that she is being elevated, she should also do what
God's love always does, namely, orient one's self downward, to that which
is nothing in itself. Consequently, the Christian is both totally free and totally
bound by needs of others. She is totally free and totally given to service for
others.

In summary, it could be said that in Luther's thinking all human efforts in

---

[44]Martin Luther *Weimarer Ausgabe* 10:1.2; 366, 18-34 (*Summer Postil*, 1526; my translation).
[45]Martin Luther *Weimarer Ausgabe* 12.489-90.
[46]Ibid., 40:1.665.

principle are meant for the service of love. Preaching the gospel, feeding the hungry and clothing the naked are sharing good as much as the rest of life in the family, society and church. "All human actions in the church and society spring up from love to protect and cultivate the life created by God."[47]

---

[47]Mannermaa, *Kaksi rakkautta*, pp. 99-100.

# 4

## The Church as Covenant
### REFORMED ECCLESIOLOGY

### The Marks of the Church

As with Martin Luther, so also with John Calvin and Ulrich Zwingli—it took time before they came to the painful realization that the Reformation withdrawal from the Catholic Church was more than a temporary one. After the collapse of the Colloquy of Regensburg in 1541, which was a last-ditch attempt to reach a compromise between Catholics and Protestants, the Reformers were slowly compelled to begin to develop their distinctive understanding of the church. Calvin is the leading figure in that company of Protestant Reformers who set themselves the difficult task of creating an ecclesiology that would be faithful to both the ancient creeds and to the ideas that brought the Reformation into existence. Calvin agreed with Luther that the marks of the true church were the preaching of the Word of God and the right administration of the sacraments.[1] However, he came to emphasize correct faith and an upright Christian life more strictly than Luther. "He accepted Zwingli's test of 'faith,' and the Anabaptists' test of 'life,' and added a sharing in the sacraments."[2] According to Calvin, "members of the church [are] those who by confession of faith, by example of life, and by partaking of the sacraments profess the same God and Christ."[3]

In opposition to Luther, however, Calvin believed that there were specific scriptural directions regarding the right order of ministry in the visible church, so that a specific form of ecclesiastical order now became an item of doctrine.

---

[1]John Calvin, *Institutes of the Christian Religion*, ed. John T. McNeill (Philadelphia: Westminster Press, 1960), 4.1.12.

[2]C. Penrose St. Amant, "Reformation Views of the Church," in *The People of God: Essays in the Believers' Church*, ed. Paul Basden and David S. Dockery (Nashville: Broadman, 1991), p. 213. See further Roland Bainton, *The Reformation of the Sixteenth Century* (Boston: Beacon, 1952), pp. 115-16 especially.

[3]Calvin *Institutes* 4.1.8; see also Calvin, *Commentary* (Grand Rapids, Mich.: Eerdmans, 1948), 1 Corinthians 11:2.

This distinctive feature of administration was the differentiation between "minister" and "elder" (presbyter). Another difference from Luther consisted of the role of discipline. Whereas for Luther questions of behavior were mostly left to the judgment of the conscience, Calvin was much more the legalist who sought to implement a specific and rather ascetic view of the norms of Christian conduct. While the statement that "every Calvinist was a monk" is certainly an overstatement, it still contains a kernel of truth.[4] He even devoted one chapter in his *Institutes* to the topic of discipline.[5] Calvin's rather strict and often seemingly one-sided emphasis on behavior and doctrine also made his view of the church depart from the ecclesiology of his counterpart Zwingli's, in which personal faith was the key.[6]

One of the most distinctive and controversial aspects of the Reformed view of the church, especially in the Calvinistic form, is the integral relationship between the state and church. During Calvin's early years in Geneva, church and state were parallel, giving mutual support and collaboration. The two powers shared a common goal. Later, however, Calvin drew a clearer boundary line between the two: church and state became two aspects of a single reality, though they cannot be identified. According to Calvin, even earthly rulers should "advance the kingdom of Christ and maintain purity of doctrine."[7]

## *The Church Visible and Invisible*

For Calvin, the church is primarily a visible community. One motif that helped Calvin to stress the visible side of the church was his growing emphasis on the public appropriation of the sacraments, especially of baptism. Calvin followed Augustine and distinguished "belief in the church" from "believing the church." He argued that the latter correctly showed the church to be the means for salvation, while the former attributes salvation to the church and not to God.[8] It was in this context that Calvin first used the expression "visible church" in a positive sense; he described the church as the "mother" of the faithful through whom one has rebirth and salvation. He also emphasized

---

[4] Bainton, *Reformation of the Sixteenth Century*, 116. Strangely enough, François Wendel, in his excellent study on Calvin, disagrees (*Calvin: Origins and Development of His Religious Thoughts* [New York: Harper & Row, 1963], p. 301).

[5] Calvin *Institutes* 4:22.

[6] See further P. D. L. Avis, "'The True Church' in Reformation Theology," *Scottish Journal of Theology* 30 (1977): 326-32.

[7] Calvin, *Commentary*, Isaiah 49:23.

[8] Calvin *Institutes* 4.1.2.

public ministry and church discipline. Although the discussion of the visible church still lacked the details on polity, the shifting emphasis from invisible to visible church was clear.[9]

Along the way Calvin developed his baptismal theology, and his idea of the church as a visible community became more nuanced. By the 1543 *Institutes* Calvin had further developed the idea of the visible church to the point that one must not separate from this church: "Therefore, just as it is necessary to believe that the church visible to God's eyes alone is invisible to us, so to this one, which is called church with respect to men, we are ordered to be reverent and observe communion."[10] Calvin considered the invisible church to be a "true" church comprised of the totality of the elect before God. He also considered the visible church to be a "true" church because it was the authentic instrument that manifested and initiated those elected in Christ. Thus, there are not two distinct churches existing side by side, but rather one church which has two parts, one part visible to God and the other part visible to humanity.[11]

This double nature of the church, wherein visible and invisible are held as one but still distinguished, was reinforced by Calvin's sacramental and baptismal discussion. He emphasized God's free offer of Christ as the nature of the substance of the sacraments. "This offer always marked the one true church: explicitly in the visible church through the sacraments, themselves a form of the word that offered engrafting in Christ; and implicitly in the invisible church because the elect were those engrafted in Christ. Baptism represented entrance into the visible church community."[12] In other words, Christ was offered to all through the visible church, and that offer, through the Word and sacraments, marked the presence of the one true church. On the other hand, only some people (the elect known only to God) truly accepted the offer of Christ. As early as 1536 Calvin had described these true believers as "the mystical body of Christ," and in the 1539 *Institutes* Calvin extensively referred to them as those elected in Christ.[13]

In the final analysis, it is very important to note that this distinction between the visible and invisible church is eschatological. The invisible church is the church that will come into being at the end of time when God administers the

---

[9]See further John W. Riggs, "Emerging Ecclesiology in Calvin's Baptismal Thought, 1536-43," *Church History* 64, no. 1 (1995): 37-38.
[10]Calvin *Institutes* 4.1.7.
[11]Riggs, "Emerging Ecclesiology," p. 41.
[12]Ibid.
[13]Calvin *Institutes* 3.22.7; Riggs, "Emerging Ecclesiology," p. 42.

final judgment. Regardless of all weaknesses and frailties, the visible church is to be honored by all Christians, so there is no Donatist tendency of withdrawing into a fellowship of believers only. In other words, the invisible church, which consists of only the elect, is an object of hope, not a reality in this life, while the visible church is the concrete form of the church of Christ on earth. Furthermore, in line with Catholics and Lutherans, Calvin did not place the holiness of the church in the individuals—although he was not indifferent to that concern—but rather on objective aspects of the gospel and the sacraments.

## A Graced Covenant Community

There are varying assessments among commentators of Calvin as to the specific role of the sacraments and the sacramental principle in Calvin's theology and ecclesiology. Recently, it has been suggested that Calvin (and Luther) represent what has traditionally been called the Catholic and Orthodox "eucharistic ecclesiology" in which the relationship between the church and the sacraments, in this case the Eucharist, is mutual.[14] Brian A. Gerrish goes so far as to say that the "entire *oeuvre* [work] of John Calvin may be described as a eucharistic theology, shot through with the themes of grace and gratitude."[15] This statement means that according to Calvin all good things come to us from their graceful source in God: "It is not enough simply to hold that God is one who should be worshipped and adored by all, unless we are persuaded also that he is the fountain of all good, so that we should seek nothing anywhere else but in him. . . . And so we should learn to look for, and to ask for, all these [good and beautiful things in the world and in our lives] from him, and when we receive them to ascribe them thankfully to him."[16] God's abundant grace, his very being imparting himself in love, is what we as creatures find all around us, and the only appropriate response is eucharistic, the meal of gratitude. The human being for Calvin in this sense is "eucharistic man."[17]

The climax of God's good gifts for Calvin is Jesus Christ. "This is the purpose of the gospel that Christ should become ours, and that we should be in-

---

[14]Owen F. Cummings, "The Reformers and Eucharistic Ecclesiology," *One in Christ* 33, no. 1 (1997): 47-54.

[15]Brian A Gerrish, *Grace and Gratitude: The Eucharistic Theology of John Calvin* (Edinburgh: T & T Clark, 1993) as paraphrased by Cummings, "Reformers and Eucharistic Ecclesiology," p. 52.

[16]Calvin *Institutes* 1.2.1.

[17]Cummings, "Reformers and Eucharistic Ecclesiology," p. 52, quoting Gerrish, *Grace and Gratitude*, p. 50.

grafted into his body."[18] This leads to mystical union between Christ and human beings. Christ as the source and mediator of the covenant becomes one with us and so, in the church, there is a union between the human and divine. This is, of course, nothing other than the use of eucharistic language. For Calvin, the proper instrument by which the gift, Jesus Christ, is given to us is the Word of God, which is in turn the instrument of the Holy Spirit.[19] Consequently, pneumatology, Christology and sacramental theology are closely related with regard to his doctrine of the church.[20]

## Tensions in Reformed Ecclesiology

As already mentioned, no Protestant Reformer started the renewal of the church with a view to developing a distinctively Protestant theology, let alone ecclesiology. Whenever Protestant ecclesiologies are studied, whether Lutheran or Reformed, it has to be acknowledged that these views represent at their best responses to existing needs; they were occasional works rather than systematic theologies of the church. Tensions and inconsistencies follow from this kind of endeavor. Two tensions are well known and worth mentioning in order to give a more concrete form to the Reformed doctrine of the church, apart from the fact that in contrast to its Lutheran counterpart, the Reformed camp had from the beginning two leading figures, Calvin and Zwingli. Even though both leaders represent in general terms the Reformed view of the church, each also has different emphases.

One tension comes to focus especially with the early Zwingli. According to him, the final ecclesiastical authority rested in the local community of believers. Zwingli preferred the German term *Gemeinde* (community, congregation), as did also the early Luther, to emphasize this aspect of ecclesiology. Very soon, however, he came to believe that this authority was exercised by the civil government allegedly acting in line with the teachings of Scripture. Still another wing of the Reformation, the Anabaptist more radical "left-wing," was more consistent with this idea of the locus of authority residing in the local community and did not let the state rule over the church. Zwingli and the Anabaptists thus came to disagree concerning the authority, and consequently, the nature of the church.[21]

---

[18]Calvin, *Commentary on the Epistle to the Romans*, 1:9.
[19]See further Calvin *Institutes* 3.1.1; 1.9.1.
[20]See further Cummings, "Reformers and Eucharistic Ecclesiology," pp. 53-54.
[21]St. Amant, "Reformation Views of the Church," p. 212.

Another unresolved emphasis of Zwingli also came to focus in his contacts with the Anabaptists and other more radical Reformers. Zwingli's stress on personal faith as the test of the elect, and therefore of those who make up the church, created an "anomaly because he also identified the church with the total community, except for a few Catholics." He disdained the logic of personal faith that would have led to a believers' church. In fact, for a short while in the 1520s he leaned toward believers' baptism, as did Luther also, and therefore toward a believers' church. But soon his views were changed and he aligned himself with the state-church model even though never giving up his insistence on the need for faith. That was one of the reasons why some of his followers, such as Felix Manz and Conrad Grebel, decided to depart from the Reformed camp and form their own group of Reformers. As is well known, Zwingli, however, retained a "weak" view of the sacraments, both baptism and the Lord's Supper, and continued to stress the need for faith. Sacraments for him were never "sacraments" in the classic meaning of the term, according to which they effect what they signify *(ex opere operato)*, which was the view of Luther and, of course, the Catholic Church.

Not only Zwingli but also Calvin stressed faith as essential to the efficacy of the sacraments. "We are not made partakers in Jesus Christ and his spiritual gifts by the bread, wine, and water, but . . . we are brought to him by the promise, so that he gives himself to us, and, dwelling in us by faith, he fulfills what is promised and offered to us by the signs." His emphasis is that Christ grants his gifts in the sacraments by faith.[22] At the same time, Calvin was not consistent in his view of the sacraments. His understanding of the Lord's Supper pointed in the one direction and his view of baptism in another. As a result, his sacramental doctrine is both ambiguous and open to different interpretations.

If the believer alone can enter into communion with Christ, such union in the Supper and baptism is the effect of faith. Nevertheless, in 1536 Calvin spoke of the faith of children in whom God acts secretly without our knowing how. Later he abandoned that view and replied to those who believed that baptism is a sacrament of faith, of which infants are not capable, by saying, "That objection is resolved in one word, if we say that they are baptized for their future faith and penitence, whereof, although we see none in appearance, nevertheless the seed is here implanted by the hidden working of the Holy Spirit."[23] Calvin clung to the practice of infant baptism despite his inability to

---

[22]Ibid., p. 215.
[23]Ibid., p. 216.

find a basis for it in Scripture. He sought to ground it in the circumcision in the Old Covenant and the blessing of children by Jesus. In addition, he referred to patristic evidence without citing the source.[24]

## Karl Barth's Revisionary Reformed Ecclesiology

If John Calvin is the theological architect of the Reformed wing of the Protestant Reformation, Karl Barth, the "church father" of the twentieth century, is its ablest and most creative interpreter for modern times. Representative of those original thinkers who stand firmly in their own tradition, yet both transcend and expand it, Barth offers to the ecumenical world the most radical criticism and reappropriation of the Calvinist-Zwinglian ecclesiological tradition. It can legitimately be said that Barth's doctrine of the church anticipates and deepens the long tradition of the Believers' church ecclesiology to be discussed in the following chapter in more detail. In a recent study on Barth's revision of Protestant ecclesiology, Craig A. Carter argues that Barth's vision of the church represents a "completion of the Reformation."[25]

However, the choice of Barth as a representative of modern Reformed ecclesiology is questioned by some for the simple reason that his view is so critical of much of the mainline Reformed understanding as explicated by Calvin, Zwingli and their successors. Many note correctly that Barth's view of the church approaches the emphases of the Free churches' doctrine of the church. A response to this objection points out that to ignore the contribution of Barth would seriously limit the diversity within the Reformed family. But since Barth's theological focus does not lie in the doctrine of the church, he is not counted among the small number of leading ecclesiologists to be discussed in part two.

Barth's doctrine of the church is conditioned by three theological loci, namely pneumatology,[26] Christology and the Word of God. "Anthropological and ecclesiological assertions arise only as they are borrowed from Christol-

---

[24]Calvin, *Institutes* 4.16.8.

[25]Craig A. Carter, "Karl Barth's Revision of Protestant Ecclesiology," *Perspectives in Religious Studies* 22, no. 1 (1995): 35-44. In this section I am heavily indebted to Carter's presentation. The main source for Bath's ecclesiological developments is to be found in the fourth volume of his *Church Dogmatics*, 4 vols., ed. G. W. Bromiley and T. F. Torrance (Edinburgh: T & T Clark, 1956-1975). In fact, each part of volume four highlights some aspects of the being of the church: "The Holy Spirit and the Gathering of the Christian Community" (part 1), "The Holy Spirit and the Upbuilding of the Christian Community" (part 2) and "The Holy Spirit and the Sending of the Christian Community" (part 3).

[26]For Barth's pneumatological ecclesiology, see further James J. Buckley, "A Field of Living Fire: Karl Barth on the Spirit and the Church," *Modern Theology* 10, no. 1 (1994): 81-102.

ogy."[27] The main definition of the church for Barth is the body of Christ.[28] In the opening subsection of volume four titled "The Word of the Holy Spirit," Barth notes that moving to ecclesiology from Christology means making the transition from the second to the third article of the creed; in fact, our ecclesiological statements are theological in that they are statements of faith.[29] But even though it is the Holy Spirit that calls the church, it is still a "phenomenon of world history,"[30] a human society. This is the gateway to the emphasis on the visible nature of the church. Barth rejects the idea that the church is invisible, labeling this view "ecclesiological docetism."[31] But rather than looking at a single unified institutional structure, he views the local congregation as the visible form of the church.[32]

It is clear that Barth advocates a congregational church government rather than episcopal or presbyterian structures of the Reformers. Accordingly, Barth defines the church in dynamic rather than in static terms. He prefers terms such as "community" and "congregation."[33] "The church is when it takes place."[34] The questions naturally arise as to who are the true Christians and how one recognizes the true church. Barth opposes two mistaken ways common in the past, namely the sacramentalism of the Roman Catholic Church and the "moralism" of Anabaptism. The first one ends up being a human action to limit the freedom of the Spirit, the latter one a presumptuous human desire to be infallible in judging who are true Christians.[35] Barth's alternative is to begin with the doctrine of election and define true Christians, and hence members of the true church, as "the men assembled in it who are thereto elected by the Lord."[36]

Barth criticizes the Reformers' view of the church as self-sufficient for lacking in missionary orientation.[37] The whole church, not just the "religious," are called to participate in God's mission. From the missionary perspective, he

---

[27]Barth, *Church Dogmatics*, 2/1, p. 149. See further Nicholas M. Healy, "The Logic of Karl Barth's Ecclesiology: Analysis, Assessment and Proposed Modifications," *Modern Theology* 10, no. 3 (1994): 254-56.

[28]See further Healy, "Logic of Karl Barth's Ecclesiology," pp. 256-57.

[29]Barth, *Church Dogmatics*, 4/1, pp. 644-45.

[30]Ibid., IV/1, p. 652.

[31]Ibid., IV/1, p. 653.

[32]Carter, "Karl Barth's Revision of Protestant Ecclesiology," p. 36.

[33]Barth, *Church Dogmatics* 6/1, p. 650.

[34]Ibid., p. 652.

[35]Ibid., pp. 694, 696.

[36]Ibid., p. 696.

[37]See further ibid., 4/3:2, pp. 762-95.

also criticizes the distinction between the invisible and visible church: rather than concerning ourselves with the distinction between the wheat and tares, we should leave judgment in God's hand and get on with the proper human work of witnessing.[38] So, for Barth the main task of the church is to be a witnessing community rather than a means of grace, which in his understanding was the Reformers' emphasis.[39]

One of Barth's emphases that has since become an ecumenical axiom—and a lived reality in many Free churches—is the insistence on the giftedness of all members of the church for ministry, not only of a few. In his view the Reformation doctrine of the priesthood of all believers will not take any concrete form unless the Pauline teaching on the gifts of the Spirit is being reaffirmed.[40] The existence of that kind of serving church requires the voluntary commitment of all members; consequently, Barth's adamant opposition to infant baptism in favor of believers' baptism becomes understandable. "His doctrine of believers' baptism leads naturally to the doctrine of the believers' church, . . . one in which only those who have freely chosen to confess Jesus Christ publicly through baptism are members."[41]

It should now be evident that for Barth any kind of union between church and state is an anathema, because the state is part of the world.[42] He argues that what the state really needs is a Free church "which as such, can remind it of its own limits and calling, thus warning it against falling into either anarchy on the one hand or tyranny on the other."[43]

---

[38]Carter, "Karl Barth's Revision of Protestant Ecclesiology," p. 38; Barth, *Church Dogmatics* 4/3:2, pp. 765, 783, 790 especially.

[39]See, e.g., Barth, *Church Dogmatics* 4/3:2, pp. 795, 797.

[40]Ibid., 4/3:2, pp. 843-901.

[41]Carter, "Karl Barth's Revision of Protestant Ecclesiology," 42; for Barth's doctrine of baptism (both water and Spirit baptism) see further Barth, *Church Dogmatics*, 14/4, pp. 6, 32, 44, 100-33, 164-95 especially.

[42]Barth, *Church Dogmatics* 4/2, p. 688.

[43]Ibid., p. 687.

# 5

# The Church as the Fellowship of Believers

## FREE CHURCH ECCLESIOLOGIES

### An Ecclesiological Transformation

Most everybody would agree today that there is a radical ecclesiological shift happening: "The understanding of the church seems to be moving away from the traditional hierarchical model to the (no longer quite so new) participative models of church configuration." Today's global developments seem to imply that Protestant Christendom of the future will exhibit largely a Free Christian form. Although the episcopal churches will probably not surrender their own hierarchical structures, they, too, will increasingly have to integrate these Free church elements into the mainstream of their own lives both theologically and practically.[1] This has been called the "process of congregationalization" of Christianity.[2] Harvey Cox expresses this mentality clearly in his book on the Latin American liberationist Leonardo Boff: "How will the church leaders deal with a restless spiritual energy splashing up from the underside of society and threatening to erode traditional modes of ecclesiastical governance?"[3] Miroslav Volf contends that whatever one thinks about these developments in the church and society, it is a fact that a Free church model is emerging as a powerful global force: "The continuing global expansion of the Free church model is without a doubt being borne by irreversible social changes of global proportions."[4]

One can, of course, simply disregard these radical changes by an attitude that dogmatically limits the ecclesiality of the church to models that still conform

---

[1]Miroslav Volf, *After Our Likeness: The Church as an Image of the Trinity* (Grand Rapids, Mich.: Eerdmans, 1998), p. 12.

[2]Russell Chandler, *Racing Toward 2001: The Forces Shaping America's Religious Future* (Grand Rapids, Mich.: Zondervan, 1992), p. 210; Volf, *After Our Likeness*, p. 13.

[3]Harvey Cox, *The Silencing of Leonardo Boff: The Vatican and the Future of World Christianity* (Oak Park, Ill.: Meyer-Stone, 1988), p. 17. I am indebted to Volf, *After Our Likeness*, p. 13, for this reference.

[4]Volf, *After Our Likeness*, p. 13.

with more traditional churches. Parodies of Free churches abound even in more recent literature, implying that these groups manifest something less than "church." For example, a statement from the top of the hierarchy of the Roman Catholic Church disqualifies the Free churches ecclesiologically by assessing these Christian communities as ones that fled to North America and "took refuge from the oppressive model of the 'State Church' produced by the Reformation . . . [and] created their own church, an organization structured according to their needs."[5] Ecumenically this kind of attitude is disastrous and sociologically naive in that a few strokes of a theologian's pen seem to attempt to discredit the fastest growing segment of Christianity—which displays many features surprisingly similar to the original form of the Christian church. Fortunately, the same document qualifies its ecclesiological assessment by admitting that

> the authentically Catholic meaning of the reality "Church" is tacitly disappearing, without being expressly rejected. . . . In other words, in many ways a conception of Church is spreading in Catholic thought, and even in Catholic theology, that cannot even be called Protestant in a "classic" sense. Many current ecclesiological ideas, rather, correspond more to the model of certain North American "Free churches."[6]

As already noted in the introduction to part one, which movements to include under the rubric *Free churches* is not self-evident. Here we will begin with what most theologians regard as the origins of Free church mentality, namely the Radical Reformation and the emerging Anabaptism. Then, along the way we will give references to the doctrine of the church as it was further developed by the Baptist tradition and its main architect, John Smyth. One of the central foci here will be the rise of what is often called the idea of the believers' church, undoubtedly the most distinctive feature of this ecclesiological tradition. Unfortunately, for the purposes of general outline and comprehensiveness, the differences between various Free church ecclesiologies cannot be highlighted, and thus theological accuracy in some cases is sacrificed for the broader pedagogical goals of the present book.

## The Radical Reformation Heritage

Church history, as any other history, is written from the perspective of those

---

[5]Joseph Cardinal Ratzinger, *The Ratzinger Report: An Exclusive Interview on the State of the Church, Joseph Cardinal Ratzinger with Vittorio Messori* (San Francisco: Ignatius, 1985), p. 46.
[6]Ratzinger, *Ratzinger Report*, pp. 45-46.

who hold power. Even at the end of the nineteenth century, most church historians still divided Western Christianity into Protestant and Catholic types without remainder. A whole array of legitimate Christian churches and communities were left out. These were mainly the descendants of the Radical Reformation. Anabaptism and later Baptist movements were on the one hand forerunners of later Free churches and on the other hand the legacy of that part of the Protestant Reformation that wanted to go further than the Magisterial Reformers went.[7] The radical Reformers were dissatisfied with the "compromises" of their mainline counterparts.[8]

Even though Free church ecclesiology was appropriated and distinctively developed by several traditions going ultimately back to the Radical Reformation, some Free churches, for example the Baptist movement, have been uneasy at times about their undeniable link with assorted radical thinkers and actors in history, most especially with the abortive Kingdom of Münster, Germany, in the sixteenth century. There were several other episodes of the Radical Reformation, for example the life and martyrdom of the apocalyptic preacher Hans Hut, that connect the later Baptist movement with the struggles of the Reformation and Counter Reformation.[9]

There is always a difference of perception between opposing groups. Whereas the Catholics and Magisterial Reformers regarded the left-wingers as dissenters, they considered themselves the true church of God on earth, the true apostolic church. Consequently, they saw a shocking difference between the apostolic church and the compromised state church. Sebastian Frank claimed boldly:

> I believe that the outward Church of Christ, including all its gifts and sacraments, because of the breaking in and laying waste by antichrist right after the death of the Apostles, went up into heaven, and lies concealed in the Spirit and in truth. I am thus quite certain that for fourteen hundred years now there has existed no gathered Church nor any sacrament.[10]

---

[7]See further James W. McClendon Jr., *Doctrine: Systematic Theology*, vol. 2 (Nashville: Abingdon, 1994); see also John J. Kiwiet, "Anabaptist Views of the Church," in *The People of God: Essays on the Believers' Church*, ed. Paul Basden and David S. Dockery (Nashville: Broadman, 1991), pp. 225-34.

[8]Michael Novak, "The Free churches and the Roman Church: The Conception of the Church in Anabaptism and in Roman Catholicism: Past and Present," *Journal of Ecumenical Studies* 2 (1965): 429.

[9]See further McClendon, *Doctrine*, pp. 341-42.

[10]Cited in Alister E. McGrath, *Christian Theology: An Introduction* (Oxford: Blackwell, 1994), p. 415.

In other words, the true church was in heaven, and its institutional parodies on earth. In this strictly defined believers' church model, the church was seen as "an assembly of the righteous" rather than a "mixed body": "In truth, those who merely boast of his name are not the true congregation of Christ. The true congregation of Christ is those who are truly converted, who are born from above of God, who are of a regenerate mind by the operation of the Holy Spirit through the hearing of the Word of God, and have become the children of God."[11]

## Unmediated Access to God

It is a historical and theological commonplace to contend that Anabaptists and other groups of the left wing of the Reformation devalued Scripture and put in its place a reliance on the Holy Spirit.[12] While there is undeniably some truth to this claim, it is also clear that this impression comes more from the often less-than-fair judgments of their opponents.[13] It is more correct to say that rather than devaluing the written Word, the Anabaptists had a distinctive view of the relationship between the Spirit and Word. It is a historical fact that even though they emphasized the Holy Spirit, they were also rigorously obedient to the Bible.[14] Scripture was the supreme authority for Anabaptists. In fact, the whole point of their often quite narrow and even exclusivist view of the church and matters relating to society was their insistence on obedience to the most literal interpretation of Scripture. Anabaptists also insisted that whoever has made the commitment to obedience and has the Spirit can read Scripture with understanding. Furthermore, far from being individualistic, they emphasized the importance of the community for the right understanding of revelation; namely, the Spirit was operative in the church even though the opponents highly doubted it. This, of course, made the common people supreme Bible interpreters in a more concrete way even than in the mainline Reformation.

Though the Free churches from early on have wanted to ground their faith in the revelation of God in the Bible, they have still wanted to claim an unmediated access to God, apart from human-made prerequisites such as special ministry, sacraments or liturgies. The Quakers, another stream of the descendants of the left-wing Reformation, are a representative, though ex-

---

[11]Ibid., p. 415.

[12]See e.g., Gary D. Badcock, *Light of Truth and Fire of Love: A Theology of the Holy Spirit* (Grand Rapids, Mich.: Eerdmans, 1997).

[13]For Martin Luther's harsh judgment against the Enthusiasts (*Schwärmerei*), see further Yves Congar, *I Believe in the Holy Spirit* (New York: Crossroad, 1983), 1:139-40.

[14]See further McClendon, *Doctrine*, pp. 117-18.

treme, example of this mindset.[15] The basic idea is a direct, unmediated access to God and salvation. There is therefore no need for sacraments or formal worship. In an important sense, the Holy Spirit is the rule of true worship. And the only "cult" is listening in silence to let the Spirit speak. In many cases, no human worship leadership is assigned in favor of letting the Spirit be the master of ceremonies.

There is no denying the fact that there is a heavy accent on individualism and the ambiguous view of the meaning of community. What makes the category of community ambiguous is that on the one hand, these little groups of Christians really held everything in common, but on the other hand, no human community, and certainly no church hierarchy, was allowed to make spiritual decisions. For Quakers and others, God continued to speak through history. Each person is capable of a personal, direct relationship with God.

## The Believers' Church

One of the self-designated names for the Free churches is the "Believers' church," which has been widely used especially among the Baptists but also others. Franklin H. Little has attempted to give more specific content to that expression. First, the Believers' church, although outwardly constituted by volunteers, is Christ's church and not theirs. The older European scholarship especially felt a lot of suspicion of what they thought was the principle of "voluntary" religion (*Freiwilligkeitskirchen*[16] in German). Second, membership in the Believers' church is in fact voluntary and witting. Consequently, the practice of believers' baptism rather than infant baptism is generally, although not exclusively, preferred. The fact that membership is voluntary has made it possible to accent the dignity and voice of each member in the church. Third, the principle of separation from the world is emphasized, although often misinterpreted both by critics and by initiates. Those who have followed Ernst Troeltsch's famous distinction between "church type" and "sect type" have often connected Free churches with Donatism and perfectionism. However, the separation between the church and the world instead relates to the distinction between those who believe and those who do not. Fourth, mission and witness are key concepts for the Believers' church and involve all members. The Anabaptist treatment of the "counsel of perfection" is illustrative.

---

[15]See further Congar, *I Believe in the Holy Spirit*, 1:141-43.
[16]Karl Holl, "Luther und die Schwärmer," *Gesammelte Aufsätze zur Kirchengeschichte*, 6th ed. (Tübingen: J.C.B. Mohr, 1932), 1:420ff.

Over against the medieval Catholic mentality according to which only a few were "religious," among the Anabaptists counsels were applied to each person in the church. Likewise, the Hutterites, the Quakers, the Congregationalists, the Baptists, the Methodists, the Moravians—all these Free churches and many others have a long and rich history of missions. Fifth, as has already become evident, church discipline and internal discipline are stressed, since the church is to consist of believers who have submitted their lives without condition to Christ. And sixth, of great importance lately has been the concept of "the secular." Opposing the idea of "cultural Christianity," the Believers' churches have opposed the identification between the church and the secular and have wanted to grant an integrity and dignity to the life outside the church. Take for example the idea of a "secular" government instead of the medieval "Christian" state in which the priest and the prince ruled together, the latter being servant to the former.[17]

Many other general characteristics have been offered by the representatives of the Free church ecclesiologies to describe their own view and doctrine of the church, such as an appeal to the New Testament rather than to tradition as the ground for church doctrine; primitivism, or the principle of restoration; and an affirmation of religious liberty.[18] Furthermore, George H. Williams has argued that a possible equivalent term for the Believers' church is the "gathered church" as over against the "given church" of the older traditions. This notion of the gathered church is opposed to the church of *corpus christianum* (the institutionalized church under the protection of the governing society) that "could turn out to be . . . the surviving nationalized vestiges of medieval Christendom . . . [amidst] any associated national, ethnic, class, and regional subcultures."[19] To accentuate the intimate nature of the gathered church, metaphors such as wedlock have been used in history; Melchior Hofmann, the Charismatic preacher behind both Musterite and Mennonite Anabaptism, likened believers' baptism to the bridal bliss of Israel (Jer 2:2). Congregationalist Puritans thought of pure congregations as the Beloved in the desert awaiting the embrace of the abiding Wisdom (Song 8:5).[20]

---

[17]Franklin H. Little, "The Concept of the Believers' Church," in *The Concept of the Believers' Church*, ed. James Leo Garrett (Scottdale, Penn.: Herald, 1969), pp. 15-33.

[18]William R. Estep Jr., "A Believing People: Historical Background," in *The Concept of the Believers' Church*, ed. James Leo Garrett (Scottdale, Penn.: Herald, 1969), pp. 57-58.

[19]George H. Williams, "A People in Community: Historical Background," in *The Concept of the Believers' Church*, ed. James Leo Garrett (Scottdale, Penn.: Herald, 1969), p. 102; Williams, "The Believers' Church and the Given Church," in *The People of God: Essays in the Believers' Church*, ed. Paul Basden and David S. Dockery (Nashville: Broadman, 1991), pp. 325-32.

[20]Williams, "People in Community," p. 118.

## The Priesthood of All Believers

As already noticed, one of the most distinctive emphases of the Free church ec-clesiologies has been the insistence on the right and gifting of each believer for ministry as equal partners. Any notion of special ministry relegated only to a few members in the church has been adamantly opposed. The Free churches have in general continued the tradition of the Radical Reformation in their cri-tique of overly inelastic church structures and the limitation of the ministry to the ordained clergy. They wanted to put into practice the idea of the priest-hood of all believers.[21] Most Free churches have ordained ministries but differ from older churches in two basic ways. Few, if any, Free churches understand ordination to be one of the sacraments as both Catholic churches do. For most of them, ordination is just a public confirmation of a divine call already active in one's life.[22]

The second different emphasis of the Free church view of ministry lies in the appeal to the priesthood of all believers, "which connotes access to God and a participation in ministry on the part of all believers."[23] The view of Dis-ciples of Christ is representative here. According to Harry Clyde Munro:

> Through Jesus Christ . . . every believer has direct and immediate access to God. He needs no human professional mediator. Or if one does lose touch with God and seems unable to re-establish this personal relationship, a brother Christian

---

[21]For a survey of older and more recent Free church views of ministry and the priesthood of all believers, see James Leo Garrett, *Systematic Theology: Biblical, Historical, and Evangelical* (Grand Rapids, Mich.: Eerdmans, 1995), 2:560-63. For the Baptists, see Robert G. Walton, *The Gathered Community* (London: Carey, 1946), p. 102; Herschel H. Hobbs, *You Are Chosen: The Priesthood of Believers* (San Francisco: Harper & Row, 1990); and Paul Beasley-Murray, "The Ministry of All and the Leadership of Some: A Baptist Perspective," in *Anyone for Ordina-tion?* ed. Paul Beasley-Murray (Tunbridge Wells, U.K.: Monarch, 1993), pp. 157-74; for the Congregationalists, see Cyril Eastwood, *The Priesthood of All Believers: An Examination of the Doctrine from the Reformation to the Present Day* (London: Epworth, 1960), pp. 164-71; for the Quakers, see Douglas Gwyn, *Apocalypse of the Word: The Life and Message of George Fox (1624-1691)* (Richmond, Va.: Friends United Press, 1986), p. 166; and for the Pentecostals, see my *Spiritus Ubi Vult Spirat: Pneumatology in Roman Catholic-Pentecostal Dialogue (1972-1989)*, Schriften der Luther-Agricola-Gesellschaft (Helsinki: Luther-Agricola-Society, 1998), pp. 332-45.

[22]See further Fisher Humphreys, "Ordination in the Church," in *The People of God*, pp. 288-98. For the view of John Smyth, the founder of the Baptist church (the oldest Free church), see the careful discussion in Volf, *After Our Likeness*, pp. 245-47. For the Pentecostal churches' view as it was defined in the International Roman Catholic-Pentecostal Dialogue, see my *Spiritus ubi vult spirat*, pp. 346-49.

[23]Balthasar Fischer, "Catholic Liturgy in the Light of Vatican II and the Post-Conciliar Reform of the Liturgy," *One in Christ* 13 (1977): 28-30.

may help him find the way back. . . . Unlike the professional priest who remains permanently as the necessary mediator between the believer and God, the pastor or lay brother who serves in this priestly way steps aside as soon as the relationship has been established and the person so helped can become his own priest.[24]

James D. G. Dunn notes that Pentecostal and Charismatic churches and other newer Free churches have been successful in giving expression to the wider experience and expression of Charismatic ministry in their churches.[25] It is perhaps true that whereas the older churches (especially Catholic churches) have typically—and according to Catholic Miguel M. Garijo-Guembe, "one-sidedly"[26]—based their understanding of the ministry, office and authority on the Pastoral Epistles, the Free churches have opted for the Corinthian model in which the charismatically empowered priesthood of all believers is more in focus.

Free churches have not hitherto explicated the theological foundation for ministry, though they have in practice fulfilled much of what the Protestant principle of the priesthood of all believers means. Members of the church, including women with little or no education, have had the opportunity to participate in all kinds of service in the church.

## *The* Notae Missionis, *"The Notes of the Mission"*

The Free churches have lived for and out of mission and evangelization. Mission has not been *a* task of the church but rather *the* purpose of all church life. A recent declaration by leading Free church theologians appeals to the importance of mission for the being of the church: "We have found ourselves agreed that the mission of the church in the world is to work out her being as a covenant community in the midst of the world. The visible community is the organ of missionary proclamation. Integration into its fellowship and style of life is the goal of the evangelistic call to individuals."[27] Bishop Stephen Neill quite correctly suggested that to the traditional Reformation marks of the church there should be added three more, namely "fire on earth" (missionary vitality), willingness to suffer for Christ and the mobility of the pilgrim.[28]

---

[24]Quoted in Garrett, *Systematic Theology* 2:561.

[25]J. D. G. Dunn, *The Christ and the Spirit*, vol. 2, *Pneumatology* (Grand Rapids, Mich.: Eerdmans, 1998), especially p. 293.

[26]Garijo-Guembe, *Communion of Saints*, p. 144.

[27]"Report of the Findings Committee" of the 1967 Louisville Conference "The Concept of the Believers' Church" in *The Concept of the Believers' Church*, ed. James Leo Garrett (Scottdale, Penn.: Herald, 1969), p. 320.

[28]Stephen Neill, *The Unfinished Task* (London: Lutterworth, 1957), pp. 19, 20.

Menno Simons, one of the pioneers, said the same when he added four marks of the church to the twofold Reformation view (the preaching of the Word and the right administration of the sacraments), namely holy living, brotherly love, unreserved testimony and suffering. John H. Yoder calls Neill's three marks the *notae missionis*. The ultimate purpose of these attributes is to carry out mission, in other words, make the church a willing instrument for God's cause in the world.[29]

Holy living has always been of great concern to the ethically oriented mentality of the Free churches. The Anabaptist churches have had "the ban," by means of which church members could be excluded from the congregation. The Polish Racovian Catechism lists five reasons for maintaining rigorous discipline within Anabaptist communities, most of which reflect its policy of radical separation from the world:

1. so that the fallen church member may be healed, and brought back into fellowship with the church

2. to deter others from committing the same offense

3. to eliminate scandal and disorder from the church

4. to prevent the Word of the Lord falling into disrepute outside the congregation

5. to prevent the glory of the Lord being profaned[30]

Menno's second mark of the true church, brotherly love, was also a concern for other Reformers, but in the radical wing this characteristic took more concrete ecclesiological form. Brotherly love belonged to each disciple's lifestyle as she or he followed the Master. The third distinctive mark of the church was witness and testimonies. The purpose of the church for Menno was to make sure "that the name, will, word, and ordinance of Christ are constantly confessed in the face of all cruelty, tyranny, tumult, fire, sword, and violence of the world, and sustained unto the end."[31] Finally, the missionary church was to be ready to suffer for Christ's and the gospel's sake. This kind of suffering is not the result of misbehavior but of conformity with the path of Christ (1 Pet 4:14-16).

---

[29]John H. Yoder, "The Church in the World: Theological Interpretation," in *The Concept of the Believers' Church*, ed. James Leo Garrett (Scottdale, Penn.: Herald, 1969), pp. 250-83.

[30]Cited in McGrath, *Christian Theology*, p. 417.

[31]Cited in Yoder, "The Church in the World," p. 267.

# 6

# The Church in the Power of the Spirit

## PENTECOSTAL/CHARISMATIC ECCLESIOLOGIES

### The Emergence and Spread of the Pentecostal/Charismatic Phenomenon

The twentieth century witnessed dramatic developments in the Christian church with the emergence and rapid growth of Pentecostalism[1] and later Charismatic movements,[2] which helped reshape the worldwide Christian church at the end of its second millennium.

Most popular written histories of Pentecostalism usually trace the origins in the American context to a revival that began on January 1, 1901, at Charles F. Parham's Bethel Bible School in Topeka, Kansas, with students speaking in (unknown) tongues after spending concentrated time studying the accounts of the book of Acts. Several years later this revival gained more publicity through an African American Holiness preacher, William J. Seymour, who preached the new message of Pentecost at the Azusa Street Mission in Los Angeles, California. From 1906 onward, the news of the "outpouring" of the Holy Spirit spread across the nation and around the world. Before long, Pentecostal revivals could be found in Canada, England, Scandinavia, Germany, Asia, Africa and Latin America.

---

[1]A short statement on the emergence of Pentecostalism and basic definitions can be found in the editorial article, "The Pentecostal and Charismatic Movements," in *Dictionary of Pentecostal and Charismatic Movements*, ed. S. M. Burgess and G. McGee (Grand Rapids, Mich.: Zondervan, 1988), pp. 1-6. Today the most prominent presentation of history and theologies of worldwide Pentecostalism is Walter J. Hollenweger, *Pentecostals* (London: SCM Press, 1972 and subsequent editions) and its sequel, *Pentecostalism: Origins and Developments Worldwide* (Peabody, Mass.: Hendrickson, 1998).

[2]Perhaps the easiest introduction to the origins and history of major Charismatic movements is Peter Hocken, "The Charismatic Movement," in *The Dictionary of Pentecostal and Charismatic Movements*, pp. 130-60. See also two recent issues of *Pneuma*: vol. 16, no. 2 (1994) and vol. 18, no. 1 (1996).

About fifty years later, the renewal began to enter into older churches. News about this renewal (which was to be called the "Charismatic renewal/ movement")[3] in the United States began to surface on the national level in 1960 with the publicity accorded to remarkable happenings in the ministry of Dennis Bennett, an Episcopal rector in Van Nuys, California. As the movement grew, it spread to other Protestant churches, the Roman Catholic Church and finally to the Orthodox churches. It brought to many churches an experience of a revitalization of spiritual life.

The formation of a Charismatic prayer group among faculty members and students at Duquesne University (Pittsburgh) in 1967 is generally looked upon as the beginning of the Charismatic renewal in the Roman Catholic Church. A Pentecostal-type revival in the Lutheran Church of America in St. Paul, Minnesota, was the starting point for the entrance of the Charismatic movement into Lutheranism; under the leadership of Larry Christenson it became later widely known.

During the twentieth century, the Pentecostal/Charismatic movement became the largest single category in Protestantism.[4] "Its growth from zero to 400 million in ninety years is unprecedented in the whole of church history," states Walter J. Hollenweger.[5] If currently Roman Catholics are the largest Christian group, then classical Pentecostals are now the second largest and gaining fast. Catholics now number about one half of all Christians, while Pentecostals make up almost a quarter.

From its beginning, Pentecostalism has been characterized by variety, and therefore any kind of classifications are at best generalizations. One obvious

---

[3]Henry I. Lederle, *Treasures Old and New: Interpretations of "Spirit Baptism" in the Charismatic Renewal Movement* (Peabody, Mass.: Hendrickson, 1988), p. xiii, gives us a handy way to see the difference, mostly in terms of origins: "the most useful distinction between Pentecostal and Charismatic is whether they have their roots, as it were, in 1906, or 1960."

[4]L. Grant McClung Jr. states, "David Barrett's description of the Pentecostal/Charismatic tradition, now numbering more than 400 million and growing by 19 million a year and 54,000 a day, is that it comes in an 'amazing variety' of 38 major categories, 11,000 Pentecostal denominations and 3,000 independent Charismatic denominations spread across 8,000 ethnolinguistic cultures and 7,000 languages. A cross section of worldwide Pentecostalism reveals a composite international Pentecostal/Charismatic who is more urban than rural, more female than male, more Third World (66%) than Western world, more impoverished (87%) than affluent, more family oriented than individualistic, and, on the average younger than eighteen" ("Pentecostal/Charismatic Perspectives on a Missiology for the Twenty-First Century," *Pneuma* 16, no. 1 [1994]: 11).

[5]Walter J. Hollenweger, "From Azusa Street to the Toronto Phenomenon: Historical Roots of the Pentecostal Movement," *Concilium* 3 (1996): 3.

reason is its multicultural, multinational beginnings and growth in so many cultural settings.[6] Actually, we need to speak of Pentecostalisms rather than Pentecostalism (as a single phenomenon).[7]

## Dynamic, Charismatic Spirituality at the Center of Church Life

Pentecostalism represents a grassroots spiritual movement rather than a novel theological construction. It has not so much produced a new theology as a new kind of spirituality and aggressive new evangelism methods.

> The salient characteristic of Pentecostalism is its belief in the present-day manifestation of spiritual gifts, such as miraculous healing, prophecy and, most distinctively, glossolalia. Pentecostals affirm that these spiritual gifts (charismata) are granted by the Holy Spirit and are normative in contemporary church life and ministry.[8]

Many observers of the movement hold that the "revalorization of the Charismata"[9]—rather than theological analysis—entails the most important contribution of Pentecostalism and later Charismatic movements.[10] Pentecostalism has (re)introduced a dynamic, enthusiastic type of spirituality to the modern church.[11] The focus of Pentecostal spirituality is experiencing God mystically as supernatural. The category of experience is essential to understanding the spirituality of Pentecostals, and thus their worship. In the words of Daniel Albrecht, the researcher of Pentecostal spirituality:

> In a very real sense the Sunday services of . . . [Pentecostal] churches are designed to provide a context for a mystical *encounter*, an experience with the divine. This encounter is mediated by the sense of the immediate divine presence. The primary rites of worship and altar/response are particularly structured to sensitize

---

[6]For a recent discussion, see A. A. Anderson and W. J. Hollenweger, eds., *Pentecostals After a Century: Global Perspectives on a Movement in Transition* (Sheffield, U.K.: Sheffield Academic Press, 1999).

[7]Robeck, "Taking Stock of Pentecostalism," p. 45. For the variety of Pentecostal theologies, see Vinson Synan, "Pentecostalism: Varieties and Contributions," *Pneuma* 8, no. 2 (1986): 34-36.

[8]Jon Ruthven, *On the Cessation of the Charismata* (Sheffield, U.K.: Sheffield Academic Press, 1993), p. 14.

[9]Synan, "Pentecostalism," p. 36.

[10]Ibid., p. 37.

[11]For a definitive description of Pentecostal spirituality, see Daniel E. Albrecht, *Rites in the Spirit: A Ritual Approach to Pentecostal/Charismatic Spirituality* (Sheffield, U.K.: Sheffield Academic Press, 1999).

the congregants to the presence of the divine and to stimulate conscious experience of God. . . . The gestures, ritual actions, and symbols all function within this context to speak of the manifest presence.[12]

For Pentecostals, "worship" is another way of saying "presence of God."[13] Their worship service is an interesting mixture of spontaneity: exercise of spiritual gifts such as speaking in tongues, prophesying, prayer for healing; and attentiveness to the mystical encounter with God. The Holy Spirit is not the center of the worship. Jesus Christ and God, in the power of the Spirit, are the center. Often called "emotionalism" or "enthusiasm" by the public and scholars alike, the expressive worship of Pentecostalism carries on the tradition of Montanists, Anabaptists, Quakers, Shakers and other revival movements. This type of worship is often accompanied by singing in tongues, applause to the Lord, the raising of hands and the shouting of loud "amens" and "hallelujahs."[14]

Empowerment through the Spirit for witnessing and service are emphasized. Personal and mass evangelism receive high priority, perhaps the main factor accounting for the phenomenal growth of the movement. Pentecostal spirituality and worship emphasize the supernatural.

The Pentecostals envision a world subject to invasions by the supernatural element. Pentecostals teach adherents to expect encounters with the supernatural. . . . Claims of signs, wonders, and miracles are not limited to the regions of the Sunday ritual. They are to be a part of daily life.[15]

The identity of a Pentecostal theology that informs and shapes its ecclesiology can be characterized with the help of their preferred label, the "full gospel." This full gospel comprises five theological motifs:

1. justification by faith in Christ

2. sanctification by faith as a second definite work of grace

3. healing of the body as provided for all in the atonement

4. the premillennial return of Christ

5. the baptism in the Holy Spirit evidenced by speaking in tongues

This last motif came to be the most distinctive feature of classical Pentecos-

---

[12]Daniel E. Albrecht, "Pentecostal Spirituality: Looking through the Lens of Ritual," *Pneuma* 14, no. 2 (1996): 21.
[13]Ibid., p. 9.
[14]Synan, "Pentecostalism," p. 37.
[15]Albrecht, "Pentecostal Spirituality," p. 23.

talism.[16] Perhaps the "prophethood" of all believers could be added to the priesthood of all believers as a sixth motif.[17] Whether this fivefold (or sixfold) description of Pentecostalism is legitimate in the final analysis cannot be established in this presentation; the central point to note is the accent on lived Charismatic spirituality rather than on discursive theology.

Hollenweger has argued that the paradigm for defining Pentecostal identity must be understood even more broadly. His classic description includes the following aspects of Pentecostalism as forming its identity:

- orality of liturgy
- narrativity of theology and witness
- maximum participation at the level of reflection, prayer and decision making, and therefore a form of community that is reconciliatory
- inclusion of dreams and visions into personal and public forms of worship, functioning as a kind of icon for the individual and the community
- an understanding of the body/mind relationship that is informed by experiences of correspondence between body and mind, the most striking application being the ministry of healing by prayer[18]

## Pentecostal Ecclesiology: Is There Any?

The Catholic Paul D. Lee, an informed analyst of Pentecostalism, raises the question of whether it is reasonable to speak about a distinctive Pentecostal ecclesiology at all:

> If Pentecostalism is a movement, is it useful or valid to talk about ecclesiology at all? What does ecclesiology mean to a Pentecostal? At first, Pentecostals were so busy spreading the "good news" of the fresh outpouring of the Spirit "in the last days" that they became unconcerned about forming a denomination. The premillennial urgency of the imminent Kingdom made Pentecostals focus on their

---

[16]Steven J. Land, *Pentecostal Spirituality: A Passion for the Kingdom* (Sheffield, U.K.: Sheffield Academic Press, 1992), p. 18.

[17]Land, *Pentecostal Spirituality*, p. 18.

[18]W. J. Hollenweger, "After Twenty Years' Research on Pentecostalism," *International Review of Missions* 75 (January 1986): 6. He has presented this kind of list in numerous other writings too, and it has been enthusiastically cited by most of the observers of the movement, both insiders and outsiders. More recently, Hollenweger ("From Azusa Street," pp. 3-14) has summarized the "roots" of Pentecostalism in these terms: (1) the Black oral root; (2) the Catholic root; (3) the evangelical root; (4) the critical root; and (5) the ecumenical root. Hollenweger, "Verheissung und Verhängnis der Pfingtsbewegung," *Evangelische Theologie* 53, no. 3 (1993): 265-88. See also my *Pneumatology: The Holy Spirit in Ecumenical, International and Contextual Perspective* (Grand Rapids, Mich.: Baker, 2002, 87-98.

readiness, through personal conversion and regeneration, thereby rendering any ecclesiological deliberation rather irrelevant or at least secondary.[19]

This is a legitimate observation, especially since Pentecostals have written surprisingly little on ecclesiology, the only substantial contribution being the classic *A Theology of the Church and Its Mission: A Pentecostal Perspective* by M. L. Hodges.[20] Peter Hocken, in his article "Theology of Church" in *The Dictionary of Pentecostal and Charismatic Movements* (written by a Catholic theologian), notes that "the process of denominationalization did not . . . produce any distinctively Pentecostal view of the church, except for those bodies seeking to restore the fivefold ministry of Ephesians 4:11."[21] Understandably, Pentecostal ecclesiology is of an ad hoc nature which leaves much room for improvization.[22] Since most Pentecostals emphasize the spiritual, thus invisible, nature of the church, much of their writing has been on ecclesiastical polity that is characterized by the restorationist desire to go back to apostolic times.[23]

Lee is correct when he says that Pentecostal ecclesiology "is not so much a thematized theology as a lived reality"; therefore, the answer to the question above "will almost certainly not be met with a theologically satisfactory answer."[24] But this does not mean in any way that ecclesiology is of little importance or that it is a luxury added to personal spirituality.[25]

Providentially, in 1972 the Pentecostals entered into an international dialogue with the Roman Catholic Church. This extended dialogue has forced Pentecostals to reflect on the church and its life and ministry. While ecclesiological topics were occasionally discussed during the earlier phases of the

---

[19]Paul D. Lee, *Pneumatological Ecclesiology in the Roman Catholic-Pentecostal Dialogue: A Catholic Reading of the Third Quinquennium (1985-1989)* (Dissertatio Ad Lauream in Facultate S. Theologiae Apud Pontificiam Universitatem S. Thomae in Urbe, Rome, 1994), p. 15.

[20]Peter Kuzmic and Miroslav Volf ("Communio Sanctorum: Toward a Theology of the Church as a Fellowship of Persons," a position paper read at the International Roman Catholic-Pentecostal Dialogue, Riano, Italy, May 21-26, 1985 [unpublished], p. 2), however, remark that the lack of writings on ecclesiology is not limited just to Pentecostals but also includes evangelicals at large. For a recent attempt to construe an evangelical ecclesiology, see George Vandervelde, "Ecclesiology in the Breach: Evangelical Soundings," *Evangelical Review of Theology* 23, no. 1 (1999): 29-51.

[21]Peter Hocken, "Theology of Church," in *The Dictionary of Pentecostal and Charismatic Movements*, ed. S. M. Burgess and G. B. McGee (Grand Rapids, Mich.: Zondervan, 1988), p. 213.

[22]Michael Harper, "The Holy Spirit Acts in the Church, Its Structures, Its Sacramentality, Its Worship and Sacraments," *One in Christ* 12 (1976): 322.

[23]Lee, *Pneumatological Ecclesiology*, p. 16.

[24]Ibid., pp. 16-17.

[25]Ibid., p. 17.

talks, the third quinquennium (1985-1989) was devoted to the theme of the church under the general title of *koinonia*.[26] It has helped Pentecostals to explicate their understanding of the doctrine of the church.

One of the perennial problems of ecclesiology has been the relationship between the Spirit/charisma and institution.[27] Understandably, the Catholic Church has emphasized more the role of hierarchy, ordained ministry, church authority and sacramental apparatus, whereas Pentecostalism, as a recent revival movement, has sought for the experience of a free flow of charisms in the church. However, Pentecostals were ready to go beyond the all-too-simplified dichotomy of "charisma *versus* institution" to a more fruitful notion of church which is *both* Charismatic *and* has structure.

The dialogue reveals to us that Pentecostal ecclesiology is not naive enough to downplay the role of authority/structures, nor is Catholic ecclesiology content with an overemphasis on hierarchy. In addition, Pentecostals do not agree among themselves concerning how church structures and institutions should be made up. The views range from congregational to episcopal,[28] but what is important is that they accept the full ecclesial status of the churches ordered in various ways. For Pentecostals there is no single criterion to indicate the "true nature" of a given church.[29] Their view is based on the observation that the New Testament does not seem to show us *the* structure but several structures.[30]

## The Church as a Charismatic Fellowship

As already mentioned, the third quinquennial Catholic-Pentecostal talks were focused on *koinonia*, the leading theme in ecumenical ecclesiology since the 1980s. Even though until recently Pentecostals have not participated in that discussion, they have always favored fellowship language for the church. Decades before ecumenical theology began to hark back to biblical and patristic

---

[26]For a detailed analysis, see Veli-Matti Kärkkäinen, *Spiritus Ubi Vult Spirat: Pneumatology in Roman Catholic-Pentecostal Dialogue (1972-1989)* (Schriften der Luther-Agricola-Gesellscahft 42; Helsinki: Luther-Agricola Society, 1998), pp. 234-330 especially; and Lee, *Pneumatological Ecclesiology.*

[27]See further Luigi Sartori, "The Structure of Juridical and Charismatic Power in the Christian Community," *Concilium* 109 (New York: Seabury, 1978), pp. 38-55.

[28]Harper ("The Holy Spirit," p. 324) argues that Pentecostals have shown, on the whole, little originality when they have come to establish ecclesial structures.

[29]"Final Report of the Dialogue between the Secretariat for Promoting Christian Unity of the Roman Catholic Church and Some Classical Pentecostals," *Information Service* 55 (1984/2-3), #84.

[30]Ibid.

roots to revive the ancient theological understanding of Christian community as *koinonia,* Pentecostals lived fellowship among Spirit-filled sisters and brothers. Pentecostal spirituality and theology have almost from the start appreciated fellowship language over "institutionalized church" (as hierarchical structure).[31] "Pentecostal soteriology and pneumatology point . . . unmistakably in the direction of an *ecclesiology of the fellowship of persons.*"[32]

The Pentecostal dialogue team sought to develop a Pentecostal view of the church as Charismatic fellowship, a pneumatologically constituted reality. This is what they see emphasized in the New Testament picture of the church: "fellowship was *a common experience of baptism into the body of Christ through the Spirit* (cf. 1 Cor 12.13)."[33] This fellowship is something to be experienced, a shared experience in the everyday life of the community. In this sense the question "Where is the church?" cannot be answered without reference to the living presence of the Spirit.[34]

According to Pentecostal ecclesiology, there are three basic models: first, the traditional Protestant "lecture room" setting where the focus is on pulpit and preaching; second, the Catholic Church as a "theater setting" where the emphasis falls on the dramatic elements of worship; third, the Pentecostal "fellowship" where the emphasis is on the community gathered together for mutual edification. Without wanting to exclude the elements of preaching and sacraments, they suggest that in the New Testament the fundamental characteristic of worship is mutual sharing in the fellowship. God communicates himself to Christians through more than just written or proclaimed word or ritual cultic activity: "he does so more by the Spirit *through one another.*"[35] Quoting Lesslie Newbigin, they say "that a real congregational life, wherein each member has his opportunity to contribute to the life of the whole body through gifts which the Spirit endows him, is as much part of the *esse* (essence) of the church as are ministry and sacraments."[36] The dynamic of the fellowship is concretely lived out through the charismata. "As fellowship should be the unalienable modus of the church's existence, so the charismata should be a permanent feature of its life."[37]

---

[31]Ibid., #10.

[32]Kuzmic and Volf, "Communio Sanctorum," p. 2, emphasis in original.

[33]Ibid., p. 14, emphasis in original.

[34]Ibid., p. 4.

[35]Ibid., p. 5, emphasis in original.

[36]Kuzmic and Volf, "Communio Sanctorum," p. 16, quoting Newbigin, *The Household of God: Lectures on the Nature of the Church* (London: SCM Press, 1953), p. 106.

[37]Kuzmic and Volf, "Communio Sanctorum," p. 16.

If every member of the community is provided with the charisms and they depend on each other in their exercise of them, then the hierarchical structures and the question of obedience to authority should be reevaluated, Kuzmic and Volf argue.[38] But the emphasis on the charismatically structured church does not mean stressing charismata at the expense of structure and institutions. "This would be," the authors note, "both sociologically and historically naive."[39] They say that history teaches us the lesson that the movements that broke through the calcified church structures soon developed their own structures and institutions.[40]

## Distinctive Features of Charismatic Movements' Ecclesiologies

Although Pentecostalism and the Charismatic movements share basic commonalities, there are also definite differences. This is understandable in view of the fact that Charismatic theologies are shaped by their respective church traditions.[41] For example, the Catholic Charismatic movement is shaped as much or more by its commitment to the Catholic Church as it is by its commitment to a type of spiritual experience.[42]

Pentecostalism represents a revival movement with a restorationist tendency and consequently a low view of history and tradition. In contrast, the Charismatic theologies usually pay much more attention to tradition and go back to the historical roots of their traditions. Catholic Charismatics especially often remind us of the fact that spiritual gifts have never been absent from the life of the church, finding examples (even of "singing in the Spirit") throughout their history.

Furthermore, Charismatic Christians usually have more focus on community than do their Pentecostal counterparts. They have a greater sense of community life, something especially true for Charismatics in more sacramental

---

[38]Ibid., p. 21.

[39]Ibid., p. 22.

[40]Ibid., p. 23.

[41]For basic documents, see Kilian McDonnell, ed., *Presence, Power, Praise: Documents on the Charismatic Renewal*, 3 vols. (Collegeville, Minn.: Liturgical Press, 1980).

[42]See further Francis A. Sullivan, "Catholic Charismatic Renewal," in *The Dictionary of Pentecostal and Charismatic Movements*, pp. 110-25; Kilian McDonnell, "Catholic Charismatic Renewal and Classical Pentecostalism: Growth and Critique of a Systematic Suspicion," *One in Christ* 23 (1987): 36-61; Kilian McDonnell, ed., *The Holy Spirit and Power: The Catholic Charismatic Renewal* (Garden City, N.Y.: Doubleday, 1975); Kilian McDonnell, *Charismatic Renewal and Churches* (New York: Seabury, 1976); Kilian McDonnell, *Charismatic Renewal and Ecumenism* (New York: Paulist, 1978).

denominations. The Spirit is seen as working through tradition, which carries and interprets divine revelation. The new experience of the Spirit is interpreted in light of Scripture and tradition. Believing that the Spirit has been at work throughout the history of the church, Charismatics search for the continuity between their new experience and the faith handed down. For example, in the Catholic renewal movement, the Spirit is also seen at work through the seven sacraments of the church, all of which depend on the grace of God and the faith of the recipient (or the faith of the parents in the case of infant baptism).

It has also been characteristic of the Charismatic movement to develop theology from the beginning. They aim to show how their experience adds to and can be a part of their traditional theology, rather than turning them against it. Congar is concerned about the fact that in many Charismatic theologies there is an unhealthy opposition between "charism" and "institution,"[43] which is certainly true of Pentecostalism.

## Salient Features of Pentecostal/Charismatic Ecclesiologies

Eastern Orthodox (then Anglican) priest Michael Harper of England has characterized the contribution of Pentecostal/Charismatic church life in these terms:

1. The important role of the Holy Spirit in giving life and power to the individual and through the individual to the Church and world.

2. The active participation of the whole assembly of God's people in acts of worship and administrations of the sacraments.

3. The release of the laity in ministry in the Church and world, and their active role in all parts of church life.

4. The importance of the local church as the gathering of the people of God, to be a corporate expression of Christ's life to the world.

5. The experience of Charismatic actions of God. A kind of quasisacramentalism, actively at work in people's lives.

6. The restoration of experiential apostolicity to the whole Church. The Roman Catholic Church has stressed its apostolic nature largely in historical terms, apostolic succession and all that. Protestant Churches moved the emphasis to doctrine in an attempt to restore the apostles' teaching to the Church. . . . The Pentecostal contribution has been in the restoration of the apostolic signs—healing, miracles, prophecy, speaking in tongues and so on.

7. The Pentecostals' greatest contribution may yet be assessed in terms of their

---

[43]Congar, *I Believe in the Holy Spirit*, especially 2:165-69.

ability to instill indigenous principles from the start in the Third World, which in part accounts for the remarkable growth. Whereas historic church missionary endeavors in the nineteenth century were carried out in the atmosphere of empire-building and the westernizing of other cultures, Pentecostal outreach has very largely been free from such taints.[44]

There is no denying the fact that with its distinctive, often controversial testimony Pentecostal/Charismatic Christianity has immensely influenced the rest of Christendom. In recent years, for example, the older churches have come to appreciate the Pentecostal dynamism and desire to capture some of it in their liturgical forms, as was evident, for example, in the WCC Assembly at Canberra (1991) and the World Missions Conference at San Antonio (1989).

---

[44]Harper, "Holy Spirit Acts," p. 323.

# 7

# The Church as One

## THE ECUMENICAL MOVEMENT ECCLESIOLOGIES

### The Challenge of Ecumenism for the Church

The purpose and agenda of the ecumenical movement in principle is simple and straightforward: it is the community of all who believe in Christ, and so it purports to promote the unity of Christians and churches.[1] If the church is the church of Christ, and since there is only one Christ, then unity belongs to the nature of the church. The third Assembly of the World Council of Churches (WCC) at New Delhi (1961) anchors the unity of the church in the unity of the triune God:

> The love of the Father and the Son in the unity of the Holy Spirit is the source and goal of the unity which the triune God wills for all men and creation. We believe that we share in this unity in the Church of Jesus Christ. . . . The reality of this unity was made manifest at Pentecost in the gift of the Holy Spirit, through whom we know in this present age the first fruits of that perfect union of the Son with his Father, which will be known in its fullness only when all things are consummated by Christ in his glory.[2]

In other words, the unity of the church is not primarily a human effort but rather is given from God and as such mandatory for all Christians. This is the very basic ecumenical conviction that guides the work for Christian unity at all levels. That is the confession of the credo of the early churches: "one, holy, catholic, and apostolic church" (Nicene Creed). "In brief, the New Testament does not speak of the church without, at the same time, speaking of its unity.

---

[1]For a classic definition of the term *ecumenism* and various facets of its meaning, see W. A. Visser 't Hooft, "The Basis: Its History and Significance," *The Ecumenical Review* 2 (1985): 86.

[2]"New Delhi Section on Unity," in *A Documentary History of the Faith and Order Movement 1927-1963*, ed. L. Vischer (St. Louis: Bethany, 1963), p. 144.

Thus the unity of the church is a matter of Christian faith and confession and not something subject to our disposition or a matter of considerations of mere utility."[3]

In its most comprehensive meaning, the term "ecumenism" refers not only to the relationships between the churches but also between religions and finally to the unity of all humankind under one God. Wolfhart Pannenberg, among others, has championed this last aspect in his insistence that the church of God on earth is a sign pointing toward the unity of all men and women at the eschaton. The Catholic Hans Küng has argued that there are two directions in ecumenical work, namely *ad intra*, in relation to other churches, and *ad extra*, in relation to other world religions.[4]

However, two conflicting sets of opinions about the status of the ecumenical movement are heard currently.[5] On the one hand, most churches demonstrate a genuine willingness to commit themselves to pursuing the oneness of the churches. On the other hand, following the enthusiasm of the first three decades or so after the establishment of the formal ecumenical venue in terms of the WCC in 1948, many influential voices openly talk about a crisis.[6] It is not

---

[3]Harding Meyer, *That All May Be One: Perceptions and Models of Ecumenicity* (Grand Rapids, Mich.: Eerdmans, 1999), p. 8. In New Testament scholarship the main orientation holds that regardless of all differences between various ecclesiologies of the New Testament, there is still a united core (e.g., Raymond Brown). Ernst Kasemann has challenged this assumption and wondered whether the witness of the New Testament gives support for the search for unity. Risto Saarinen, *Johdatus Ekumeniikkaan* (Helsinki: Kirjaneliö, 1994), pp. 22, 23. See also James Dunn, *Unity and Diversity in the New Testament* (London: SPCK, 1977).

[4]Hans Küng, *Theologie in Aufbruch: Eine Ökumenishce Grundlegung* (Munich: Kaiser Verlag, 1987), p. 246.

[5]The best introduction to various facets of ecumenism and the ecumenical movement is *The Dictionary of the Ecumenical Movement*, ed. Nicholas Lossky et al. (Geneva, Switzerland: WCC Publications, 1991). For the history, see *A Documentary History of the Faith and Order Movement: 1927-1963*, ed. Lukas Vischer (St. Louis: Bethany, 1963); and *A Documentary History of Faith and Order: 1963-1993*, ed. Gunther Gassman (Geneva, Switzerland: WCC Publications, 1993). For a collection of the most important ecumenical documents, see *Growth in Agreement and Agreed Statements of Ecumenical Conversations on a World Level*, ed. Harding Meyer and Lukas Vischer (New York: Paulist, 1984). For the key texts, see *The Ecumenical Movement: An Anthology of Key Texts and Voices*, ed. Michael Kinnamon and Brian E. Cope (Grand Rapids, Mich.: Eerdmans, 1997).

[6]A new book on the ecumenical movement by one of the leading ecumenists has this to say: "The signs of a deterioration of the ecumenical urgency are immense. There is a palpable decrease of common interest in ecumenical themes, events, and publications. The underlying loss in ecumenical motivation is connected with a disdain for the ecumenical achievement and an uncertainty of ecumenical orientation. Reservation and resistance, with which the ecumenical movement had always to struggle, gain new power" (Meyer, *That All May Be One*, p. 152). For a position paper produced at the Institute for Ecumenical Research in Strasbourg, France, see *Crisis and Challenge of the Ecumenical Movement: Integrity and Indivisibility* (Geneva, Switzerland: WCC Publications, 1994).

easy to come to a right understanding of the nature and current state of the ecumenical movement since it is not, and never was, a unified and homogenous
phenomenon. Diverse motivations sustain it and they find expression in differing ways of seeking unity, "in differing 'movements,' all of which together
constitute 'the' ecumenical movement."[7]

Overall, there has been a radical scaling down of what unity implies.[8] Since
the proposal from Oscar Cullman of unity through diversity—in which the
New Testament metaphor of the members of the body is taken out of the context of the local congregation and applied to present denominations[9]—we
have heard expressions like "ecumenism in oppositions" (*Ökumene in Gegensätzen*)[10] and, most paradoxical of all, "ecumenism without unity."[11]

What complicates and challenges the ecumenical work is the fact that, understandably, Christians and churches introduce into the ecumenical movement their own specific understanding of the church and the kind of unity they
find theologically and ecclesiastically correct. Ecclesiology determines one's
view of ecumenism: what one believes about the church and its ecclesiality carries over into one's approach to the challenge of unity. However, it is important
to see that this confrontation of different understandings of unity takes place
within the ecumenical movement. This means that the differences in the understandings of unity do not necessarily prevent the commonality of the ecumenical effort.[12] To these different perceptions of unity we turn next.

## Different Perceptions of the Unity of the Church

For the oldest Christian church, the Orthodox Church, it is not easy to define
an official ecumenical standpoint for the simple reason that we lack any official
pronouncements. What is determinative, however, is the pain of existing
schisms in the church. The unity of the church has been broken time after

---

[7]See further Meyer, *That All May Be One*, p. 2.
[8]A succinct introduction to ecumenical models and ways of unity is offered by Thomas Best,
"Models of Unity," and "Ways to Unity," in *The Dictionary of the Ecumenical Movement*, pp.
1041-43 and 1043-47 respectively.
[9]Oscar Cullman, *Einheit durch Vielfalt* (Tübingen: Mohr, 1986).
[10]Erich Geldbach, *Ökumene in Gegensätzen*, Bemsheimer Heft 66 (Göttingen: Vandenhoek &
Ruprecht, 1987).
[11]Reformed ecumenist Henry I. Lederle of South Africa calls this model the "cheapest," without any meaning ("The Spirit of Unity: A Discomforting Comforter: Some Reflections on the
Holy Spirit, Ecumenism and the Pentecostal-Charismatic Movements," *The Ecumenical Review* 42, nos. 3-4 [1990]: 291).
[12]See further Meyer, *That All May Be One*, p. 7.

time.[13] The very minimum for Orthodox Christians to overcome these painful divisions is the apostolic succession of the episcopacy and sacramental priesthood, and the apostolic tradition as formulated in the ancient creeds.[14] The Orthodox Church also argues that "the unity of the church [is] grounded in its foundation by our Lord Jesus Christ and in the communion of the Holy Trinity and in the sacraments." Where can this unity be found? According to the Orthodox interpretation, this "unity is expressed through the apostolic succession and the patristic tradition and has been lived up to the present day within the Orthodox Church."[15]

Another ancient Christian family, the Roman Catholic Church, has definitively defined its understanding of Christian unity in the Second Vatican Council (1962-1965). According to *Lumen Gentium* (Dogmatic Constitution on the Church) and *Unitatis Redintegratio*, (Decree on Ecumenism), the Eucharist is the visible expression of Christian unity, and the Spirit is the principle of the church's unity. The unity comes to visible manifestation under these conditions:

> It is through the faithful preaching of the Gospel by the Apostles and their successors—the bishops with Peter's successor as their head—through their administrating the sacraments, and through their governing in love, that Jesus Christ wishes his people to increase under the action of the Holy Spirit; and he perfects its fellowship in unity; in their confession of faith; in the common celebration of divine worship; and in the fraternal harmony of the family of God.[16]

Bishops, among whom the Bishop of Rome (the Pope) has the primacy, are the guardians of the unity of the church in the Catholic understanding of ecumenism.[17] The Roman Catholic Church makes the bold claim that the unity of the church already "exists" within herself, and therefore expects that other churches will "return" to that church. Even though this mentality of the "return of separated brethren" was qualified by Vatican II, it still is part of the Catholic ecumenical view. "The unity, we believe, subsists in the Catholic Church as something she can never lose, and we hope that it will continue to increase until the end of time."[18]

---

[13]For a recent, helpful survey, see Meyer, *That All May Be One*, pp. 15-36. I am also indebted to Saarinen, *Johdatus ekumeniikkaan*, pp. 81-110, 113-21.

[14]See further C. G. Patelos, ed., *The Orthodox Church in the Ecumenical Movement* (Geneva, Switzerland: World Council of Churches, 1978).

[15]The statement of The Third Panorthodox Pre-Conciliar Conference in Chambesy, Switzerland, 1986, in *Episkepsis* no. 369 (December 1968).

[16]*Unitatis Redintegratio* 2.

[17]See further *Lumen Gentium*, especially 23.

The churches of the Reformation have also stipulated a very minimum for Christian unity, namely, the preaching of the Word of God and the right administering of the sacraments. This is the position of the Lutheran Church as formulated in the Augsburg Confession #7 (the same principle is to be found also in the Reformed Second Helvetic Confession #17):

> It is also taught, that one holy Christian church must always be and remain, which is the assembly of all believers, among whom the gospel is purely preached and the holy sacraments are administered according to the gospel. For it is sufficient for the true unity of the Christian church, that the gospel harmoniously is preached and the sacraments administered according to the Word of God. And it is not necessary for the true unity of the church, that everywhere the same ceremonies established by human beings be observed.

As long as there is basic unanimity in the understanding of the gospel, then church structures, liturgies, leadership patterns and other outer things may differ. Even though the personal faith of individuals is not a matter of indifference, unity can never be based on it.

For the Anglican Communion, as explicated in the "Thirty-nine Articles" (#19 and #34) of 1563 and 1571, the unity of the churches is also based on the preaching of the Word of God and the sacraments. However, the later "Chicago-Lambeth Quadrilateral" from 1870 went further in its specifications regarding unity and outlined four aspects: Scripture, the Apostles' Creed, the two sacraments and the episcopate.[19] Whereas the Reformation churches leave the leadership question open, for Anglicans the unity of the church requires the presence of a bishop.

The youngest Christian churches, the Free churches, have entertained many kinds of suspicions, even doubts, concerning the idea of ecumenism. The guiding principle for them has been the idea of "spiritual union" according to which the God-given unity already exists between either "true" churches or at least "true" individual believers. The Free churches have not located unity in either creeds or even the Bible, although for most of them these two have been very important, but rather in the believing hearts of individuals.[20]

---

[18]*Unitatis Redintegratio* 4.

[19]*The Book of Common Prayer*, Historical Documents of the Church, Lambeth Conference of 1888, Resolution 11.

[20]For the understanding of unity among the largest Free church, the Pentecostals, see Veli-Matti Kärkkäinen, *Spiritus ubi vult spirat: Pneumatology in the Roman Catholic-Pentecostal Dialogue 1972-1989*, Schriften der Luther-Agricola Gesellschaft 42 (Helsinki: Luther-Agricola

The Unions of Baptist Congregations in Austria and Switzerland and the Union of Evangelical-Free churches in Germany defined their understanding in the following way:

> The Christian experiences the communion of the community above all in the local assembly of the faithful. In it baptism for the confession of faith is performed, and the one bread, bestowed by the one Lord, is broken and shared. That is why the local parish understands itself as the manifestation of the one body of Christ, filled with the one Spirit and fulfilled with the one hope.[21]

Four aspects of this unity are highlighted in the Free churches: first, the personal faith of every Christian; second, the local church as the focus; third, the priesthood of all believers; and fourth, reservations with regard to the idea of visible unity.[22]

In summary, the various views of unity among Christian churches have a common foundation with regard to two main aspects: All churches want to ground the unity of the church in the unity of the triune God and the apostolic tradition as conveyed to us in the Bible and creeds. On the other hand, the churches are divided about two aspects: There are churches that regard episcopacy (and sacramental ministry) as essential (Orthodox and Catholics). Some churches regard episcopacy in general (Orthodox and Anglicans) or the papacy in particular (Roman Catholics) as mandatory, while Protestant churches leave the question of leadership open. Furthermore, the Free churches think that the personal faith of individuals is the key to unity, whereas all other churches—while not denying the role of personal faith—ground unity in the church and tradition.

The most hotly debated ecumenical question has been, and in many quarters continues to be, the nature of unity, whether it would be visible or defined in some other terms.

## Visible Union: Doubts and Potential

With the exception of most Free churches, almost all other Christian churches currently regard visible unity as the desired goal of ecumenism. Understand-

---

Society, 1998), chap. 5. For the Baptists, see William L. Pitts, "The Relation of Baptists to Other Churches," in *The People of God: Essays on the Believers' Church*, ed. Paul Basden and David S. Dockery (Nashville: Broadman, 1991), pp. 235-50.

[21]Bund Evangelisch-Freikirchlicher Gemeinden in Deutschland, ed., *Rechenschaft vom Glauben* 2, no. 7 (1977). This issue was edited by the Unions of Baptist Congregations in Austria and Switzerland and the Union of Evangelical-Free churches in Germany to define their understanding of unity.

[22]Meyer, *That All May Be One*, pp. 24-27.

ings of what makes unity visible may differ, but the overall goal is clear; this goal has been called the "ecumenical imperative." Since 1975, the WCC has defined as its first function and purpose "visible unity in one faith and in one eucharistic fellowship expressed in worship and in common life in Christ."[23] Even though this idea is not novel, it has gained importance during the past two or three decades.

Several reservations and misunderstandings exist about the nature of the desired visible unity. Some fear that the concept of "visible unity" is nothing more than a unified church organization. Others think that visible unity is distinct from or an alternative to "invisible," "spiritual" unity. Still others believe that the one church of Christ has already reached the visible realization of unity in at least their own church and therefore the unity sought is rather in the form of "reuniting" separated churches.[24]

To rightly understand this goal of ecumenism, one must keep in mind the fact that this concept seeks to preserve the distinction between God-given unity as gift and the human response to God's action and desire. Consequently, it is not the task of the ecumenical movement—or any other human organization for that matter—to create unity between the churches, but rather to give form to the unity already created by God. In other words, since God has created one church of Christ on earth, let Christians then live up to that fact in empirical life.

In addition, visible unity should not be confused with uniformity. The *Porvoo Common Statement* between Lutherans and Anglicans, for example, expresses this truth in no unclear terms:

> Unity in Christ does not exist despite and in opposition to diversity, but is given with and in diversity. Because this diversity corresponds with the many gifts of the Holy Spirit to the Church, it is a concept of fundamental ecclesial importance, with relevance to all aspects of the life of the Church, and is not a mere concession to theological pluralism. Both the unity and the diversity of the Church are ultimately grounded in the communion of God the Holy Trinity.[25]

## Communion Ecclesiology

"We believe in the Holy Spirit, the holy catholic church, the communion of

---

[23]Ibid., p. 10. The present constitution on Faith and Order (#2) says the same.

[24]Meyer, *That All May Be One*, pp. 13-15.

[25]*The Porvoo Common Statement*, Conversations between the British and Irish Anglican Churches and the Nordic and Baltic Lutheran Churches, 1992 (London: Council for Christian Unity of the General Synod of the Church of England, 1993), p. 23.

saints." With this quote from the Apostles' Creed begins a recent ecumenical document, "Toward a Lutheran Understanding of Communion"[26] which elaborates the Lutheran World Federation's (LWF) self-understanding as a "communion of churches." The *Final Report* (1985-1989) of the International Dialogue between the Roman Catholic Church and Pentecostal churches opens with an important mutual affirmation (#29):

> Both Pentecostals and Roman Catholics believe that the *koinonia* between Christians is rooted in the life of Father, Son and Holy Spirit. Furthermore, they believe that this trinitarian life is the highest expression of the unity to which we together aspire: "That which we have seen and heard we proclaim also to you, so that you may have fellowship with us; and our fellowship is with the Father and with his Son Jesus Christ" (1 Jn 1:3).

At the same time, the unity/communion of the persons of the Trinity is the highest expression of unity for Christians. This is the "deepest meaning of *koinonia*," the *Final Report* (1985-1989, #70) states, echoing the foundational sayings of *Unitatis Redintegratio* and *Lumen Gentium*.[27]

These two recent examples are but the tip of the iceberg. They show evidence of the fact that the leading theme in the ecclesiologies of the ecumenical movement has been *koinonia*-ecclesiology. "*Koinonia* is the fundamental understanding of the Church emerging from the bilateral dialogues," summarizes a recent WCC document.[28] In fact, it is amazing that living as we are in a pluralistic age, a specific paradigm such as *koinonia* is able to establish itself as the dominant ecumenical perspective. This is one of the few orientations most Christian churches have gladly embraced in recent years, from the Orthodox, to the Roman Catholic, to the Lutheran and other Protestant

---

[26]"Toward a Lutheran Understanding of Communion: A Contribution by Working Group on Ecclesiology," #1 in *The Church as Communion*, ed. Heindrich Holze, Lutheran World Federation Documentation No. 42, 1997 (parallel edition in German: *Die Kirche als Gemeinschaft: Lutherische Beiträge zur Ekklesiologie*) (Geneva, Switzerland: LWF Publications, 1997), pp. 13-30. For a careful analysis of Luther's understanding of *koinonia*, see Simo Peura, "Die Kirche als geistliche Communio bei Luther," in *Der Heilige Geist: Ökumenische und Reformatorische Untersuchungen*, ed. Joachin Heubach, Veröffentlichungen der Luther-Akademie Ratzeburg 25 (Erlangen: Martin-Luther Verlag, 1996), pp. 131-56.

[27]See the opening paragraphs of *Lumen Gentium* (The Dogmatic Constitution on the Church); *Unitatis Redintegratio* (The Constitution on Ecumenism), #2.

[28]*Fifth Forum on International Bilateral Conversations: Report* (Geneva, Switzerland: WCC Publications, 1991), p. 46. For a recent survey, see Risto Saarinen, "The Concept of Communion in Ecumenical Dialogues," and "East-West Dialogue and the Theology of Communion," in *The Church as Communion*, ed. Heindrich Holze (Geneva, Switzerland: LWF Publications, 1997), pp. 287-337.

churches, to even some Free churches.[29]

Both the New Testament and the patristic tradition attests to the centrality of the idea of communion for the understanding of the church.[30] In its
basic meaning, the term *koinonia/communion* denotes "a sharing in one reality held in common." Synonyms for *koinonia* are *sharing, participation,
community,* and *communion.* The church is a communion in the Spirit since
it is the Spirit of Christ that unites all Christians together into one church.
The centrality of a pneumatological perspective in the New Testament
communion ecclesiology is well illustrated in the title of a book by Catholic
ecclesiologists Michael Lawler and Thomas J. Shanahan: *Church: A Spirited
Communion.*[31]

One of the essential characteristics of *koinonia*-ecclesiology—a perspective
crucial to the pursuit of the oneness of the church—is the avoidance of an all-
or-nothing proposition. It allows for degrees. "It zeroes in on unacceptable division, while at the same time acknowledging the measure of unity that does
exist within diversity."[32] This is exactly what *Unitatis Redintegratio* (#3) of Vatican II admits when it speaks of "a certain but imperfect communion" between
the Roman Church and other churches. This observation carries with it enormous ecumenical potential:

> The recognition of this reality opens the way for working toward greater unity,
> without demanding uniformity, along with the train of impoverishment that a
> simple fusion of Churches entails. To put it crassly, *koinonia* packs enough punch
> to uncover the present division of the Church as a scandal, and enough biblical
> realism to do something about it.[33]

### Proselytism and Common Witness

Proselytism has become one of the "hot topics" of ecumenical ecclesiology

---

[29]For a brief but helpful survey, see "The Church as Communion," in *The Catholicity of Reformation,* ed. Carl E. Braaten and Robert W. Jenson (Grand Rapids, Mich.: Eerdmans, 1996),
pp. 1-12.

[30]For a full list of *koinonia* texts and exegesis in the New Testament, see George Panikulam,
*Koinonia in the New Testament: Expression of Christian Life* (Rome: Biblical Institute, 1979).

[31]Michael Lawler and Thomas J. Shanahan, *Church: A Spirited Communion* (Collegeville,
Minn.: Liturgical Press, 1995); for pneumatological elaborations of New Testament ecclesiology, see also "Toward a Lutheran Understanding of Communion," #8-11.

[32]George Vandervelde, "Koinonia Ecclesiology: Ecumenical Breakthrough," *One in Christ* 29
(1993): 133.

[33]Ibid., p. 133; so also Catholic Susan Wood, "Communion Ecclesiology: Source of Hope,
Source of Controversy," *Pro Ecclesia* 2, no. 4 (1993): 428.

and missiology in recent years. It is, understandably, a concern of older, more established historic churches. Usually proselytizing charges come from the older churches who claim for themselves the right to define what *proselytism* means. Often younger churches, those regarded by others as "proselytizers," have not been invited to participate in discussions on the subject, nor is it readily apparent that they are particularly concerned to address the subject themselves. The evangelizing activities of, for example, many Free churches and their numerous outreach organizations have been effective to the point that older churches have become concerned about losing numerous members as a result.

The Santiago Faith and Order meeting issued probably the most adequate explanation in relation to newer groups and charges against their proselytizing action: "[We] believe that most groups and persons who are engaged in such activities do so out of a genuine concern for the salvation to whom they address." The same statement, however, continues with a plea for dialogue in order for some methods and intentions to be challenged by other churches.[34]

Already in 1954 the WCC originated a study, "Proselytism and Religious Freedom." Two years later, an influential document, *Christian Witness, Proselytism and Religious Freedom*, was drafted and recommended to member churches in the 1961 meeting. The earlier Toronto declaration, *The Church, the Churches and the World Council of Churches* (1950), was one of the first ecumenical attempts to define proselytism among the WCC member churches and in relation to the Roman Catholic Church. In the 1960s, the Roman Catholic Church drafted the Vatican II document *Dignitatis Humanae*, which addresses, among other topics, religious freedom and proselytism. In 1970 the WCC produced another joint document, *Common Witness and Proselytism*.

Of the older churches, the Roman Catholic Church has been the most active to begin discussing this delicate topic in mutual dialogues with other churches: the Orthodox Church[35] and younger Christian families such as

---

[34]*On the Way to Fuller Koinonia: Official Report of the Fifth World Conference on Faith and Order*, ed. T. F. Best and G. Gassmann, Faith and Order Paper No. 166 (Geneva, Switzerland: WCC Publications, 1994), p. 257.

[35]"Uniatism, Method of Union of the Past, and the Present Search for Full Communion," Joint International Commission for the Theological Dialogue between the Roman Catholic Church and the Orthodox Church: Seventh Plenary Session, Balamand School of Theology, Lebanon, June 17-24, 1993, *Information Service* 83 (1993): 95-99.

evangelicals,[36] Baptists[37] and Pentecostals.[38] At the multilateral level, the Joint Working Group between the Roman Catholic Church and the WCC has recently (in 1996) published a study document entitled *The Challenge of Proselytism and the Calling to Common Witness.*

According to the joint document *Common Witness and Proselytism,* the concept of proselytism covers all inappropriate attempts at conversion that violate the individual's right to religious freedom and prevent him or her from making a religious decision in freedom.[39] The document encourages the avoidance of actions and attitudes that might be rightly considered proselytism: every kind of violence, moral constraint, pressure, use of material benefits, other kinds of inducements and so on.[40] It is noteworthy that rather than speaking extensively about the negative sides of proselytism, the document begins by explaining the positive qualities of witness: witness must proceed from the Spirit of love, it must be concerned for the good of God and human beings, not for that of a single community, and it must leave the addressee with full freedom to make a personal decision.[41] The document titled *Common Witness,* produced by the Joint Working Group (1982), develops and makes more concrete these basic guidelines. In the Orthodox-Catholic *Balamand Report,* the division of the churches is presented as a "situation which is contrary to the nature of the Church" ("Uniatism," #6). The importance of *koinonia* is emphasized (#13) as well as the principle of religious freedom (#15). The joint document urges the churches to forgive the past misgivings and move toward unity and common witness (#20ff.).

In opposition to what many Christians believe (especially the newer, more evangelistically minded Christian churches and groups), the discussion on proselytism is not meant to downplay or hinder evangelization but rather to

---

[36]"Evangelical and Roman Catholic Dialogue on Mission, 1977-1984: A Report," *International Bulletin of Missionary Research* 10, no.1 (1986): 2-21; available in book form in *The Evangelical Roman Catholic Dialogue on Mission, 1977-1984,* ed. John R. Stott and Basil Meeking (Grand Rapids, Mich.: Eerdmans, 1986).

[37]"Summons to Witness to Christ in Today's World: A Report of the Baptist-Roman Catholic International Conversations, 1984-1988," *Information Service* 72 (1990/1991): 5-14.

[38]"Evangelization, Proselytism and Common Witness." Final report from the fourth phase of the International Dialogue 1990-1997 between the Roman Catholic Church and some classical Pentecostal churches and leaders.

[39]"Common Witness and Proselytism: A Study Document of the Joint Working Group of the Roman Catholic Church and the World Council of Churches," *Information Service* 14 (1971): 18-23, #4-8.

[40]Ibid., #26-27.

[41]Ibid., #22ff.

help it. This point was made clear in the Roman Catholic-Pentecostal International Dialogue in which Catholics and Pentecostals mutually concluded that "proselytism is an unethical activity that comes in many forms," including

- all ways of promoting our own community of faith that are intellectually dishonest, such as contrasting an ideal presentation of our own community with the weaknesses of another Christian community;
- all intellectual laziness and culpable ignorance that neglect readily accessible knowledge of the other's tradition;
- every willful misinterpretation of the beliefs and practices of other Christian communities;
- every form of force, coercion, compulsion, mockery or intimidation of a personal, psychological, physical, moral, social, economic, religious or political nature, etc.[42]

This agreement between the current two largest Christian families—the one representing one of the oldest Christian traditions, the other one of the youngest—should allow better understanding about the common task of evangelization. Mission and evangelism belong to the essence of the church. If the church's desire to share its faith is missing, it does not deserve its name.

## Concluding Reflections on Ecclesiastical Traditions

The two ancient ecclesiological traditions, Eastern Orthodoxy and Roman Catholicism, share a common heritage that goes back to the early church, namely the ideas of apostolicity and catholicity. *Apostolicity* means faithfulness to the life and tradition of the apostles, and *catholicity* here indicates fullness of doctrine, the idea of not lacking in anything needed for salvation. The Reformation churches also claim apostolicity; their focus is on the Word preached, the apostolic message. All of these churches claim to stand on the foundation of the apostles and thus represent the church of God on earth. They not only include those who have made conscious confession of faith, but also those to be nurtured in the faith in the hope that later on they will confess Christ.

The emergence of a Free church tradition—including the newcomers: Pentecostals and Charismatics—was a result of the concern for holy living for *all* members of the church. While the older churches never dismissed the call for holiness, in the eyes of the younger churches they did not emphasize it enough. So the idea of the believers' church arose. These churches also claim apostolicity

---

[42]*Evangelization, Proselytism and Common Witness*, #6.

in terms of living up to the apostolic life of commitment and evangelization.

Older churches usually emphasize community and the communal dimension of the Christian life, while the newer churches pay more attention to the individual's responsibility and role. These emphases have carried over also into the concept of ministry. Older churches, understandably, often focus more on the structures of the church and consider sacraments as essential means of grace. The younger churches, though regarding neither one of these as irrelevant (for example, sacraments are exercised by virtually all Christian groups), place more emphasis on the response of faith and on flexibility of church models. Reformation churches in most cases stand in the middle of these two extremes and try to hold to both the Eastern and Western Catholic Churches' and the younger Free churches' orientations.

Ecclesial history is a sad testimony of the lack of love and sensitivity. Struggles, poisoned attitudes, even persecutions have taken place between various denominations depending on who happened to be most powerful. Sadly enough, the noble mindset of Christian love did not always prevail. Strife and wars arose between the Catholic and Reformation churches and among the right- and left-wing Reformation churches.

The rise of the ecumenical movement sheds a ray of hope on this sorrowful picture. Even though the ecumenical movement in the form of the World Council of Churches is quite young, only half a century in age, it has already shown its potential. Whatever one's view of the goal of ecumenism—"visible" unity or unity at some other levels—the Christian message itself points to the unity of all people of God under one God. It is left to be seen what the ecclesiological implications of those developments will be.

Much of the thinking about the church currently comes from theologians who are more or less tightly linked to their respective traditions. On the one hand, they represent their traditions; on the other hand, they also serve as critics. The discussion we turn to next will consider the ecclesiologies of some of these leading theologians.

# Leading Contemporary Ecclesiologists

The theologians selected for a closer examination here fall quite naturally in two groups: some of them—John Zizioulas, Jürgen Moltmann and Wolfhart Pannenberg—are such that no further justification is needed, while the rest—Hans Küng, Lesslie Newbigin, James McClendon Jr. and Miroslav Volf—are each less self-evident names, particularly in a book like this. Zizioulas is undoubtedly the leading current Eastern Orthodox theologian, whose influence extends far beyond his own church through an active ecumenical career. Moltmann's *The Church in the Power of the Spirit* in the late 1970s gave rise to a resurgence of ecclesiological thinking and echoed much of the theological, sociological, cultural and intellectual protest and contribution of the time. While Pannenberg did not produce a major work on ecclesiology until the publication of his magnum opus, his three-volume *Systematic Theology*, beginning in the late 1980s, the theological guild was impatiently looking for his final system. Expectations were not disappointed, and it is left to the beginning years of the third millennium to take stock of the implications of this major work.

The other group of theologians selected here under the rubric "Leading Contemporary Ecclesiologists" needs some more elaboration. Hardly anyone questions Küng's groundbreaking ecclesiological contribution in his widely acclaimed *The Church*, especially in view of the fact that he brought to fulfillment many of the themes of Vatican II, of which he himself was one of the architects. But in light of the fact that soon after the publication of this work he first fell into disfavor and finally broke with the hierarchy of his church, many wonder if he is the right theologian to represent *Catholic* ecclesiology. Justification for his inclusion in this book is twofold. First of all, during the time his major ecclesiological work was published, he was still in good standing with the Catholic Church and in fact was one of the leading voices of modern Catholic theology. Second, if Küng is not selected, one may ask, who then? There is, of course, no want of Catholic theologians who have written on the church. But even theological luminaries such as Karl Rahner have not majored on the church but on some other areas. True, theologians such as Yves Congar and Henri de Lubac have contributed significantly to Catholic ecclesiology, but their writings are much less accessible to a wider audience and are often regarded more as fitting in more narrowly defined ecclesiological topics. American figures such as Avery Dulles have written extensively on the church, but their contribution has been more on the side of careful analysis of existing views rather than in constructive presentation of new views.

The late missiological veteran Newbigin's presence among leading contemporary ecclesiologists is not self-evident either. His inclusion reflects my leanings toward highlighting the importance of missiology to theology. While it is true that Newbigin has written on the church, as his early work *The Household of God* indicates, his main importance lies in the careful consideration of the missionary nature of the church, especially in the changing cultural milieu of our world.

The inclusion of two Free church ecclesiologists in this book, McClendon and Volf, also reflects my conviction that the future of Christian theology in general and ecclesiology in particular lies to a significant measure in that segment of the church. Not only the numbers but also the fact that so much of traditional church life and ecclesiology has been transformed by the Free churches' influence seem to support this thesis. The late McClendon had established himself on the American scene as a leading ecumenical Free church theologian coming from a Baptist background. Before his recent death he had gathered most of his theological system into a coherent form. Volf, coming originally from Eastern Europe and now teaching at Yale University, has already established his fame as a creative theologian especially with two works: *Exclusion and Embrace*, which looks at the relationship between the church and world, and *After Our Likeness*, a study in the inner life of the church in critical correlation with Orthodox and Catholic ecclesiologies (Zizioulas and Ratzinger respectively). McClendon and Volf both represent Free church orientations, though very different from each other, and in a conciliar way corresponding to the way Pannenberg and Moltmann, each in his own distinctive way, offer their interpretations of ecumenical Protestant doctrines of the church.

# 8

# John Zizioulas

## COMMUNION ECCLESIOLOGY

### Being as Communion

John Zizioulas, the titular bishop of Pergamon and perhaps the ablest ecclesiologist of the Eastern Orthodox Church, builds critically on the long tradition of Eastern ecclesiology. His main ecclesiological work is the highly acclaimed collection of essays *Being as Communion: Studies in Personhood and the Church.*[1] While sympathetic to the works of Vladimir Lossky and others, he sees as problematic the ideas of a distinct "economy of the Spirit" and a distinction between "objective" and "subjective" structures of the church.

Undoubtedly, the leading theological motif in Zizioulas is the idea of *koinonia,* "communion." It shapes and informs everything he says about the church:

> From the fact that a human being is a member of the Church, he becomes an "image of God," he exists as God Himself exists, he takes on God's "way of being." This way of being . . . is a way of *relationship* with the world, with other people and with God, an event of *communion,* and that is why it cannot be realized as the achievement of an *individual,* but only as an *ecclesial* fact.[2]

There is no true being without communion; nothing exists as an "individual" in itself. Communion is an ontological category; even God exists in communion. Zizioulas criticizes the ancient Greek ontology in which God first is God (his substance), and then exists as Trinity, as three persons.[3] His idea is,

---

[1]John Zizioulas, *Being as Communion: Studies in Personhood and the Church* (Crestwood, N.Y.: St Vladimir's Seminary Press, 1985), especially pp. 124-25. A fine recent study on Zizioulas' ecclesiology, in critical dialogue with Catholic and Free church ecclesiologies, is offered by Miroslav Volf, *After Our Likeness: The Church as the Image of the Trinity* (Grand Rapids, Mich.: Eerdmans, 1998), part 2.
[2]Zizioulas, *Being as Communion,* p. 15.
[3]The basic philosophical and theological orientation is given in ibid., chap. 2.

rather, that of the Greek fathers who claimed that God is the person as the community of three persons. Outside the Trinity there is no God. In other words, God's being coincides with God's communal personhood.

The ecclesiological significance of the person comes to the fore in distinction from our merely biological existence in which we exist as disconnected individuals: in the church we are made persons, persons in communion. Through baptism and faith, biological existence gives way to existence in *koinonia*.

Being in communion does not, however, mean downplaying the distinctive personhood of each individual. "The person cannot exist without communion; but every form of communion which denies or suppresses the person, is unadmissable."[4] We could express this by stating that the concrete locus of deindividualization and personalization is the church.[5] This is based on the fact that, on the one hand, God is only person in communion within trinitarian persons, and on the other hand, Christ is the person *par excellence*. Christ is not merely individual but rather a person, since his identity is constituted by a twofold relation, namely, his relationships as Son to the Father and as head to his body.[6]

### Eucharist and Communion

Zizioulas is an Orthodox theologian. For him, therefore, the Eucharist is the foundational act of the church—in fact, the act that makes the church. "For Orthodoxy, the church is in the Eucharist and through the Eucharist."[7] The communion is made possible and lived out in the eucharistic *koinonia*. He bases his theology of the Eucharist in the Pauline saying that makes an explicit connection to koinonia: "The cup of blessing that we bless, is it not a sharing [communion, *koinonia*] in the blood of Christ? The bread that we break, is it not a sharing [communion, *koinonia*] in the body of Christ? Because there is one bread, we who are many are one body, for we all partake of the one bread" (1 Cor 10:16-17). This is the realization of the principle "One in many," and conversely "many in One." Many Christians are incorporated into the One Christ, and the One Christ is the representative, corporate personality of many Christians.[8] On the basis of this reflection, Zizioulas makes the profound observa-

---

[4]Ibid., p. 18.
[5]Volf, *After Our Likeness*, p. 83.
[6]See further ibid., pp. 84-88.
[7]Zizioulas, "Die Welt in eucharistischer Sachau und der Mensch von heute," *Una Sancta* 25 (1970): 342
[8]Zizioulas, *Being as Communion*, pp. 145-49 (quote on p. 145).

tion that when Paul and the early fathers talk about the "church of God" (*ekklesia tou theou*) or the "whole church," or even the "catholic church," they refer primarily to the concrete eucharistic community. So the local eucharistic gathering is the church of God.[9]

According to Zizioulas, there is one necessary condition for the local church to be able to celebrate the Eucharist which actually makes that celebrating church a church, and that is the presence of a bishop. Why so? To understand this we have to notice his understanding of ordination. Ordination, rather than being primarily a transfer of power or authority, means a fundamental change of status. It makes an individual person, the one being ordained, a "relational entity" and connects him to the local community in a very concrete way.[10] The person ordained does not come into possession of something over against the community but rather "becomes something within the community."[11] He becomes an "ecstatic" entity; in other words, a person who is able to transcend his individuality and represent the whole congregation. And since the eucharistic gathering is an icon of Christ, so also the bishop as its head is the icon of Christ. The bishop as the presider of the celebration does visibly what the head of the church, Christ himself, does invisibly; so much so that this "presiding head thus himself acquires the prerogatives belonging to Christ."[12]

But there is also a place for the laity. Zizioulas considers all members of the church to be ordained by virtue of baptism, especially since in Eastern theology baptism is inseparable from confirmation, which occurs in the context of the Eucharist. The person baptized is not only made into a Christian through baptism, but also ordained. In confirmation, hands are laid upon the person and there is *epiclesis*, prayer for the Spirit.[13] The role of the laity at the Eucharist is to say "Amen" and so to receive the act of celebration.

It should not come as a surprise that, for a theologian with such focused attention to personhood, all notions of objectification of the Eucharist are foreign. He does not want to make the Eucharist an instrument through which we receive the grace of God almost automatically. For Zizioulas the Eucharist, the main liturgical act, is an "assembly, a community, a network of relation, in which a [person] 'subsists.'"[14] The more so since in each eucharistic celebration the

---

[9]Ibid., pp. 148-49
[10]Zizioulas, "Ordination et communion," *Istina* 16 (1971): 9.
[11]Volf, *After Our Likeness*, p. 110.
[12]Zizioulas, "La Mystère de l'Église dans la tradition orthodoxe," *Irénikon* 60 (1987): 321-35.
[13]Zizioulas, *Being as Communion*, pp. 215-16; Volf, *After Our Likeness*, pp. 113-14.
[14]Zizioulas, *Being as Communion*, p. 60.

church receives the person of Christ in its totality. But what does that bold statement mean to him? This brings us to the heart of his eucharistic theology. He
conceives the eucharistic presence and appropriation of Christ in the closest possible correspondence to his pneumatically understood Christology: "To eat the
body of Christ and to drink his blood means to participate in him who took
upon himself the 'multitude' . . . in order to make of them a *single body, his body*."[15]
In other words, in the celebration of the Eucharist, the body of the One (Christ)
and the body of the many (the church) are identical.[16]

The Eucharist is also a place that transcends time. On the one hand, it is an
*anamnesis*, a remembrance, a re-calling of Christ, but on the other hand, it is
also—paradoxically—*an anamnesis of the future*, a remembering of things to
come.[17] In this way it also transcends all divisions, natural or social or whatever.

## Pneumatology and Christology as the Dual Foundation of the Church

Zizioulas acknowledges the critique expressed by Eastern theologians about
the lack of a pneumatological dimension in the Roman Catholic Vatican II ex-
plication of the church in *Lumen Gentium*. (Several Eastern theologians have
accused the Western church of bringing the Holy Spirit into ecclesiology after
the church had already been construed in christological terms.) However, Zizioulas admits that even Eastern ecclesiology falls short of a proper balance between Christology and pneumatology.[18] Zizioulas explicitly attempts to work
for a proper synthesis between Christology and pneumatology as the basis for
ecclesiology.[19] He rightly notes that the New Testament presents the mutuality
of both rather than the priority of either one. On the one hand, the Spirit is giv-
en by Christ (Jn 7:39), on the other hand, there is no Christ until the Spirit is at
work either at his baptism (Mark) or at his birth (Matthew and Luke). Both of
these views could coexist in the one and the same canon. A confusion came
early on the liturgical level due to the separation of baptism and confirmation.

---

[15]Zizioulas, "The Ecclesiological Presuppositions of the Holy Eucharist," *Nicolaus* 10 (1982):
   333-49.
[16]See further Volf, *After Our Likeness*, pp. 97-99.
[17]Zizioulas, *Being as Communion*, p. 254.
[18]Ibid., pp. 124-26.
[19]See further J. Zizioulas, "Die Kirche als Gemeinschaft," in *Santiago de Compostela 1993*, Fün-
   fte Weltkonferenz für Glauben und Kirchenverfassung, Beiheft zur Ökonomischen Rund-
   schau 67, ed. G. Gassmann and D. Heller (Frankfurt: Verlag Otto Lembeck, 1994), p. 100;
   John D. Zizioulas, "Die pneumatologische Dimension der Kirche," *Internationale Katholische
   Zeitschrift "Communio"* 2 (1973): 134-38.

As long as these two rites were united, it could be argued that confirmation (pneumatology) and baptism (Christology) form one entity.[20]

Zizioulas makes the obvious yet brilliant observation that in the New Testament the church is called the body of Christ (1 Cor 12:27; Eph 1:22-23; 4:15-16). Never is the church labeled the "body of the Spirit," and never are Christians said to be "members of the Spirit."[21] Therefore, the traditional christological grounding of the church seems plausible, but not to the exclusion of the Spirit.

According to Zizioulas, there are two kinds of Christologies. First, we can understand Christ as an individual, and secondly, as a "corporate personality"[22] in his relationship with his body, the church. In his terminology, in the former case we speak of Christ as "individual," in the latter as "person." The role of the Spirit comes to the fore here: "Here the Holy Spirit is not one who *aids* us in bridging the distance between Christ and ourselves, but he is the person of the Trinity who actually realizes in history that which we call Christin. . . . In this case, our Christology is *essentially* conditioned by pneumatology, not just secondarily as in the first case; in fact it is *constituted* pneumatologically."[23]

Zizioulas argues that such a pneumatologically constituted Christology is biblical since in the Bible Christ becomes a historical person only in the Spirit (Mt 1:18-20; Lk 1:35). He is even ready to say that "Christ *exists only pneumatologically.*" In line with the Eastern trinitarian sensitivity, he adds that to speak of Christ means to speak at the same time of the Father and the Holy Spirit. He also says, "Thus the mystery of the Church has its birth in the entire economy of the Trinity and in a pneumatologically constituted Christology."[24]

Consequently, Zizioulas speaks of the church as "instituted" by Christ and "constituted" by the Spirit.[25] He contends that it is not enough to speak of pneumatology in relation to the church but rather to make pneumatology, along with eschatology,[26] constitutive. In other words, pneumatology must

---

[20]Zizioulas, *Being as Communion*, pp. 126-29.

[21]Cf. Zizioulas, "Die pneumatologische Dimension der Kirche," p. 133. See also Zizioulas, "Implications ecclésiologiques de deux types de pneumatologie," in *Communio Sanctorum: Mélanges offerts à Jean-Jacques von Allmen* (Geneva, Switzerland: Labor et fides, 1982), pp. 141-54.

[22]Zizioulas's term, *Being as Communion*, p. 130.

[23]Ibid., pp. 110-11, emphases in the text.

[24]Ibid., pp. 111-12, emphases in the text. See further Risto Saarinen, "Die moderne Theologie und das pneumatologische Defizit," in *Der Heilige Geist: Ökumenische und Reformatorische Untersuchungen*, ed. J. Heubach (Erlaugen, Germany: Martin-Luther-Verlag, 1996), pp. 246-51.

[25]Zizioulas, *Being as Communion*, pp. 132, 136, 140.

[26]For the role of eschatology in ecclesiology, see ibid., pp. 131-32.

qualify the very ontology of the church. The Spirit is not something that ani-
mates a church that already exists. "Pneumatology does not refer to the well-
being but to the very being of the Church." In other words, pneumatology is
an ontological category in ecclesiology.[27]

As already mentioned, the corporate personality of Christ is conceived
pneumatologically. It is significant that since the time of Paul, the Spirit has
been associated with the notion of *koinonia*. Pneumatology contributes to Christology (and consequently, to ecclesiology) the dimension of communion.[28]

What then are the main consequences of a proper pneumatological orientation for the life of the church? First of all, it guards from overinstitutionaliza-
tion. Where there is pneumatological deficit, one result is a hierarchical,
centralized concept of the church. Second, it rehabilitates the local church as
the primary entity. If pneumatology is not ontologically constitutive of Christology, this can mean that there is first one church and then many churches.
However, if pneumatology is made constitutive of ecclesiology, the body of
Christ is ontologically constituted by the Spirit. In other words, the Pentecostal
event is an ecclesiologically constitutive event.[29] Third, all pyramidal notions
disappear in a pneumatological ecclesiology where the "One" and the "many"
coexist as two aspects of the same being.[30] Fourth, according to Zizioulas,
pneumatology helps ecclesiology open up to the eschatological perspective.
Incorporating the eschatological perspective avoids both "meta-historicism,"
in which the doctrine of the church is divorced from historical reality (sometimes attributed to Eastern tradition) and "historization" of ecclesial institutions, in which the doctrine of the church says nothing more than what the
church has been as a historical reality (a danger within Western churches).[31]
Fifth, the pneumatological orientation has consequences for our view of ministry. The ministry of the church is the ministry of Christ. But when Christology is pneumatologically constituted, the Spirit constitutes the relation be-

---

[27]Ibid. Quote on p. 132.
[28]See further Zizioulas, "Die Kirche als Gemeinschaft," pp. 95-104.
[29]Zizioulas, *Being as Communion*, 132-33. Zizioulas, however, sees as problematic the older
   Eastern emphasis on the local church that, in his assessment, led to a sort of "congregationalism." This was the fault of the Eucharistic ecclesiology of Afanasiev and others, since
   there was priority on pneumatology rather than a balance between pneumatology and
   Christology (p. 133).
[30]Ibid., p. 139.
[31]Zizioulas, *Being as Communion*, pp. 139-40. For the significance of eschatology and pneumatology to ecclesiology, see the seminal work of Gerhard Ebeling, *Dogmatik des Christlichen
   Glaubens* (Tübingen: Mohr, 1979), 3:5-32.

tween Christ and the ministry. This, in fact, agrees with what Paul argues in 1 Corinthians 12. The life and ministry of the body of Christ are conceived pneumatologically, in terms of the gifts of the Spirit. Be it the question of ordination or that of the role of the laity, the proper context is the *koinonia* of the Spirit among the members of the body of Christ. The charismatic life is constitutive of and not derivative from the church's being.[32]

Interestingly enough, Zizioulas remarks that the Orthodox Church's freedom from some of the experiences of the Western churches—such as the problems of clericalism or anti-institutionalism, or the Charismatic movement—may be taken as an indication that for the most part pneumatology has saved the life of Orthodoxy up to now.[33] Whatever one thinks of the accuracy of this statement in the real life of Orthodox churches, I believe it contains a theological insight worth pondering.

### *Local Church, Universal Church and Communion*

As has become clear, for the eucharistic ecclesiology of Zizioulas each local church is a whole church, since it has the whole Christ. The church can be found in all its fullness wherever the Eucharist is being celebrated. The church is essentially a local church. In contrast to Roman Catholic ecclesiology, for Zizioulas all other church structures, universal church included, derive from the local. For Roman Catholic theology, the local church receives its ecclesiality from the universal, but not so for Zizioulas. In fact, he says explicitly that a "metropolis, an archdiocese or a patriachate cannot be called a church itself, but only by extension, i.e., by virtue of the fact that it is based on . . . local churches which are the only ones . . . properly called churches."[34]

Not only is the local church a church by virtue of the celebration of the Eucharist, it is also a catholic church insofar as it involves the coming together of the whole church at a specific place. If the whole Christ is present at the Eucharist—and according to Zizioulas he is—then it becomes understandable that catholicity of the church is guaranteed by Christ's presence. This is also the key to the relationship between the local and universal church. Volf summarizes it accurately: "The larger church is present in the local eucharistic *synaxis*; in a reverse fashion, the eucharistic *synaxis* is an act not only of the concrete eucharistic communion, but also of the larger church. Thus every Eucharist

---

[32]Zizioulas, *Being as Communion*, pp. 210-12, 217 n. 20.
[33]Ibid., p. 140.
[34]Ibid., pp. 252-53.

anticipates the eschatological gathering of the *whole* people of God."[35]

The catholicity of the church in every local place, even though it is not a result of human efforts but comes by the presence of Christ, is however a foundational challenge to human beings. In order for the church to be catholic—the term derives from the Greek *katholos*, literally "according to whole, i.e., undivided"—it has to transcend all natural divisions and obstacles. Says Zizioulas:

> A eucharist which discriminates between races, sexes, ages, professions, social classes etc. violates not certain ethical principles but its eschatological nature. For that reason such a eucharist is not a "bad"—i.e. morally deficient—eucharist but no eucharist at all. It cannot be said to be the body of the One who sums up all into Himself.[36]

For Zizioulas, then, catholicity also means universality in that Christ incorporates into himself all Christians. If so, then no local churches, even though they all are whole churches, are permitted to live in an isolated, self-enclosed fashion, but rather must live in communion with all other churches. Local churches do not receive their ecclesiality from other churches, but by virtue of being eucharistic gatherings that receive the whole Christ, they are turned toward others.[37]

---

[35]Volf, *After Our Likeness*, p. 104, emphases in original.
[36]Zizioulas, *Being as Communion*, p. 255.
[37]See further Volf, *After Our Likeness*, pp. 106-7.

# 9

# Hans Küng

## CHARISMATIC ECCLESIOLOGY

### The Church in Need of Renewal

The nature given to the Church through God's eschatological saving act in Christ was given it as a responsibility. This nature must be constantly realized anew and given new form in history by our personal decision of faith. The historical Church cannot do without this constant renewal of its form. Renewal of form implies change of form by means of human decision and responsibility. God does not present us with the nature of the Church as an objective fact, nor does he overwhelm it with mystic inevitability, nor work in it by organic development. . . . It is impossible simply to preserve the Church for all time in the original form it enjoyed as the primitive Church. Changing times demand changing forms. Yet in spite of all changes in form the basic structure of the Church given to it in Christ by God's saving act must be preserved, if it is to remain the true Church. Not every change in form is therefore in accordance with the Church's nature. Through the failure of men in their free responsibility, discrepancies between nature and form can occur: mistakes and misconceptions, errors of judgment and false developments.[1]

Hans Küng has been not only one of the most productive and creative post-conciliar theologians of the Roman Catholic Church, but also the most disputed figure in his church. While officially he was stripped of his teaching credentials as a Roman Catholic theologian, he was able to retain his post at the University of Tübingen, Germany, until his retirement, and his relentless voice for renewal of the church and Christian faith has been heard both within and outside his own faith community. Küng's monumental *The Church*—launched in the aftermath of the Second Vatican Council, for which he, along with his colleague Karl Rahner and others, was influential in the preparatory

---

[1]Hans Küng, *The Church* (1967; reprint, New York: Image Books, 1976 [orig. 1967]), p. 341.

work—marks a watershed not only in the Catholic but also in contemporary ecumenical ecclesiology. With Jürgen Moltmann's *The Church in the Power of the Spirit*,[2] Küng's magnum opus transformed theological thinking about the church toward a more participatory, charismatically structured, open model in which the whole church of God, not only its hierarchy, is placed under the Word of God and given participation in God's mission in the world. While in his later theological career Küng has moved to interreligious dialogue and related issues, his continuing interest in various aspects of ecclesiology has never died, although he has continued to trouble the hierarchy of his own church especially in his criticism of the infallibility of the pope.[3]

Several features make *The Church* distinctive in its approach to the systematic treatment of the church. Perhaps the most distinctive feature is its extraordinarily extensive engagement with the biblical text. No other systematic theology of the church covers such a wide scope of biblical terrain as this book. In a very legitimate sense, *The Church* could also be characterized as a biblical theology of the church. The basic thesis is simple: "One can only know what the Church should be if one also knows what the Church was originally."[4]

Another persistent theme, in line with the rest of Küng's theology, is his call for renewal and reform of the church. The church can always err, Küng maintains, and therefore it must also be prepared to orient itself anew, to renew itself. In fact, sometimes the church's evil "un-nature" becomes so evident that it conflicts with the true nature of the church (p. 51). In its desire to renew itself, the church on the one hand attempts to adapt itself to the world as it actually is, but it also looks to its own origins, to the events that gave it life (pp. 13, 14, 16).

## The Church as It Is

Being a reformer of the church, Küng, however, wants to avoid the cardinal sin, as he sees it, of resorting to an overidealized, vague view of the church. In fact, for him the "essence" of the church is not a matter of "metaphysical stasis, but exists only in constantly changing historical 'forms.' " The historical form

---

[2]Jürgen Moltmann, *The Church in the Power of the Spirit* (London: SCM Press, 1977).
[3]Küng, *Infallible? An Inquiry* (Garden City, N.Y.: Doubleday, 1971).
[4]Küng, *Church*, p. 11; see also e.g., p. 13: "God's word is always there to lead the Church." Hereafter in this chapter, most page references to *The Church* will be given in parenthetical references.

of the church as it now shows itself to us is the starting point for reform rather than "the abstract celestial spheres of theological theory." In other words, "The real essence of the real Church is expressed in historical form" (p. 23). If the church really sees itself as the people of God—and it does in Küng's thinking—it can never be a static and supra-historical phenomenon, which exists "undisturbed by earthly space and historical time" (p. 176).

The history of the church, and also the history of the church's self-understanding, began not after but in the New Testament and has continued since (p. 37). An abstract and idealistic ecclesiology divorced from the realities of present life will tend to either overlook the "un-nature" of the church or end up just expressing pious wishes (p. 52). Commensurate with this realistic attitude, Küng criticizes the way the distinction between the invisible and visible church is often depicted, for example by the Protestant Reformers. A real church made up of real people cannot possibly be invisible. The visible church is the true church, not the false church. Nevertheless, the church is simultaneously visible and invisible. The visible aspects of the church are quickened, formed and controlled by the invisible aspects (pp. 59-64; 342).

As a real church, the faith community is composed of sinful men and women and it exists for sinful men and women. Küng's view comes close to that of Luther, who regarded the church as the community of sinners (p. 140). Therefore, the *communio sanctorum* (the communion of the saints) as *communio peccatorum* (the communion of sinners) is always in need of forgiveness and repentance (p. 230).

A hard look at the real church need not, however, lead to pessimism or hopelessness. Admirers and critics of the church alike must be aware that in the final analysis the church is an object of faith. Küng's brilliant interpretation of the creeds' reference to belief in the church makes a distinction between "believing *in*" God and in the Holy Spirit, on the one hand, but on the other hand, "believing the church." For Küng, to say that we do not "believe in the church" but rather that we "believe the church" means that *we* are the church, the fellowship of believers.

Küng reminds us that faith can never be distinguished from love. Faith is never a matter of adherence to dogmas but "is the sacrifice and self-giving of one person to another" (p. 55). So one's participation in and love for the church should affect even the way one criticizes the church. Therefore, only those inside the household of faith are entitled to express criticism toward the church.

## The People of God

As already mentioned, Küng was instrumental in the theological and ecclesiological reforms of the Second Vatican Council. One of the main concepts of postconciliar thinking about the church has been the "people of God." Küng devotes a long section in *The Church* to discussing various aspects of this concept; he both echoes the main orientations of *Lumen Gentium*, The Dogmatic Constitution on the Church, and also elaborates its teaching.

Very early the emerging Christian church possessed certain peculiar forms that pointed to developments beyond the "Old People of God," the Jews, such as baptism, the communal service of prayer, the commemoration of the eschatological meal and the living fellowship of love.

Küng argues that what makes the people of God distinctive is that every member belongs to it through God's call; there must be no attempt to make the church private and exclusive. It can never be merely a free association of like-minded religious people. "The Church is always and everywhere dependent on the free choice and call of God, who wills the salvation of all men" (p. 171). Over against the dominant tendency in much of Free church ecclesiologies, Küng argues that if the church is really the people of God, it is impossible to see the origins of the church in individuals, in believing Christians. This misconception reduces the church to something private, to an agglomeration of pious individuals.

Incorporation into the church through baptism—in which one surrenders oneself to the baptizer and so to the whole church and to the sustaining of Christian life through participation in the Eucharist—demonstrates that the individual is incorporated into a community and does not exist simply as an individual.[5]

> But the essential difference and superiority of the Christian message, when compared to other oriental religions of redemption, is that its aim is not the salvation of the individual alone and the freeing of the individual soul from suffering, sin and death. The essential part of the Christian message is the idea of salvation for the whole community of people, of which the individual is a member. (p. 172)

As soon as Küng has asserted the initiative of God in the ecclesiality of the church, he adds a qualifier: we all belong to the people of God through our human decision. As the people of God the church can never be merely a super-entity poised above real human beings and their real decisions. "The Church is

---

[5]For the importance of sacraments as ways of linking the individual to the church, see Küng, *Church*, pp. 266-92.

always and in all cases dependent on free human assent" (pp. 173-74). In churches that practice infant baptism, there should be awareness that this action should not be seen as a means of circumventing this personal decision of faith.

As the people of God, the community of faith is a pilgrim people, another dominant feature of the Vatican II understanding of the church. "The Church is essentially *en route*, on a journey, a pilgrimage" (p. 176).

What was distinctive of the "New People of God," the Christians, was that all the faithful belong to the people of God, and therefore there must be no clericalization of the church. "If we see the Church as the people of God, it is clear that the Church can never be merely a particular class or caste, a group of officials or a clique within the fellowship of the faithful. The Church is always and in all cases the *whole* people of God, the *whole* ecclesia, the *whole* fellowship of the faithful. Everyone belongs to the chosen race, the royal priesthood, the holy nation" (p. 169, emphases in the original). Consequently, Küng is critical of the unhealthy distinction between clergy and laity which attempts to remove the decisive activity and initiative away from the laity in the church.[6] "The legalistic mind basically mistrusts the free operation of God's spirit in the Church because the Spirit blows where it wills and does not wait for official permission."[7] Küng makes the accurate exegetical observation that in the New Testament the word *laos* does not indicate a distinction within the community between priests and people. Rather, the distinction it implies is between the people of God and the "non-people," those outside of faith (p. 170).

Every church member's priestly function is derived from the "final, unrepeatable and hence unlimited sacrifice of the one continuing and eternal high priest" (p. 469). Thus, the entire church is joined to Christ and offers sacrifices acceptable to God: "The abolition of a special priestly caste and its replacement by the priesthood of the one and eternal high priest has as its

---

[6]*Lumen Gentium* 10. In Küng's spirit, Catholic ecclesiologists and sacramentologists Michael Lawler and Thomas J. Shanahan (*Church: A Spirited Communion* [Collegeville, Minn.: Liturgical Press, 1995], especially pp. 73-83) criticize sharply their own church for the lack of a theology of the laity and the continued overemphasis on the ordained ministers/hierarchy, which means downplaying the (original) unity of God's people in ministry and mission. The "secular" sphere of the laity does not mean demeaning their role in the church as opposed to the "sacred" sphere of the orders. The idea of "mono-ministry or ministerial autocracy," that is, of all the most important gifts concentrated on one man or in a select group, is totally unsustainable both from the Pauline viewpoint of the charisms and the needs of the present church, they claim.

[7]Hans Küng, "The Charismatic Structure of the Church," in *The Church and Ecumenism, Concilium* #4, ed. Hans Küng (New York: Paulist, 1965), p. 41.

strange and yet logical consequence the fact that all believers share in a universal priesthood" (p. 473). Echoing the mindset of his colleague Karl Rahner, Küng maintains that the locus of true worship is not only in the sanctuary but also in the world; the sacrifices "are not part of worship in a sanctuary, but worship in the world, in the middle of everyday life, the loving service of God" (p. 478).

## The Body of Christ

Still another favored image of the church in Küng is the ancient biblical concept of the body of Christ, which has played such a decisive role in much of Catholic ecclesiology. Küng's approach to the concept revolutionizes the older Catholic canons and comes close to contemporary Protestant views, as well as the ecumenical consensus. In fact, there is close connection with the conceptions of the people of God and the body of Christ in Pauline theology. Temporal categories play an important role in the idea of the people of God; as the people of God the church is making a journey from the Old Testament election through the present toward the future. Spatial categories also dominate the notion of the body of Christ as the union of the church with its Lord. Both concepts in their own distinctive way seek to express the union of the church with Christ and among its members (pp. 292-93).

Each local community as the body of Christ is a full church, Küng contends, going against the tendency of preconciliar Catholic ecclesiology in which the ecclesiality of the local community derives from the universal church. The Pauline emphasis refers to local communities as the body of Christ. But another Pauline usage, in Colossians and Ephesians, refers to the whole church as the body of Christ. Christ is present in the whole church and the church never exhausts or contains Christ anymore than the Spirit (pp. 299-308).

## The Church as the Creation of the Spirit

The Spirit of God is the principle of freedom (2 Cor 3:17). Freedom is demanded of the church precisely because freedom has been given to the church. The church of the Spirit is the church of freedom. Ultimately, not because it has to be struggled for and won is freedom granted, but rather, because freedom has been granted it can and must be lived. True freedom is not rooted in the human being's own existence, but comes to him or her from outside. The Spirit is also an eschatological gift and so frees the people of

God into God's future. This liberating work was already evident at the day of Pentecost when, as a result of the pouring out of God's Spirit on all flesh, social barriers were removed.[8]

In line with his realistic ecclesiology, Küng also emphasizes the fact that the Spirit of God who indwells the church is no "obscure and nameless power" as in Hellenistic gnosticism or much of later theology, but is the concrete presence of God in Christ and derivatively in the church.[9] In other words, the Spirit is the earthly presence of the glorified Lord in the church.

Even though the church is the locus of the Spirit, it never possesses the Spirit; rather, the church lives under the reign of the Spirit. The church is subordinate to the Spirit. Just as we cannot identify the church with Christ, as happened in the "Church as the continued incarnation of Christ" view of the Catholic ecclesiology of the nineteenth century, neither can we identify the church with the Spirit, as was the tendency of the Catholic ecclesiology of M. J. Scheeben at the same time. The church is the church of the Spirit, but the Spirit is not the Spirit of the church but the Spirit of God and Christ (p. 229). In fact, the Spirit precedes the church. The Spirit is not an external bonus added to the church as though it could exist without the Holy Spirit. The Spirit of God comes first, and through the Spirit, God in his freedom creates the church (p. 232).

The Spirit of God is totally free to work when, where and how the Spirit wills. The Spirit cannot be restricted by the church. The Spirit is at work not only in the offices of the church but also in the whole people of God. "He is at work not only in the 'holy city,' but where he wills: in all churches of the one Church. He is at work not only in the Catholic Church, but where he wills: in Christianity as a whole. And finally he is at work not only in Christianity, but where he wills: in the whole world" (p. 232).

## The Charismatic Structure of the Church

According to Küng, there seem to be two reasons why the Catholic Church has had such a hard time in acknowledging the Charismatic structure of the

---

[8]Küng, *Church*, pp. 215-18 especially, but see also pp. 201-24. The heading of this section is the title of this chapter in Küng. He is well aware of the different orientations of various New Testament authors to the understanding of the Spirit, but his main argumentation is not influenced by this inner-biblical variation; see pp. 217-21 especially.

[9]Ibid., pp. 217, 220. A powerful contemporary "realistic pneumatology" that echoes many concerns of Küng's thinking about the Spirit is that of Michael Welker, *God the Spirit* (Minneapolis: Fortress, 1992).

church.[10] The first reason has been the clericalism and legalism hinted above. Regarding the second reason, Küng notes that the Catholic Church's ecclesiology has been founded exclusively upon the Pastoral Letters, which fail to express the pneumatic nature of the church's structure as does, for example, 1 Corinthians.[11]

What then is a charism? How do we account for it theologically? A theological description of the charisma "is God's call to the individual person in view of a specific service within the community, including the ability to perform this service."[12] Küng argues that the charismata are not primarily extraordinary but common; they are not of one kind, but manifold; they are not limited to a special group of persons, but are meant for the whole church (p. 58). To defend his proposal that the charismata are not limited to a special group of persons, Küng offers three arguments. First, he notes that in 1 Corinthians 12:28-31 Paul's ordering of church "hierarchy" places clergy near the end of his list. Second, the church is in the intermediate stage between the "not yet" and "already," which implies that no one person possesses all the charismata. And third, Scripture plainly states that the Spirit has gifted every person (1 Cor 12:7).[13]

An element of service is always attached to the charism. The true charism is not simply a miracle; it is something in the service of the community (1 Cor 12:7). Since the needs of the community are many, there is correspondingly a variety of charisms. A common misunderstanding presumes some kind of uniformity in gifting, especially related to ordination. This view finds no basis in Paul's theology. But since there are different spirits and spiritual phenomena, it is essential that there should always be the gift of "discernment of spirits" (1 Cor 12:10).[14]

---

[10]The ecumenical groundwork for the rehabilitation of the Charismatic structure of the church was done by several scholars; following are some of the most important. Hans von Campenhaus (*Ecclesiastical Authority and Spiritual Power in the Church of the First Three Centuries* (London: Black, 1969 [orig. 1953], pp. 68-71 especially) restated the emphasis of Rudolph Sohm by insisting that for Paul the Spirit is the organizing principle of the church and that ministry is the employment of a gift that the Spirit bestows. Ernst Käsemann ("Ministry and Community in the New Testament," in *Essays on the New Testament Themes* [Naperville, Ill.: Allenson, 1964], pp. 63-94) attempted even more vigorously than Campenhausen to transcend the antithesis of charism and office by viewing them in dialectical relationship. For the New Testament foundations, see J. D. G. Dunn, *The Theology of Paul* (Grand Rapids, Mich.: Eerdmans, 1998), pp. 567-68.

[11]Küng, "Charismatic Structure of the Church," p. 47.

[12]Ibid., p. 59; see also Küng, *Church*, p. 247.

[13]Küng, "Charismatic Structure of the Church," pp. 55-57.

[14]Küng, *Church*, pp. 239-46.

Amidst this variety of gifts and the freedom of the Spirit, there is though the principle of unity. Küng outlines three guiding principles from Paul that point to the need and possibility of unity. First, every church member has his or her own specific charism from the Spirit of God. Second, there is the principle of "with another for one another." The charisms are for the edification of the whole church. The Christian is not to use his or her charism as a weapon with which to seize power and position in the church but as a gift for the service of others and of the community. Third, obedience to the Lord means living in harmony with others in the church. All charisms have their origin in one and the same giver, God himself through Christ in the Spirit. The charismatically oriented ordering of the church therefore means neither enthusiasm, which ends in anarchy and disorder, nor legality, which petrifies into mediocrity and uniformity. Even the emerging hierarchical structures of the early church (the appointing of elders) does not necessarily indicate a clerical ruling system, but can be seen against the background of the fundamentally Charismatic structure of the church (pp. 248-49).

## The Church Is One

In the creeds, the church is identified as "one," as well as holy, apostolic and catholic. Could we find an ecumenical approach to the doctrine of the church that would allow us to acknowledge the one church of God on earth as a visible church, not just an invisible idea? This question has been one of the driving forces behind much of Küng's thinking about the church.

Küng freely admits that there is nothing in Catholic theology opposing the Reformers' twofold description of the basic ecclesiality of the church, namely the preaching of the Word and the right administration of the sacraments. The only problem is that these two criteria are too vague; they do not really distinguish the true church from the false, or from the "non-church." Almost anybody, heretics included, would affirm these two principles. The validity of these two criteria, however, depends on the fourfold classical "marks" of the church referred to above (pp. 342-48).

For Küng, the work for the unity of the one church of Christ does not mean suppressing the variety of existing churches. In the final analysis, the unity of the church is not based in the unity of the members among themselves, but rather on the unity of God. "It is one and the same God who gathers the scattered from all places and all ages and makes them into one people of God" (p. 353). Consequently, the multiplicity of churches is not a bad thing in itself.

Küng summarizes his local-church-oriented, unity-in-diversity view of ecumenism in the following way:

> If, however, every local Church is a community, if every local Church is in its own
> way the ecclesia, the people of God, a creation of the Holy Spirit, the body of
> Christ, can the multiplicity of the Churches be a bad thing in itself? The unity of
> the church should not be sought only outside the local gathering of the commu-
> nity. Precisely the unity of the local Church, which implies something self-con-
> tained but not isolated, involves a multiplicity of Churches, since this local
> Church cannot be unique. The unity of the Church presupposes, therefore, a com-
> mon life shared by all the local Churches. (pp. 354-55)

Thus the unity of the church presupposes a multiplicity of churches. The
various churches do not need to deny their origins, their specific situations,
their way of life and thought, or their structures. The same thing is not suitable
for everyone. The unity of the church not only presupposes a multiplicity of
churches, but even makes it flourish anew. From the time of the New Testament on, there have been fundamentally different historical forms of the one
church, all of them legitimate. The coexistence of different churches does not
in itself jeopardize the unity of the church; only the hostile confrontation en-
dangers unity. In other words, though excluding and exclusive differences are
harmful, our differences in and of themselves can now be seen as assets (pp.
356-57).

# 10

# Wolfhart Pannenberg

## UNIVERSAL ECCLESIOLOGY

### The "Churchly" Nature of Systematic Theology

It might come as a surprise to the students of Wolfhart Pannenberg's theology that even though the third volume of his massive *Systematic Theology*[1] may well be the most distinguished recent contribution to the ecumenical doctrine of the church, he had not previously produced a full-scale study of ecclesiology. His *The Church*,[2] a collection of essays and translation of a larger German work, *Ethik und Ekklesioloie*,[3] only touches some of the crucial issues but does not aim at presenting an outline of a doctrine of the church. An earlier essay, "The Kingdom of God and the Church," is pregnant with several ecclesiological themes but only in an embryonic form.[4] Even more surprisingly, his involvement with the issues related to ecclesiology has been mainly of a practical nature. To anyone familiar with his general approach to theology, this observation seems to run against the grain of Pannenberg's work; he has devoted almost all his productive life to developing a methodology of theology with superb analysis of theoretical issues of various sorts. Perhaps the most lasting ecclesiological contribution of Pannenberg before *Systematic Theology* is his important role in the drafting of *Baptism, Eucharist, and Ministry* of the WCC, one of the most influential ecumenical documents in recent decades.[5]

In order to gain a perspective on his ecclesiology, one has to acknowledge the fact that for Pannenberg theology, and consequently ecclesiology, is a pub-

---

[1]Wolfhart Pannenberg, *Systematic Theology*, vol. 3 (Grand Rapids, Mich.: Eerdmans, 1998).

[2]Wolfhart Pannenberg, *The Church* (Philadelphia: Westminster Press, 1981).

[3]Wolfhart Pannenberg, *Ethik und Ekklesiologie* (Gottingen: Vandenhoeck & Ruprecht, 1977).

[4]Wolfhart Pannenberg, "The Kingdom of God and the Church," in *Theology and the Kingdom of God* (Philadelphia: Westminster Press, 1969), pp. 72-101. Pannenberg's *The Apostles' Creed in Light of Today's Questions* (Philadelphia: Westminster Press, 1972) also touches some ecclesiological themes.

[5]Faith and Order Paper no. 111 (Geneva, Switzerland: WCC Publications, 1982).

lic discipline rather than an exercise in piety. He adamantly opposes the widespread privatization of faith and theology so prevalent especially in the modern Protestant thought culminating in Schleiermacher and others. Theology has to speak to common concerns, since there is no special "religious truth." To its detriment, modern theology has by and large left behind the truth question, but Pannenberg himself has not been willing to surrender the quest for the one truth.

Stanley J. Grenz, one of the interpreters of Pannenberg's theology,[6] has aptly noted that Pannenberg's theology has a "churchly" nature. This comes to focus in several distinctive features that Pannenberg's approach to ecclesiology displays.[7] Three of those may be noted here by way of introduction. First, there is a pronounced pneumatological orientation to the doctrine of the church. The most distinctive feature of Pannenberg's pneumatology is its aim of continuity; the same Spirit of God who is operative in creating and sustaining life in creation and human beings, and in creating new life in the believers, is the Spirit operative in the church and moving the world and the church toward the final fulfillment.[8] Second, unlike most systematic theologies that discuss the reception of salvation in the individual believer's life before the treatment of ecclesiological themes, Pannenberg places the soteriological discussion into the doctrine of the church. In other words, he does not want to see the faith first received into an individual heart and then the church added as an afterthought. Rather, Pannenberg insists that even though appropriation of faith is a highly personal response, it can only be done in the church, the bearer of the Spirit of God and God's grace. The relationship between the individual believer and the church is mutual and perichoretic: "The church can only try to fulfill its function as a sign pointing to God's kingdom but in distinction from it, in this way mediating to believers assurance of their participation in eschatological salvation, and thus itself being able, in its liturgical life, to be the place of the Spirit's presence already on this side of the eschatological consummation."[9] Third, the doctrine of election is joined to ecclesiology rather than to the first part of systematic theology, the doctrine of God or the human being, as is conventional.

---

[6]Stanley J. Grenz, *Reason for Hope: The Systematic Theology of Wolfhart Pannenberg* (New York: Oxford University Press, 1990), p. 150.
[7]See further ibid., p. 150.
[8]See further Veli-Matti Kärkkäinen, *Pneumatology: The Holy Spirit in Ecumenical, International and Historical Perspective* (Grand Rapids, Mich.: Baker, 2002), pp. 117-25.
[9]Pannenberg, *Systematic Theology*, 3:xv. Hereafter in this chapter, most page references to volume 3 of Pannenberg's *Systematic Theology* will be given in parenthetical references.

## Ecumenism in the Service of the Unity of Humankind

In writing a major contribution to the doctrine of the church, Pannenberg has aimed for the whole worldwide church rather than any specific denomination—even his own, the Lutheran Church. To be more precise, he is not even satisfied to write to the church and Christians alone but to the rest of humanity as well, since in his view the church is an anticipation and a sign of the unity of all people under one God. Ecumenical sensitivity could well be the most distinctive feature of Pannenberg's doctrine of the church. He makes the brilliant observation that hardly any other factor obscures the truth of the gospel of Jesus so much as the fact of church division and its accompanying phenomena, especially the pursuit of power by ministers of the church in combination with a limited outlook with regard to the unity of the church (p. xv).

But Pannenberg is not content to only promote ecumenism for its own sake; for him the ecumenical endeavors point to the final goal of the church, the unity of all people of God under one God.[10] "If Christians succeed in solving the problems of their own pluralism, they may be able to produce a model combining pluralism and the widest moral unity which will also be valid for political life."[11]

Pannenberg engages in a lively conversation with the description of the church as the "sign" and sacrament in conciliar Roman Catholic theology.[12] Vatican II expressed the concept of the church as a sign and tool for the most inward union with God and for the unity of all people. Even though Pannenberg basically agrees with the Protestant criticism of exaggerated sacramentalizing of the biblical concept of "mystery" (because Eph 3:4 links the mystery to Christ rather than to the church), he still sees it helpful theologically to maintain that the church in Christ is a sign of the coming unity of all people under one God. But he is quick to point out that in itself the church is not immediately seen as the sacrament of unity in which the unity of humanity in the kingdom of God finds anticipatory representation and is historically at work for human reconciliation. The reason is obvious: in the church's historical form the divine mystery of salvation achieves only broken manifestation. Perversions and power plays abound. It is only by virtue of the fellowship with

---

[10]See further Wolfhart Pannenberg, "Unity of the Church—Unity of Mankind: A Critical Appraisal of a Shift in Ecumenical Direction," *Mid-Stream* 21 (October 1982): 485-90.

[11]Wolfhart Pannenberg, "Christian Morality and Political Issues," in *Faith and Reality* (Philadelphia: Westminster Press, 1977), p. 38.

[12]For the Vatican II view of the church as a sacrament (sacramental sign), see *Lumen Gentium* [The Dogmatic Constitution on the Church], 3.

Christ—albeit not identification—that the church mediates its function as sign. "As the body of Christ the church is the eschatological people of God gathered out of all peoples, and it is thus a sign of reconciliation for a future unity of a renewed humanity in the kingdom of God" (p. 43).[13]

The idea of the church as sign, pointing beyond itself to the final purposes of God, is a designation greatly preferred by Pannenberg, for whom the idea of the church mainly as the vehicle for the reception of individual salvation is too limited a goal. This goal is too limited for two reasons: First of all, Pannenberg's theology is very corporeal, especially his eschatology. There is no individual attainment of final salvation without the rest of the community. Second, the church with all its importance in the economy of God in the world is never an end in itself but always serves higher purposes: God's future rule in the arrival of God's kingdom. Pannenberg is also a theologian of hope, although in a very distinctive way, and thus even ecclesiology is always looking forward to the final culmination of God's purposes. The task of the sign is to point beyond itself, and therefore the idea of "sign" accurately captures this leading aspect of his doctrine of the church.

Pannenberg's overall program of seeing the church and ecumenism in the service of the unity of all people also shapes his view of church leadership. Unlike Protestant theologians in general, Pannenberg sees justification for the ministry/minister in the unity of Christianity as a whole. He asks whether, in addition to leadership at the local and regional levels, a ministry for the unity of Christians is also needed at the universal level of the church as a whole, not merely in the synodical form of ecumenical councils by bishops, but also by the "ministry of an individual who can be active as a spokesperson for Christianity as a whole." Even with his reservations about the current Roman Catholic claim for such ministry by the pope, Pannenberg basically gives a positive answer to his own query. He defends his non-Protestant standpoint as follows:

> It is a fact of Christian history that with the end of the primitive Jerusalem church the church of Rome became the historical center of Christianity. If any Christian bishop can speak for the whole church in situations when this may be needed, it will be primarily the bishop of Rome. In spite of all the bitter controversies resulting from chronic misuse of the authority of Rome in power politics, there is here no realistic alternative. . . . We ought freely to admit the fact of the primacy of the Roman Church and its bishop in Christianity. (pp. 420-21)

---

[13]See further Pannenberg, *Systematic Theology*, especially 3:38-44.

Pannenberg maintains that the Lutheran Reformation never rules out in principle a ministry to protect Christian unity on the universal level as a whole. According to the Lutheran faith, the church as a whole cannot err by reason of Christ's promise (Jn 10:28). Therefore, the universal teaching office—and teaching is the essence of Pannenberg's view of the universal ministry of the bishop of Rome and of ecumenical councils—submits itself to the service of unity (pp. 423-24).

## *The Kingdom of God, Society and the Church*

The church's relation to and dependence on God is a corollary feature of Pannenberg's approach. In his theology, God is the object and determining reality of all theology: God is the power that determines everything. If the idea of God must be able to illumine not only human life, but also experience of the world, then ecclesiology should also.

The church, then, is the anticipation of the kingdom of God; therefore its essence is constituted by the kingdom, of which it is the sign (pp. 30-33). This fact explains the integral connection between ecclesiology and eschatology, so visible in Pannenberg's systematic delineation of Christian faith. Surprisingly, Pannenberg places not only the church but also society under the kingdom. In other words, he sets God's rulership over all human orders (pp. 49-57). The church has been given a noble task: "It serves both as a sign, pointing to a future society of peace and justice that no political system can bring into existence and as a reminder of the transience of all social orders in contrast to the finality of God's rule."[14]

As any other German theologian, Pannenberg constantly engages in critical dialogue with Karl Barth. Even though Pannenberg finds several faults in Barth's approach to the doctrine of the church (for example, his virtual identification of the church and Christ), Pannenberg applauds the idea of seeing the kingdom as directed beyond itself to the unity of humankind under one God. If the sign and the thing signified are not distinguished clearly enough, then even the future hope of Christian faith is compromised: "If the church fails to make this distinction clearly, then it arrogates to itself the finality and glory of the kingdom, but by the poverty and all too human character of its own life it also makes the Christian hope incredible." As Jesus in his earthly proclamation humbly distinguished himself from the Father and

---

[14]Grenz, *Reason for Hope*, p. 153.

the future of his kingdom,[15] so the church must distinguish itself from the kingdom and its future (p. 32). But even though the church is not identical with the kingdom of God, the future of God is already present in it and is accessible to people through the church, through its proclamation and its liturgical life. Christians are already translated into the kingdom of God's dear Son by the Spirit of the Father (Col 1:13) (p. 37).

By now it should be clear that as a sign and tool of the coming kingdom of God the church has its end not in itself but in the future of a humanity that is reconciled to God and united by common praise of God in his kingdom. For Pannenberg, in keeping with the universal relevance of God's reconciliation in Christ, the most fundamental truth about the nature of the church is its goal of all humanity being united under one God. Therefore, the church is essentially missionary (p. 45).

Pannenberg's view of the overarching nature of God's kingdom also informs his view of justice and its realization in the world. Opposite what modern Western culture has imagined since the time of classical liberalism, human means cannot reach the kingdom, nor its justice. The concept of justice is anchored in religion rather than human capacity. The coming of the kingdom, which at the eschaton will take place through the sovereign intervention of God, will usher in justice and peace. Whatever noble activities Christians and other people carry out toward that goal are not irrelevant, but neither are they instrumental in its realization. Pannenberg always insists that the fulfillment of human destiny—like the destiny of the rest of creation—cannot be found in the political order but comes only in the kingdom of God. He is critical of that aspect of the official ecumenical movement that attempts to achieve justice and peace majoring on a "purely ethical interest in promoting a unity of humanity . . . without regard for religious differences between people and their cultures" (p. 47). The unity and peace among Christians and between them and their God is a proleptic sign of the renewed humanity.[16]

Furthermore, Pannenberg argues strongly that, notwithstanding the political content of Christian hope in the coming of God's kingdom, Jesus addressed his proclamation of the imminent rule of God to individuals and did not announce any kind of political program of liberation. "Only in the faith of

---

[15]For the central idea of self-distinction (of the Son from the Father) in Pannenberg's trinitarian doctrine, see Wolfhart Pannenberg, *Systematic Theology* (Grand Rapids, Mich.: Eerdmans, 1991), 2:375-79.
[16]See further Grenz, *Reason for Hope*, p. 157.

individuals who, responding to the summons of Jesus, subordinated all other concerns in life to the imminence of the divine rule does this future already become the present" (p. 98).

Having said this, however, Pannenberg does not deny the potential political implications of the church's life. Even though the fellowship of the church is "spiritual" (2 Cor 3:6) because membership in the church does not rest on physical descent but on baptism as a sign of fellowship with Christ and of membership of his body (1 Cor 12:13), there is always the possibility that the relationship of Christians with and by Christ works itself out not only in the sanctification of their individual lives but also in that of every sphere of their common life, including the political and economic forms of this life. Pannenberg contends that especially when the fellowship of Christians is not just a minority in a non-Christian society, then the "Christian spirit ought to govern the political and economic forms of the common life." There may well "be envisioned and expected an overthrowing and restructuring of all forms of social life that are not controlled by the Christian spirit" (p. 479). Yet at the same time, Christians are aware that all such restructuring of forms of social life can have only provisional significance and will always in principle be open to revision; at best it can be only a provisional sign of the future of the kingdom to come. Hence the eschatological fellowship of Christians cannot take fully adequate shape in any this-worldly political order. Neither can the fellowship of Christians or its individual members unreservedly identify themselves with any model of political order (pp. 478-83).

## The Communion of Saints

Pannenberg is a Lutheran theologian. Sometimes it is not easy to say whether he is Lutheran in the sense that he draws from the best Reformation sources or in that he is anxious to offer a corrective criticism toward his own tradition. Nowhere in his ecclesiology is this feature more prevalent than in his discussion of the inner life of the church. He builds on the classical concept of the church as the communion of saints, not unlike Luther, but in a very distinctive way, often critical of Luther's and Lutheran appropriations of the concept. His favored overall designation for this aspect of the church is messianic fellowship, a term widely used by his German colleague Jürgen Moltmann, but with a distinctive slant.

Basically, Pannenberg defines the inner life of the church as the fellowship *(koinonia)* of believers and the body of Christ. However, the term "assembly of believers" does not mean merely a gathering or society of individual Christians. This is true even of Protestantism, he notes, since according to *Confessio Augustana* (#7) the church is not an arbitrary association of believing individuals but the fellowship in which the gospel is purely taught and the sacraments are rightly administered as instituted. Thus the teaching of the gospel and the sacraments form the basis of the fellowship of Christians and mediate this fellowship. This also lays the foundation, and, indeed, the only condition for the unity of the church. The mediation of the fellowship of believers by Word and sacrament links the personal sense of the formula *communio sanctorum* to the sacramental sense of communion in holy things, that is, in the saving gifts of Word and sacrament. This participation in holy things is none other than participation in Christ himself. The Eucharist in particular represents this connection, which is constitutive for the church, "between the fellowship of individual believers with the Lord who is present in Word and sacrament and their fellowship with one another that rests thereon" (pp. 101-2). Thus, the concept of the "body of Christ" is directly related to the real presence of Jesus Christ at the celebration of the Eucharist.

In Pannenberg's ecumenical ecclesiology, which always attempts both to overcome the Catholic-Protestant cleavage and integrate the differing traditions into a coherent one, the dual conception of the church as the body of Christ and as the fellowship of believers comes to focus in a mutually conditioned relationship:

> Calling the church the body of Christ is no mere metaphor nor is it just one of the biblical ways of depicting the nature of the church. Instead, the realism of the inseparable union of believers with Christ that finds expression in the idea of the church as the body of Christ is basic to an understanding of the church as a fellowship of believers and hence also as the people of God. The church is a fellowship of believers only on the basis of the participation of each individual in the one Lord. (p. 102)

Pannenberg rightly contends that the Reformation view of the church as the communion that is united with Christ stands in a tradition reaching back to patristic theology and finding its basis in the New Testament (1 Cor 10:16-17; Eph 4:15-16). For Pannenberg the unity or communion of the whole church of Christ finds manifestation at each local liturgical celebration where Christ is present. In other words, at each celebration of baptized Christians all Christianity is present. "The church is thus a *communio* that consists of a network of local churches." It is not in the first place a universal institution; the reality of the church is manifested in local communities gathered around the Word and sacrament, in other words, a fellowship of believers (p. 103).

## Pneumatological Ecclesiology

As already mentioned, the most characteristic feature of Pannenberg's theology and pneumatology is its holistic, comprehensive approach. [17] Creation, salvation, church and eschaton belong together. It is the same Holy Spirit of God who works united in all of these spheres: "the doctrine of the Spirit as an eschatological gift . . . aims at the eschatological consummation of salvation" (p. xiii).[18] The same Holy Spirit of God who is active in salvation is active in creation and in the consummation of God's eternal plan:

> The same Holy Spirit of God who is given to believers in a wholly specific way, namely, so as to dwell in them (Rom 5:9; 1 Cor 3:16), is none other than the Creator of all life in the whole range of natural occurrence and also in the new creation of the resurrection of the dead. . . . The work of the Spirit of God in his church and in believers serves the consummating of this work in the world of creation. (p. 2)

Pannenberg starts his third volume, the theme of which is ecclesiology and pneumatology, with the chapter title "The Outpouring of the Spirit, the Kingdom of God, and the Church." Pannenberg's ecclesiological vision sees an integral, dialogical relationship between the Spirit and Son. "The christological constitution and the pneumatological constitution do not exclude one another but belong together because the Spirit and the Son mutually indwell one another as trinitarian persons."[19] Everywhere the work of the Spirit is closely related to that of the Son, from creation to salvation to the consummation of creation in the eschaton.

The reciprocity, rather than asymmetry (usually in the form of Christology taking precedence), is accentuated by the fact that in the New Testament[20]

---

[17]See further my "Spirit, Christ, and Church," *One in Christ* 4 (2000): 343-46.

[18]See also especially, Pannenberg, "The Working of the Spirit in the Creation and in the People of God," in *Spirit, Faith and Church*, ed. W. Pannenberg, A. Dulles and C. E. Braaten (Philadelphia: Westminster Press, 1970), pp. 13-31.

[19]Pannenberg, *Systematic Theology*, 3:16-17 especially; this emphasis is evident throughout his discussion of the foundations of the church in the earlier part of vol. 3.

[20]Pannenberg (ibid., pp. 6-7) rightly notes that the concepts of the Holy Spirit in the New Testament are by no means uniform. While Paul (but also 1 Pet 3:18) traces the resurrection of Jesus to the Spirit, Luke and John say nothing on the theme. Other differences could be added; suffice it to say here, however, that according to Pannenberg the different concepts of the Holy Spirit simply express different aspects that have their basis in the Old Testament and obviously belong together in this context.

Jesus Christ himself is seen as a recipient of the Spirit and his work in conception (Luke), baptism (Mark) and resurrection (Rom 1:4; 8:11).[21] According to
John, the Spirit is given to Jesus Christ "without measure" (Jn 3:34), whereas
for believers the Spirit is a gift related to their becoming sons and daughters
by fellowship with Jesus Christ (Rom 5:15; 6:3-5) (see p. 9). Since the risen Lord
is wholly permeated by the divine Spirit of life, he can impart the Spirit to others insofar as they have fellowship with the Lord.[22]

The gift of the Spirit is not just for individual believers but aims at the building up of the fellowship of believers, "at the founding and the constant giving
of new life to the church" (p. 12). The Spirit thus unites believers with Christ
and into fellowship with others. The story of Pentecost (Acts 2) expresses that
the Spirit does not simply assure each believer individually of his or her fellowship with Jesus Christ, but that he thereby founds at the same time the fellowship of believers (p. 3).

Pannenberg rightly notes that in Paul, Jesus Christ is the foundation of the
church (1 Cor 3:11), whereas in Luke the church seems to be founded by the
"power" of the Holy Spirit. In constructing a systematic appraisal of the New
Testament teaching it is important that we neither see these various ideas as
alternatives nor suppress the differences by harmonizing. Each theological
concept of the church must integrate into itself the material aspects articulated
by these different orientations in the same canon. To this effect the Johannine
statements are helpful because they share with Luke an interest in the Spirit as
an independent entity, and yet at the same time they deal with the theme of the
link between his work and Jesus Christ. The Spirit's work is to glorify Jesus (Jn
16:13-14), but as that takes place Jesus himself through the Spirit's work is one
with the Father (Jn 14:20) (pp. 15-16).

In short, the church is thus the creation of both the Spirit and the Son.
Therefore, Pannenberg argues, a one-sided christological grounding for the
church has to be judged as lacking, and distorting the full reality. It leads, as
the history of the Western church shows, to an overemphasis on official church
structures derived directly from Jesus Christ (pp. 17-19). Christology, on the
one hand, and the integral relation of pneumatology to creation and to eschatology on the other hand, together help avoid a defective constriction of pneumatology from a christological angle that finds the Spirit's work only in the
fellowship of believers. This limitation of the Spirit's work Pannenberg further

---

[21]Pannenberg, *Systematic Theology,* 1:316; 2:84; 3:4-5.
[22]Pannenberg, *Systematic Theology,* 1:269.

sees as exaggerating this side of the Spirit's work, which manifests itself in a harmful enthusiasm evident throughout church history (pp. 19-20).

Pannenberg affirms the classical twofold description of the church as the body of Christ,[23] which highlights the christological orientation, and as the fellowship of believers, which highlights the pneumatological (pp. 99-110). It is the Spirit who by his work builds up the body of Christ as he testifies to Jesus Christ in the hearts of believers (p. 151). The Holy Spirit is the agent who makes possible for individual believers the immediacy of Jesus Christ in the church that is his body (pp. 122-35).

The same Spirit is not merely the basis of the Christian's immediacy with Christ but also the basis of the fellowship of believers in the unity of the body of Christ.

From all this Pannenberg draws an all-important ecclesiological principle, namely, that the work of the Spirit releases and reconciles the tension between the fellowship and the individual in the concept of the church, and hence, the underlying anthropological tension between society and individual freedom. The work of the Spirit lifts individuals ecstatically above their own particularity, not only to participation in the sonship of Christ, but at the same time also to the experience of the fellowship in the body of Christ that unites individual Christians to all other Christians. Furthermore, the Spirit's work is ecstatic not merely in individual Christians but also in the life of the church (pp. 33-34). The Spirit's role in the church is also accentuated in the Lord's Supper in which the Spirit mediates Christ's presence among his people gathered at the table (pp. 304-24).

## An Elected Community

As already mentioned, one of the distinctive features of Pannenberg's ecclesiology is the inclusion of the topic of election. For him, obviously, election is a highly corporeal reality rather than a choosing of some individuals for salvation (or, conversely, for damnation). The discussion of election and its relation to history forms the needed bridge between ecclesiology and eschatology.

Following Melanchthon, Pannenberg reinterprets election corporeally and historically. He takes note of the fact that even biblical history oscillates be-

---

[23]For Pannenberg the body of Christ is no mere metaphor nor it is just one of the biblical ways of depicting the nature of the church. Instead, it reveals the realism of the inseparable union of believers with Christ (*Systematic Theology*, 3:102).

tween an individual and a corporeal orientation to God's election. For Pannenberg, the main emphasis is corporeal rather than an "abstract" Augustinian concept of election. This abstract view can only lead to either determinism or Pelagianism, both pitfalls that Pannenberg wants to avoid at any cost. It also detaches election from real history and relegates it to choices by God in the past.[24] This abstract theory makes the notion of "calling" highly problematic and almost nonexistent; if God in the distant past has already made effective choices, what could possibly be the role of inviting people?[25]

In the Old Testament, and over against the mainstream of the classical Christian doctrine, election related God's eternal choice to the whole people of God. Individuals were chosen or called in order to serve the people. Even the New Testament, though individuals come more to the fore as objects of divine election, does not follow a line that leads to an abstract conception because the founding of the church created an opportunity for all peoples to be included in God's saving mission. Election was extended beyond the people of Israel to the Gentiles (pp. 443-44; 456-57). Precisely as the "people of God" the elected community exists as an exemplary anticipation and advance representation of the eschatological fellowship for which humanity is destined in the kingdom of God.[26]

What Pannenberg is not ready to give up, however, is the election of individuals as part of the community. Pannenberg's soteriology and ecclesiology have this built-in tension between individual responsibility on the one hand and God's election of the community and the coming of the kingdom of God by its own force on the other. Pannenberg brings this tension into focus in a somewhat complicated manner in his preface to the doctrine of election:

> By their eschatological reference, and in the case of baptism by anticipating the death of the baptized against the background of the eschatological future of God, the significatory acts of the church give advance notice of the whole course of life of those to whom they apply. The lives of the participants became a repeating of that which is represented in advance by the acts. In the repeating there is a place for the free action of the participants, though in such a way that it is always a repeating. The grace that is present in the sacramental signs, and that is imparted to the recipients, always precedes the repeating of what the sings represent. (p. 435)

---

[24]Ibid., pp. 439-47; see also Grenz, *Reason for Hope*, pp. 173-74.

[25]For calling and its relationship to election, see Pannenberg, *Systematic Theology*, 3:447-55.

[26]For an extensive treatment of the concept of the "people of God" and its relation to election and history, see Pannenberg, *Systematic Theology*, 3:463-70; on its relation to Israel as the "old" people of God, see ibid., pp. 470-77.

In other words, there is a mutual relationship between the individual and corporeal election. In a sense, God's election of the whole people of God is the basis for the election of individuals; but if the individual's "yes" to God's invitation is missing in the form of faith and reception of the sacraments, election remains ineffective.

# 11

# Jürgen Moltmann
## MESSIANIC ECCLESIOLOGY

## A Contextual Ecclesiology

Jürgen Moltmann's first three contributions to theology were *Theology of Hope* (1964), [1] *The Crucified God* (1972) and his main ecclesiological work, *The Church in the Power of the Spirit* (1975). His later series consists of *The Trinity and the Kingdom of God* (1981), *God in Creation* (1985), *The Way of Jesus Christ* (1990) and his main pneumatological work, *The Spirit of Life* (1992). A Protestant counterpart to Hans Küng's *The Church*, Moltmann's *The Church in the Power of the Spirit* is one of the defining ecumenical works on the doctrine of the church in recent decades.

Ecclesiological discussions are not limited to this main work, however. In *Theology of Hope* the eschatological promise given in the resurrection of Christ creates a missionary church, a church of dialectical hope which is shaped and conditioned by the death of Christ and the resurrection of Christ and us. The church is called to serve the world, including having political involvement. In *Theology and Joy* [2] the missionary church celebrates the festival of freedom, anticipating the joy of the new creation. *The Crucified God* [3] adds to dialectical hope dialectical love; the church identifies itself with those with whom the crucified Christ identified himself.

Moltmann himself characterizes his theology as having a biblical foundation, an eschatological orientation and a political responsibility. [4] To these, one

---

[1] Jürgen Moltmann, *Theology of Hope: On the Ground and the Implications of a Christian Eschatology* (London: SCM Press, 1967).
[2] Jürgen Moltmann, *Theology and Joy* (London: SCM Press, 1973).
[3] Jürgen Moltmann, *The Crucified God: The Cross as the Foundation and Criticism of Christian Theology* (London: SCM Press, 1974).
[4] Jürgen Moltmann, *History and the Triune God: Contributions to Trinitarian Theology* (London: SCM Press, 1991), p. 182.

element has to be added, namely a trinitarian emphasis. Especially in his later works, he has come to highlight the importance of the doctrine of the Trinity for other theological loci. The trinitarian structure is also evident in *The Church in the Power of the Spirit,* whose main divisions, after the introductory discussions, follows a trinitarian plan: "The Church of Jesus Christ" (chap. 3), "The Church of the Kingdom of God" (chap. 4), and "The Church in the Presence of the Holy Spirit" (chap. 5) and "The Church in the Power of the Holy Spirit" (chap. 6). In this trinitarian perspective, he situates the church in the concrete realities of life and speaks for a church that is faithful to its calling: this church he identifies as the church of Jesus Christ, the missionary church, the ecumenical church and the political church.[5]

For his creative work, he draws from various sources: his ecumenical contacts and work in the WCC and in relation to the Eastern Orthodox Church (one of the distinctive features of Moltmann's theology is his extended dialogue with the Eastern spirituality and theology); his extensive travel in the third world; his interest in the Pentecostal/Charismatic movements; and his contacts with churches other than the German state-churches, namely the "voluntary religion" of Protestant Free churches, liberation theologies of Latin America and elsewhere, and Catholic base communities in Latin America. The fact that he draws from so many different sources makes his theology not only contemporary but also contextually relevant. Moltmann's voice has been heard also outside the confines of the Western academy, and a growing number of two-thirds-world theologians have interacted with his proposals.[6]

## *Christological Focus*

Moltmann describes his doctrine of the church as a messianic and relational ecclesiology. "Messianic" means essentially "christological"; the christological foundation always points toward the eschaton, so his view is "a christologically founded and eschatologically directed doctrine of the church" (p. 13). The church is the church of Jesus Christ, subject to his lordship alone. Consequently, for Moltmann ecclesiology can only be developed from Christology

---

[5]Moltmann, *The Church in the Power of the Spirit* (London: SCM Press, 1977), pp. 1-18. Hereafter in this chapter, most page references to *The Church in the Power of the Spirit* will be given in parenthetical references.

[6]A very helpful overview of Moltmann's ecclesiology is offered by Richard Bauckham, *The Theology of Jürgen Moltmann* (Edinburgh: T & T Clark, 1995).

(p. 66). But it is important to notice that statements about Christ also point be-yond the church to the kingdom, the future reign of Christ, the Messiah. Thus Christ's church has to be a "messianic fellowship." As the church of Christ, she lives "between remembrance of his history and hope of his kingdom"; the church is not the kingdom but its anticipation (p. 75).

As the church of Jesus Christ, the church is bound together with the history and destiny of her Lord. The dialectic of suffering and joy characterizes the ex-istence of the church; the cross and resurrection set the tone for its life. The church participates in the passion of Christ, "sighings of the Spirit," until God's kingdom of joy and peace will arrive. God has made Godself vulnerable to the sufferings of the world, and the church is drawn to that: "God's pain in the world is the way to God's happiness with the world" (p. 93). The dialectic of suffering and joy also becomes apparent in the dual nature of the church. The church is both the "church under the cross" and also the "church of the festival of freedom and joy."

While the christological focus in Moltmann's systematic theology has been especially determinative in his doctrine of the church, in his later works, trin-itarian and especially pneumatological perspectives on the church have gained more importance. A trinitarian outlook was already evident in *The Church in the Power of the Spirit,* but as a whole the doctrine of the Trinity has captured his interest more and more. His continued dialogue with Eastern Or-thodox theology has had a determining influence in this shift.

## A Fellowship of Equal Persons

For Moltmann, the church is a free society of equals, an open fellowship of friends. Mirroring the egalitarian relationships between the trinitarian per-sons, the church is a communion of equals. Moltmann argues that one's doc-trine of the Trinity directly carries over to ecclesiology. Where there is a hierarchical notion of the Trinity, a hierarchical view of the church follows. With an open Trinity, one finds relationships of affection with respect and loy-alty. Not only is the Trinity open, but so was Jesus' friendship. It was not closed and exclusive, but inclusive, even revolutionary: "Open and total friendship that goes out to meet the other is the spirit of the kingdom in which God comes to man and man to man. . . . Open friendship prepares the ground for a friend-lier world" (p. 121).

An open church is a voluntary fellowship of committed Christians rather than a "cultural" state church. Moltmann clearly opts for a "Free church" model and is sharply critical of the state church model with infant baptism.[7] As a voluntary fellowship of Christians the church members submit their lives under Christ's lordship. The state church is "a pastoral church for the people"; "a public institution to administer the religion of society" that preserves the status quo; a clerical institution, only narrowly interested of religious needs.[8] That is, the state church is a church without community and commitment. Moltmann's favorite way of talking about the church is "the mature and responsible congregation" that consists of committed discipleship in the service of the kingdom and fellowship in freedom and equality, mutual acceptance and care, in solidarity with the poor and oppressed. In this kind of church, baptism is not so much a "believer's baptism" as it is a baptism to Christian calling, discipleship and service.

## A Church for Others

Yet another designation for Moltmann's doctrine of the church is "relational ecclesiology." The church never exists for itself but is always in relation to God and the world; therefore it is a serving, missionary church: "The church cannot understand itself alone. It can only truly comprehend its mission and its meaning, its roles and its functions in relation to others" (p. 19).

There is a *theological* foundation for Moltmann's relational ecclesiology: everything, including God, only exists in relationships. Moltmann's view of the Trinity may be described as an "open Trinity": in creation, God opens Godself to the world, and also makes Godself vulnerable to happenings in history.[9] Consequently, ecclesiology always has to be developed in relation to Christology, pneumatology and eschatology. Relationality means openness to the world and to God's future: the church is to be "open for God, open for men and open for the future of both God and men. The church atrophies when it

---

[7]Jürgen Moltmann, "The Challenge of Religion in the 1980s," in *Theologians in Transition: The Christian Century "How My Mind Has Changed" Series*, ed. J. M. Wall (New York: Crossroad, 1981), p. 110.

[8]Jürgen Moltmann, "Theology in Germany Today," in *Observations on "The Spiritual Situation of the Age": Contemporary German Perspectives*, ed. J. Haberman (Cambridge, Mass.: MIT Press, 1984), p. 189.

[9]See further Moltmann, *History and the Triune God* and *The Crucified God*. There is no doubt about the panentheistic orientation of Moltmann's theology, which means that God and world are brought "closer" to each other than in classical theism, in a sort of mutual relationship. The term *panentheism* has to be differentiated from *pantheism*, which means total identification of God and the world. Moltmann's view lies somewhere between classical theism and pantheism.

surrenders any one of these opennesses and closes itself up against God, men or the future" (p. 2). The English title of the popular version of his main ecclesiological work clearly brings this aspect of his doctrine of the church into focus: *The Open Church*.[10]

One way the church lives for the world and for others is by participating in the "offices" of Christ. Following traditional Reformed dogmatics, Moltmann talks about the three offices of Christ as prophet (ministry), priest (death) and king (resurrection/rule). The church participates in all of these in its response to God's invitation to be an instrument of salvation. In its prophetic task, the church participates in Jesus' messianic proclamation and his setting people free. This is the liberating ministry of the church. Participating in Jesus' passion, the church lives and ministers under the cross, in suffering solidarity with the weak. And being part of Jesus' exaltation, the church lives as the fellowship of freedom and equality in the Spirit. To these traditional offices, Moltmann adds two more, namely Christ's transfiguration, which highlights the aesthetic dimension, the worship and "festival of freedom," and Christ's friendship, by which the church opens up itself into an open friendship and inviting fellowship.[11]

The church does not live for itself but rather exists for the world. Therefore, the church lives for and out of mission. But even mission has to be shaped by the principle of openness. "Israel, the world religions, and the economic, political, and cultural processes of the world" are partners in history "who are not the church and will never become the church" (p. 134). In other words, the mission of the church is not to "spread the church but to spread the kingdom"; the church is not self-serving but serving the world and the kingdom (p. 11). The church as an "anticipation" of the coming of the kingdom and "representation" of the kingdom is a fragmentary and preliminary "part" of the coming "whole." This brings the ministry of the Spirit into focus in terms of the mediations and ministries of the Spirit: "As the mediations and powers of the Holy Spirit, they lead the church beyond itself, out into the suffering of the world and into the divine future" (p. 198).

Moltmann is also a political theologian. His political, social and ecological concern is visible also in his view of the church. Even though the church's mission is based on the gospel and the history of Christ, political involvement is a necessary part of the church's ministry to the world.

---

[10]Jürgen Moltmann, *Invitation to a Messianic Lifestyle* (London: SCM Press, 1978); American edition: *The Passion for Life: A Messianic Lifestyle* (Philadelphia: Fortress, 1978).
[11]See further Moltmann, *Church in the Power of the Spirit*, part 3.

### The Church in the Power of the Spirit

Moltmann's revived interest in the Holy Spirit has come to highlight the importance of pneumatology to messianic eschatological ecclesiology; he sometimes even calls it "Charismatic ecclesiology." In trinitarian history the Holy Spirit mediates the eschatological future to us as the church lives between the history of Jesus and the anticipation of the coming of the kingdom; the Spirit serves the coming of the kingdom of Son. In that sense, the church participates in the mission of the Spirit. But since the work of the Spirit is not confined to the church, the Spirit works everywhere in creation. For this reason the church cannot absolutize itself, but is always provisional in nature.

As the creation of the Spirit, the church is also a "Charismatic fellowship" of equal persons. There is no division between the office bearers and the people (p. 298). The church for Paul (1 Cor 12—14)—and for Moltmann—is where the Spirit's self-manifestation takes place in overflowing powers, charismata. Consequently, the people of God see themselves in their existence as being "the creation of the Spirit": "The Spirit calls them into life; the Spirit gives the community the authority for its mission, the Spirit makes its living powers and the ministries that spring from them effective; the Spirit unites, orders and preserves it" (p. 294). Consequently, the ministry of the church is Charismatic in essence. For Moltmann, "ecclesiology becomes hierarchology if we do not start from the fact that every believer, whether he be an office-bearer or not, is a member of the messianic people of God." The ministry is turned into an insipid, "spiritless, kind of civil service, and the charisma becomes a cult of the religious genius, if we do not make the one charismatically living community our point of departure" (pp. 289-90).

Moltmann wants to emphasize the role of charismata in the church, but he does so by expanding the often too-narrow understanding of spiritual gifts. Traditionally, the charismata have been divided into two groups: "supernatural" (1 Cor 12:8-10) and "natural" (Rom 12:6-8). But both groups have operated within the confines of the church and individual piety. Moltmann insists that the Holy Spirit gives spiritual gifts for service in the world, for example, prophetic speech in liberation and ecology movements. "If charismata are not given to us so that we can flee from this world into a world of religious dreams, but if they are intended to witness to the liberating lordship of Christ in this world's conflicts, then the Charismatic movement must not become a nonpolitical religion, let alone a de-politicized one."[12]

---

[12]Moltmann, *Spirit of Life*, p. 186.

The church was born on the day of Pentecost, and glossolalia was the sign of its birth.[13] As the creation of the Spirit, this church of Christ is dependent on the Charismatic powers of the Spirit. The church participates in the passion of Christ and the "sighings of the Spirit" until God's kingdom of joy and peace arrives. Glossolalia, speaking in tongues, is "such a strong inner grasp of the Spirit that its expression leaves the realm of understandable speech and expresses itself in extraordinary manner, just as intense pain is expressed in unrestrained crying or great joy in jumping and dancing."[14]

As an anticipation of the kingdom, the church celebrates the sacraments in the power of the Spirit:

> When it listens to the language of the messianic era and celebrates the signs of dawn and hope in baptism and the Lord's Supper, the church sees itself in the presence of the Holy Spirit as the messianic people destined for the coming kingdom. In the messianic feast it becomes conscious of its freedom and its charge. In the power of the Holy Spirit the church experiences itself as the messianic fellowship of service for the kingdom of God in the world. (p. 289)

## Community of the Holy Spirit

One of the most distinctive and creative features of Moltmann's theology in general and ecclesiology in particular is his thoroughgoing ecological concern. This ecological orientation has come to full maturity in his more recent work on pneumatology. Moltmann adamantly opposes what he sees as a limited doctrine of the Spirit in the past. In both Protestant and Catholic theology and devotion, there is a tendency to view the Holy Spirit solely as the Spirit of redemption. Its place is in the church, and it gives men and women the assurance of the eternal blessedness of their souls. This redemptive Spirit is cut off from both bodily life and the life of nature. It makes people turn away from "this world" and hope for a better world beyond. Theology has been content with talking about the Holy Spirit in connection with God, faith, the Christian life, the church and prayer, but seldom in connection with the body and nature.[15] The results have been tragic. This limited view of the Spirit has impoverished and emptied the churches while the "Spirit emi-

---

[13]Moltmann, "The Spirit Gives Life: Spirituality and Vitality," in *All Together in One Place: Theological Papers from the Brighton Conference on World Evangelization*, ed. H. D. Hunter and P. D. Hocken (Sheffield, U.K.: Sheffield Academic Press, 1993), p. 26.

[14]Ibid., p. 27.

[15]Moltmann, *Spirit of Life*, p. 8.

grates to spontaneous groups and personal experiences."[16]

Moltmann wants to rehabilitate the biblical view of the Spirit as the Spirit of life, the divine energy of life, which according to the Old Testament interpenetrates all living things. His firm conviction is that wherever there is passion for life, there the Spirit of God is operating: life over against death, liberation over against oppression, justice over against injustice, and so on. Therefore, the only legitimate attitude is that which affirms life.

The term "community of the Holy Spirit" has been used in theology to refer to the church. Moltmann radically expands this traditional notion to encompass the whole "community of creation" from the most elementary particles to atoms to molecules to cells to living organisms to animals to human beings to communities of humanity.[17] Any kind of community of creation is the fellowship of the Holy Spirit. To capture this, a holistic doctrine of the Spirit is needed.[18]

The Holy Spirit has been understood as the Spirit of sanctification; the very name "*Holy* Spirit" makes this clear. Commensurate with how the doctrine of justification has been understood in traditional theologies, the doctrine of sanctification has referred to the development of spiritual life in an individual believer. Moltmann's point of departure is the observation that since all life is meant to continue, to grow, sanctification has to do with the furtherance and facilitation of growing life. Sanctification in this more comprehensive perspective encompasses several aspects. It means rediscovering the sanctity of life and the divine mystery of creation, and defending them from life's manipulation, the secularization of nature and the destruction of the world through human violence. The earth belongs to God and therefore is something to be protected. Out of this attitude grows "reverence for life." The church as an anticipation of the coming kingdom of peace and harmony is called to participate and champion the sanctification of life that includes the search for the "harmonies and accords of life."[19]

---

[16]Ibid., p. 2.
[17]Ibid., pp. 225-26.
[18]Moltmann actually explicitly labels his pneumatology "holistic" in ibid., p. xiii.
[19]Ibid., pp. 171-74 (quote on p. 173).

# 12

# Miroslav Volf

## PARTICIPATORY ECCLESIOLOGY

### The Church as the Image of the Trinity

The Croatian-born theologian who became a professor at Yale University, Miroslav Volf has outlined a trinitarian ecclesiology in a critical interaction between Roman Catholic, Orthodox and Free church ecclesiologies.[1] Taking his point of departure from a critical dialogue with the views of Cardinal Joseph Ratzinger of the Roman Catholic Church and John Zizioulas of the Eastern Orthodox Church, he purports to offer a viable Free church ecclesiology partly based on the thoughts of the first Baptist theologian, John Smyth from seventeenth-century England. Volf sympathizes with feminist theologians' insistence on the church as a fellowship of free, equal persons. While Volf wants to counter the tendencies toward individualism in Protestant ecclesiology in general and Free church ecclesiology in particular, he seeks to suggest a viable understanding of the church in which both person and community are given their proper due. "The ultimate goal is to spell out a vision of the church as an image of the triune God" (p. 2).

With feminists and Free churches, Volf contends that the presence of Christ in the Spirit, which constitutes the church, is mediated not simply (and in Volf's case, not even primarily) through ordained ministers but through the whole congregation. Consequently, the whole church is called to engage in ministry and make decisions about leadership roles.

Unlike too many ecclesiological treatises, even more recent ones, Volf listens carefully not only to the tradition, but also to the emerging voices of thriving, growing churches both in the West and especially outside. His work is

---

[1]Miroslav Volf, *After Our Likeness: The Church as the Image of the Trinity* (Grand Rapids, Mich.: Eerdmans, 1998). Hereafter in this chapter, references to this book will be made in parentheses in the text.

also distinctive in that it is one of the first theologically responsible, constructive works from a Free church perspective. Standard ecclesiologies tend to either totally ignore younger churches, which are usually theologically less sophisticated, or at their best just offer some passing comments on their growth or numbers. Volf queries, "The Churches of the Future?" (p. 11), and Free churches may be just that.

## Christ's Presence and the Ecclesiality of the Church

Volf asks two interrelated questions, both of which relate to the ecclesiality of the church, namely, "What is the church?" and "Where is the church?" To address these questions theologically, Volf sees God's eschatological new creation as the all-embracing framework for an appropriate understanding of the church. The future of the church in God's new creation is the mutual personal indwelling of the triune God and of his glorified people according to the vision of the apocalyptic seer in Revelation 21—22. The participation in the very life of the triune God is not only a future hope but also a present experience (1 Jn 1:3). Taking notice of the ancient rules of Ignatius (that the ecclesiality of the church could be secured by reference to Christ's presence)[2] and that of Irenaeus (who linked ecclesiality with the Spirit of Christ),[3] Volf makes the necessary distinction between the general and particular presence of the Spirit (pp. 128-29) and concludes:

> Wherever the Spirit of Christ, which as the eschatological gift anticipates God's new creation in history (see Rom 8:23; 2 Cor 1:22; Col 1:11-20), is present in its *ecclesially constitutive* activity, there is the church. The Spirit unites the gathered congregation with the triune God and integrates it into a history extending from Christ, indeed, from the Old Testament saints, to the eschatological new creation. This Spirit-mediated relationship with the triune God . . . constitutes an assembly into a church. (p. 129)

This for Volf answers the question of the identity of the church. What about the second question: "Where is the church?" The Catholic and Orthodox suggestion that the sacraments and the bishop (the latter is needed to secure the sacraments) are the guarantors of the Spirit's presence is not an acceptable idea to Volf. Neither is he totally happy with the suggestion of John Smyth and others from Free churches who contend that the prerequisites for the constitutive presence of Christ are obedience to Christ's commandment and a right (in

---

[2]Ignatius *Letter to the Smyrneans* 8:2.
[3]Irenaeus *Adversus Haereses* 3.24.1.

their understanding, "biblical") organization of the church. Consequently, as far as the conditions of ecclesiality are concerned, the episcopal and Free church traditions differ especially in three respects: (1) According to the Catholic and Orthodox traditions, Free church ecclesiology lacks a bishop to ensure the presence of Christ, while according to the Free church tradition, such a bishop is not permitted. (2) In the episcopal model, Christ's presence is mediated sacramentally; in contrast the Free churches speak of Christ's unmediated, "direct" presence in the entire local communion. (3) According to the episcopal tradition, the church is constituted through the performance of objective activities, and Christ's constitutive presence is not bound to the subjective disposition (even if the latter is not unimportant); whereas the Free churches have come to emphasize subjective conditions, namely faith and obedience, to the point that where these are missing, despite the presence of the objective aspects, serious doubt arises regarding ecclesiality (pp. 133-35).

Volf attempts to transcend this ecumenical impasse by suggesting that the only condition for the ecclesiality of the church is the presence of Christ amidst the gathered community as mentioned in Matthew 18:20: "for where two or three are gathered in my name, I am there among them." This ecclesiological rule goes back to Ignatius,[4] Tertullian[5] and (with some qualifications) to Cyprian.[6] On the basis of "theological" exegesis of Matthew 18:20, Volf comes to the conclusion that "where two or three are gathered in Christ's name, not only is Christ present among them, but a Christian church is there as well, perhaps a bad church, a church that may well transgress against love and truth, but a church nonetheless" (p. 136).

## The Church as an Assembly

The church is first an assembly of those gathered in Jesus' name. As a local church it is the people who in a specific way assemble at a specific place. However, the church continues to be the church even when it is not assembled; it lives on as a church in the mutual service its members render to one another and in its common mission to the world. The church nowhere exists "above the locally assembled congregation, but rather 'in, with, and beneath' it."[7] A con-

---

[4]Ignatius *Letter to the Smyrneans* 8:2.
[5]Tertullian *De echortatione castitatis* 7.
[6]Cyprian *De unitate* 12.
[7]Here Volf, *After Our Likeness*, p. 138, quotes from Otto Weber, *Versammelte Gemeinde: Beiträge zum Gespräch die Kirche und Gottesdienst* (Neukirchen, Austria: Buchhandlung des Erziehungsvereins, 1949), p. 33.

gregation is the body of Christ in the particular locale in which it gathers to-gether.

How can we recognize what kind of assembly is a legitimate church? Volf is too good a theologian to imply that any kind of free association of likemind-ed people would produce a church. "A church is an assembly, but an assembly [of any kind] is not yet a church." An indispensable condition for ecclesiality is that the people assemble in the name of Christ. Gathering in Christ's name is the precondition for the presence of Christ in the Spirit. Gathering in the name of the Lord also connects the church with the whole history of Jesus Christ; in the New Testament the church is the church of Jesus Christ (Rom 16:16). The purpose of this identification of the assembly with Christ is not only cognitive acceptance of the life and history of Jesus Christ but also com-mitment to his will. In other words, there need to be both cognitive specifica-tion and personal identification. Confession of faith in Christ, although a highly personal act, is far more than personal; it is done before other believers and the whole world (pp. 145-50, esp. p. 145).

Confession of faith also opens up Volf's understanding of the roles of sac-raments and office in relation to the question of ecclesiality. Here again Volf steers a middle course between the episcopal churches (Roman Catholic and Eastern Orthodox), which hold that sacraments and office are indispensable conditions for ecclesiality, and the Free churches, for whom the sacraments at their best contribute to the well-being of the church and for whom the question of ministry patterns is more a practical than an ontological question in ecclesiology.

Volf does not see the office of minister as a constitutive element of the church: "Christ does not enter the church through the 'narrow portals' of or-dained office, but rather through the dynamic life of the entire church. The presence of Christ is not attested merely by the institution of office, but rather through the multidimensional confession of the entire assembly." In other words, ordained office belongs not to the *esse* (essence) but to the *bene esse* (well-being) of the church. In contrast, the sacraments—baptism and the Lord's Supper—belong to the necessary conditions of the church as long as they are understood as a form of the confession of faith and an expression of faith. This is indeed what the sacraments are in the New Testament, Volf con-tends. They are a public representation of the confession of faith. In baptism, the person baptized publicly professes faith in him in whose name baptism oc-curs, and as for the Lord's Supper, the ecclesial praise of God and of God's salvific activity constitutes it (pp. 152-54, esp. 152).

## Church and Churches

What is the relation between the local assembly and the totality of the eschatological people of God? In other words, what is the primary sense of the term
*ekklesia*? For Catholic theology, *ekklesia* refers to the universal church; Orthodox
theology argues for the identity of every local church with the universal
church. The Free churches have traditionally insisted on the primacy of local
churches almost to the exclusion of the concept of the universal church. If one
starts with the priority of the local church in keeping with the general tone of
Free church ecclesiology, then the universal church is the sum of all local
churches. But how then, Volf asks, can every individual local congregation already be "the prolepsis" (an anticipation) of the eschatological people of God?
For him, the key concept is "anticipation." The local church, rather than being
a "concrete realization of the existing universal church" (Catholic theology), is
"the real anticipation or proleptic realization of the eschatological gathering of
the entire people of God." There is a mutual relationship between the local and
the universal:

> It is precisely as partially overlapping entities that both the local church and the
> universal church are constituted into the church through their common relation
> to the Spirit of Christ, who makes them both into the anticipation of the eschato-
> logical gathering of the entire people of God. This is why every local church can
> also be completely the church even though it encompasses only a part of the uni-
> versal church. (pp. 140-41)

The mutual interdependence of local and universal church also comes to
the fore in Volf's understanding of the ecclesial mediation of faith in the form
of their common confession of faith. Each time a congregation professes faith
in Christ, it also does so before the world. And never can the confession be an
idiosyncratic act of a local church. As a constitutive act for the church, "every
church must be constituted by the same confession." In other words, confessions of faith connect every church with all other churches (p. 154).

Since the confession of faith mediates Christ's presence, each local church
is a legitimate church by virtue of that presence. In that sense, each local
church is "independent." Of course, the Free churches have too often interpreted their independence in a way that has made the local church not only independent but also totally self-sufficient to the point that they have not
recognized a total disregard for other churches as a violation of the principle
of ecclesiality. Volf offers a corrective here: even though each local church
"stands on its own spiritual feet" as a result of the presence of Christ, its "in-

dependence" does not mean that other churches are in every instance denied the right to intervene in the life of a local church or that the local church can dismiss other churches and their ecclesiality. On the one hand, other churches can intervene in the affairs of a local church if (and only if) the ecclesiality of this church is threatened as a result of a distortion of the confession of faith or through permanent resistance in practice to Christ's rule. On the other hand, each local church is to be open toward other churches; Volf holds this as an indispensable interecclesial condition of ecclesiality.

This principle he calls an "interecclesial minimum." No church, to be a true church, can on its own, in isolation from all other churches, claim to be a church without acknowledging all other churches. Through this openness to other churches, a church necessarily sets out on the path to its future, a path in which it is able to express and deepen its communion, that is, "differentiated unity" with all other churches (pp. 155-58).

## The Charismatic Church

According to Volf, the question "Where is the church?" cannot be answered without reference to the living presence of the Spirit.[8] The basic idea of the Charismatic structure of the church can be summarized in five principles.[9] First, the thesis that the church is constituted by the way of the entire called and charismatically endowed people of God presupposes that the exalted Christ himself is acting in the gifts of the Spirit.[10] The second identifying feature of the charismata is their universal distribution (1 Cor 12:7; Rom 12:3; Eph 4:7; 1 Pet 4:10). In the community as the body of Christ, there are no members without charisma. Thus the division into those who serve and those who are served is ecclesiologically unacceptable. Universal distribution implies common responsibility for the life of the church as well as mutual subordination. The third characteristic feature for the charismata is their fundamental interdependence (Rom 12:6; cf. 1 Cor 12:7-11). Consequently, the life of the church members must be characterized by mutuality. Fourth, the sovereign Spirit of

---

[8]Peter Kuzmic and Miroslav Volf, "Communio Sanctorum: Toward a Theology of the Church as a Fellowship of Persons," Pentecostal position paper read at the International Roman Catholic-Pentecostal Dialogue, Riano, Italy, May 21-26, 1985, p. 14.

[9]Volf, *After Our Likeness*, 228-33. The basic outline was already presented earlier in Volf, "Kirche als Gemeinschaft: Ekklesiologische Überlegungen aus freikirchlicher Perspektive," *Evangelische Theologie* 49 (1989): 52-76.

[10]Volf builds here on E. Käsemann, "Amt und Gemeinde im Neuen Testament," in *Exegetische Versuche und Besinnungen* (Göttingen: Vandenhoeck & Ruprecht, 1970), 1:109-34.

God allots the charismata "as the Spirit chooses" (1 Cor 12:11). "The Spirit works *when* the Spirit chooses; the church cannot determine at which time the Spirit is to bestow its gifts" (p. 232, emphasis in the original). Finally, Volf speaks for the synchronic and diachronic plurality of charismata. Charismata can vary from time to time and from person to person.

Volf emphasizes that his interpretation is nothing new in theology or church life. "This model involves . . . only *reinterpretation* of what is already actually happening in churches" (p. 227, emphasis in the original). He argues that the model according to which the Spirit constitutes the church through officeholders (Catholic and Orthodox) obscures the ecclesiologically highly significant fact that in all churches faith is mediated and kept alive by ordinary people. He further notes that the ecclesiological obscuring of the role of the laity in constituting the church is one of the most important theological factors contributing to lay passivity, resulting in the model of the "church in passivity" (p. 227).

## Toward a Theology of the Laity

Volf calls his approach a "participatory ecclesiology." He believes that the Free churches' real ecclesiological challenge for other churches calls them to flesh out the implications of the priesthood of all. Other churches, Volf claims, must in a new way discover theologically and learn to live out today what they have already known and in part lived out from the beginning: the active priesthood of all believers, a priesthood that they originally understood not only soteriologically but also ecclesiologically.[11] The churches have to come to acknowledge the fact that in accordance with their being called and endowed by the Spirit of God, all members of a church depict and offer the manifold grace of God through their actions and words (1 Pet 4:10-11). The church comes into being and comes to life through the communication of salvation by mutual service with the pluriform gifts of the Spirit.

All members of the church create the "plausibility structures" in which the communication of faith and life in faith first become possible. "Thus the Spirit does not constitute the church exclusively through those who bear office, but through all members, who serve the others with their gifts."[12] He notes that a step toward countering the problem of the passivity of the laity is a theological revaluation of the laity as the medium through which the church is constituted

---

[11]Volf, "A Protestant Response to 'We Are the Church: New Congregationalism,' " *Concilium* 3 (1996): 37.
[12]Ibid., p. 38.

by the Spirit of God. As the church comes into being through the presence of Christ in the Holy Spirit, it means that the exalted Christ himself acts in the gifts of the Spirit. "Since . . . all Christians have charisms, Christ also acts through all members of the church, and not just those who hold office."[13]

Volf notes the fact that many churches have criticized the overemphasis of the *BEM*-document on the representation of Christ by the ordained ministry (alone).[14] Not until a proper theology of the laity is developed is there any hope of overcoming the perennial problem of the bipolarity of person in office versus community. When laity are seen as the medium through which the church is constituted by the Spirit of God, then spiritual activity and receptiveness are no longer divided into two groups of persons, but represent two basic activities of each individual: each individual acts in the person of Christ and each is a recipient of this action.[15] Understandably, Volf is critical of *Lumen Gentium* (#10), which, with all its emphasis on the role of the laity, still holds that the "common priesthood" and "hierarchical priesthood" do differ not only in degree but also "essentially."

The churches have to come to acknowledge the fact that in accordance with their being called and endowed by the Spirit of God, all members of the church depict and offer the manifold grace of God through their actions and words (1 Pet 4:10-11). This leads not to underestimating the outstanding importance of those who are "in office," Volf reminds us, but to the conviction that the whole life of the church is not ordered around official ministers. In this way only, the problem that Volf targets—a problem that Bernard Cooke refers to as the "distancing of God" from the laity in the congregational life[16] and Jaroslav Pelikan labels an "aristocracy of the Spirit"[17]—can be overcome.

---

[13]Ibid., pp. 39-40.

[14]Ibid., p. 40.

[15]Ibid., pp. 40-41.

[16]B. J. Cooke, *The Distancing of God: The Ambiguity of Symbol in History and Theology* (Minneapolis: Fortress, 1990).

[17]Jaroslav Pelikan, *The Emergence of the Catholic Tradition*, vol. 1, *The Christian Tradition* (Chicago: University of Chicago Press, 1971), p. 107.

# James McClendon Jr.

## BAPTIST ECCLESIOLOGY

### The Church and the Practice of Doctrine

In shaping its teaching, the church seeks to be simply the church, so that Christians may be a people who find in Christ their center, in the Spirit their communion, in God's reign their rule of life. The convictions that make such a common life possible fall into three broad, overlapping categories, those that inform Christian living (moral convictions), those that display the substance of Christian faith (doctrinal convictions), and those that open out into a Christian vision or worldview (philosophical convictions).[1]

The theological vision of the late James Wm. McClendon Jr., whose life and thinking were embedded in an ecumenical Baptist heritage going back to Anabaptist, Mennonite and Radical Reformation forefathers, took a synthetic and integrative approach. Nothing less than a holistic Christ-centered theology, rooted in the rich classical tradition of both the East and West, at the same time contemporary and often creative in its constructive proposal, was sufficient to the one we can perhaps call the premier theologian of the Free church wing of the church. His Baptist vision of the church is an integral part of his theological and ethical system and can be understood only against the whole.[2]

McClendon's understanding of the church is tied to his view of theology and doctrine. Christian doctrine is something that is practiced in the church; even when it is not "practical" in the popular sense of the world, its power and legitimacy comes from the praxis in the church. In his simple, profound style, McClendon defined doctrine as "a church teaching as she must teach if she is

---

[1]James Wm. McClendon Jr., *Doctrine: Systematic Theology,* vol. 2 (Nashville: Abingdon, 1994), p. 21.
[2]Ibid., p. 327, states this explicitly even though it is evident in the structure and argumentation of his systematics. He acknowledges the fact that for some his treatment of the church at the end of *Doctrine* may come too late.

to be the church here and now."[3] He was not content with earlier approaches to doctrine, neither the Catholic traditions in which the doctrine consists in revealed truth imparted to the church, nor the Liberal Protestant view according to which the religious feeling (Schleiermacher and others) is the core; McClendon's view, of course, took its point of departure in both classical approaches but went beyond them by asserting that learning and studying doctrine is the task given to the whole church, the gathered fellowship. "The Christian gospel summons all to be students in the school of Christ (*mathetai*, learners, disciples). In the broad sense in which the church is itself a teacher, each member is a teacher as well" (p. 29).[4] In other words, his idea is that of a disciple church engaged in its doctrinal or teaching task, centered on the study of Scripture, which for McClendon is the objective content and character of doctrine (pp. 34-35).

McClendon also calls the church a narrative[5] community, the home of doctrine. The local community of readers of Scripture, the narrative of and concerning Jesus Christ, meet and work together and face the interpretive task from a shared context of witness in a particular place. Even though national and denominational structures do have meaning, the essence of Christianity, in contrast with, for example, Adolf von Harnack's "fatherhood of God" idea, is this communitarian view of the church as narrative *koinonia*. This communitarian approach finds that essence in no hierarchical body or single theological tradition, but in the faithful church, where *church* means first of all "congregation, the local assembly of disciples."[6]

Talk about the doctrine of the church is no luxury, but rather a task, a responsibility given to Christian theology. The reason is obvious: Christians exist only as Christians of some tradition or denomination. They are not only "Christians" but also Greek Orthodox, German Baptist, Scandinavian Pentecostals, African Reformed and so on. Moreover, the plethora of Christian denominations, partly based on doctrinal disputes, underscores the responsibility of working on the doctrine on the church (p. 332).

---

[3]Ibid., p. 24. Hereafter in this chapter, all page references to *Doctrine* will be given in parenthetical references.

[4]For his understanding of doctrine, see pp. 23-34 especially.

[5]See further the most creative and challenging work of McClendon, *Biography as Theology: How Life Stories Can Remake Today's Theology*, 2nd ed. (Philadelphia: Trinity Press International, 1990 [orig. 1974]).

[6]See further J. McClendon and John Howard Yoder, "Christian Identity in Ecumenical Perspective," *Journal of Ecumenical Studies* 27 (1990): 773-81.

## A Gathering Church

For McClendon's Baptist ecclesiology, the doctrine of the church begins with—but does not end with!—the actually meeting, "flesh-and-blood disciples assembly." The character of the church is tangible, local, gathering. Being an ecclesiology of a believers' church (a gathering in a particular location) does not, however, make it particularist. "A Baptist ecclesiology must in this sense be catholic in order to be faithfully Baptist" (pp. 327-28). It is also catholic in the sense of being communal rather than individualistic. It has become almost a commonplace to charge believers' churches with overindividualism, and we can find legitimate reasons to do so if we observe the actual life of many Free churches. But for McClendon, that is to work against the Baptist vision. Christian faith for him expresses the idea of community (p. 329).

The principle of gathering church also determines other matters as well. Over against those, like Paul Tillich and Millard Erickson, who define the church in terms of its functions, McClendon emphasizes its nature as the "coming together of believers." A predominantly functional approach to the church runs the danger of making it too instrumental.

The gathering church, however, does not imply any kind of gathering, such as the coming together of members of a club. The church gathering is God's gathering, and it has a definite purpose even when it is not seen as something primarily functional. It is the place to live out the "New Way" of Christian discipleship. In McClendon's theological vision, salvation is understood as revolution (pp. 105-22). Soteriology is included under the reign of God, and this rule is eschatological in nature. Christian theology had to create a new conceptual apparatus to express the radical nature of salvation in Christ. Revolution had taken place and was continuing in the lives of the disciples and in the church. The aim of this revolution was to establish right relations among believers and Christ, and to define the new way of life, the way of discipleship. The church, "The Fellowship of the Spirit,"[7] is the locus of this discipleship life.

McClendon illustrates the distinctive nature of the Baptist gathering community by referring and making some adjustments to the well-known typology of Lesslie Newbigin analyzed in more detail below. In addition to Newbigin's first two categories, the Catholic and Protestant type, McClendon adds the Baptist type, and he includes Pentecostals in that category. The third type includes those churches, now called Free churches, that stem from the Radical

---

[7]McClendon's title for part three of *Doctrine*, which deals with the doctrine of the church.

Reformation through Anabaptists, Mennonites, Brethren and others. Building on Newbigin's analysis, McClendon comes to the surprising conclusion that this type, "local, Spirit-filled, mission-oriented, its discipleship always shaped by a practice of discernment" is almost too good to be true (p. 343). Even though these churches unfortunately have often fallen short of this pattern, the driving force is the requirement that the church now be seen in the frame of the New Testament church.

But in actual church life that kind of church hardly exists, or it only exists occasionally, in glimpses. Therefore, Christian ecclesiology is always a provisional ecclesiology; not unlike Christian eschatology, it looks forward to a fulfillment not yet achieved. This insight also carries enormous potential. Ecumenical dialogue and exchange of gifts always takes place on the way, not with fixed, final positions or a maturity already achieved (pp. 344-45).

Christian ecclesiology not only looks forward to a more refined understanding of what the church is but also looks into the past. In McClendon's creative, often surprising flow of argument, the relationship between the old people of God and the new— the Jews and Christians—gains a programmatic significance. To that topic we now turn.

## *Believers' Church and the Jewish Heritage*

Lumping together the two parts of this section's title does not necessarily reveal their integral connection in the foundations of McClendon's ecclesiology. One may wonder what difference it makes to look at the age-old problem of the Jewish-Christian relationship from a distinctively believers' church perspective. McClendon claims that the idea of the believers' church has the potential of making a difference. His argument rests on this premise:

> The local-church approach made here frees us from an initial dilemma others face: Those who begin with a "church universal" often find it difficult to allow any divine redemptive purpose outside the church. For example, some have even expanded the definition of the church to include historical Israel, a move that seems at once presumptuous and historically mistaken. Yet "universal church" universality seems to require something like it. Another historical Christian approach is to say that the church is "the new Israel," displacing the old—an outlook that appears nowhere in the New Testament. (p. 347)

McClendon takes note of various Christian approaches to the Jews (esp. pp. 347-54). Paul van Buren, an American Episcopalian, after his experiment with the "secular gospel," turned later to the topic of Judaism. In a theology based on revelation, the primary medium of revelation is Israel's history and Scripture, even after the closing of the canon. Israel's distinctive testimony has been with regard to creation and the strong link between creation and covenant. The Catholic feminist Rosemary Ruether has claimed that deeply rooted anti-Semitism spews from the very heart of the Christian gospel; it is almost "the left hand of Christology." For her, historical Christianity is a "divine invader" to messianic Jewish theology. The Anabaptist John Howard Yoder's analysis offers the best starting point for McClendon. For Yoder, the parting of the ways between these two cousin religions was not inevitable even though it seems to be so; and for a few crucial decades in the beginning it did not occur! It was only after A.D. 135 or later that the separation became almost final. This second-century split was for Yoder the original "fall of the church." Yet Yoder now sees surprising parallels between the believers' church ecclesiology with its strong sense of standing in need of restoration because of its previous deformation at the hands of establishment Christianity, on the one hand, and the need after the Holocaust to recover a somehow lost understanding of the proper relation between Christianity and Judaism. McClendon wonders whether there could be not only a parallel here, but a connection.

Yoder begins with Abraham, who represented for biblical writers that which was meant to bless others, namely the faithfulness of Abraham. This heritage places the God of the Bible in contrast with the gods of the nations, whose typical gifts are wealth and security. Thus Jews inherited, not another religion, but a precious gift of God to share with rest of the world. With Jesus there came a new definition of God, one who ordained a servant peoplehood, such as Joseph was in Egypt with his total obedience to God and disloyalty to earthly rulers. Faithfulness entails obedience. Yoder claims that Jews then, like Baptists now, questioned the direction being taken by mainstream religion.

McClendon's view, as already mentioned, builds on and moves beyond Yoder's insights. All agree, McClendon says, that Jews and Christians are uniquely related. For him, however, Jewishness begins not with Abraham but with Jeremiah, the refugee during the time of exile. Because of the exile, the majority of the Jews went into the Diaspora and substitutes replaced all the old localized Hebraic institutions. Still, the Jews became in exile a witness among the nations to a Deity not made with human hands. This separate peoplehood, according to McClendon and many specialists on Judaism, gave rise to anti-Semitism with Jews being selected as scapegoats with fatal results.

Now the challenge to the Christian church and theology is to repent and return to the Jewish people in humility and dialogue. This is the way of Jesus for McClendon.

> What kind of community will make it impossible for believers in Jesus to be at the same time enemies of his brothers and sisters according to the flesh (Matt 25:40)? What kind of community will reject the link with the state's coercion that led so many Christians into the maelstrom of violence? What kind of Christian community can reclaim its heritage from before the time when "the parting of the ways" denied the Jewish footing of Christian community? (p. 360)

It is the task of the Baptist vision, and so McClendon's ecclesiology, to outline the main features of this kind of ecclesiology, which however is also provisional.

## The Peoples of God and the People of God

The broad requirements for Christian community that would signify the gospel of Christ and also act as a reconciling agent toward the old people of God are the following: The community must be suited to Christian life together. It has to be in consonance with the future God promises and the creation God provides, as well as with the social pattern displayed in the cross of Jesus. It must be a community at once redeemed and redemptive. It must center upon the present living Jesus Christ in the power of the Holy Spirit. Though all too brief, this summarizes the leading ideas of McClendon's system insofar as they build the foundation for his ecclesiology.

McClendon argues that for Paul, especially with reference to the last part of Galatians 6:16, the "Israel of God" did not mean *a* people but *two peoples*. After the life, death and resurrection of the Messiah, the old people were not, of course, discarded, but according to Romans 9-11 a new plant, the seed of Abraham in Jesus Christ, was grafted onto the old tree. Here, then, is a first-century picture of peoples still being formed into one people. McClendon prefers to call it "people-in-formation," the Israel of God, not to exclude either Jews or non-Jews, Samaritans or Romans, or anybody else. "It is a people made out of peoples, a future-oriented, gift-created, plural community of destiny, whose canon or entrance standard is in every case new creation" (p. 364).

In other words, this is a people made up of peoples. The implications abound: Christians and Jews together as a people. Catholics, Orthodox, Reformed, Lutheran, Baptists, Pentecostals, you name it. Or an Anglican people, a Swedish Lutheran people, a Mennonite people, for example.

Furthermore, in McClendon's local church-oriented vision, everything goes back to local gatherings of this people of God. Even though a church cannot—and should not—be a church in isolation from the rule of God or from the rest of God's people, yet in each local church the "wonder of community formation in Christ has occurred" (p. 366).

So, in the final analysis, what now makes a church God's church in this Baptist vision? What constitutes authentic Christian community today? McClendon proposes three elements, all interrelated. The rule of God requires church members who are subject to that rule; the centrality of Jesus Christ demands church leaders led by Christ; and the fellowship of the Spirit implies a common life whose practices suit the age to come, a community at once redeemed and redemptive. Even though, in the light of the recent New Testament scholarship, there cannot be any single pattern of church life, there are "the long continuities of Christian teaching," such as God's rule, Christ's centrality and the Spirit's koinonic presence, which tie the church members together into a people. For example, from the rule of God comes membership that consents to that rule. "In Baptist parlance, that has meant receiving the Spirit, obeying the gospel, receiving Christ, taking up discipleship. It implies a disciple church, shaped by its distinctive conversion-baptism" (p. 367). From the centrality of Christ comes leaderships that say *no* to social control of the old age and *yes* to the fellowship of the Risen One. From Spirit-gathered community practices come the "vector of a community that lives between the times, adapting, adjusting, transforming, interpreting so that the church can be the church even as it helps the world to see itself as world" (p. 367).

## A People Set Apart

The concept of the ministry of the church flows out of the idea of the believers' church, a gathered people. For McClendon, the understanding of ministry and leadership is a critical theological issue, "like a knife separating joint and marrow," that divides the church's worldly self-understanding from the self-knowledge given it by the Spirit of God. Whereas all religions have always had priests, a class of special people among the whole people of that religion, Jesus adopted the central theme of Israel's covenant existence, namely that of the whole people of God as a nation of priests (Ex 19:5-6), and made it central for his followers: "You know that among the Gentiles the recognized rulers lord it over their subjects, and the great make their authority felt. It shall not be so with you" (Mk 10:42-43 REB). Not only did Jesus renounce worldly standards of leadership for his followers, but also for himself; the Son of Man did not come to receive but to give service to others (Mk 10:44-45). Consequently, the distinction between "lay" and "clerical" has no clear New Testament roots. Those churches that find such distinctions essential to the being of the church are not building on the testimony of the New Testament but rather on the emerging worldly standards of the postapostolic age (pp. 367-68).

Here, then, is a place in the church for radical reformation, McClendon argues. This requires the abolition of the concept of "the laity," a passive, second-rank Christian class, and the re-introduction of the biblical concept of "the discipleship." A dynamic concept of the discipleship is present in the Pauline concept of gifts to each member in the church. First Corinthians 12, dealing with a contest within a church over place and honor, offers lists of various gifts. What is remarkable about that list is that (Paul's own) gift of apostleship is listed alongside "helping others" and "speaking in tongues" (pp. 367-70).

> Leadership, ecstasy, and the humblest service are alike gifts of the one Spirit of God. The same can be said with regard to the letter to the Ephesians. The fullness of Christ (4:13) does not refer to individuals as in Greek thought, but to the whole body of Christ. This is, then, the challenge of radical reformation in ministry: not a set-apart ministry of those who work for God while others work for themselves, but a people set apart for God. The whole people of God. (p. 369)

For this people set apart for God, worship is an encounter between God and God's people. God acts and enables people to answer. "In the broadest sense this elicited answer is their reasonable worship (Rom 12:1)" (p. 376). What makes Christian worship distinctive is the fact that unlike, for example, affective worship in which the worshipers are expected to be changed by way of their feelings, or magical worship in which the worshiper means to control God, the divine initiative is primary (pp. 374-77).

Christian worship does not limit the presence of Christ to the Eucharist, for instance, but looks up to the Living Christ who was also present during those forty days after his resurrection (Acts 1:1-5). The obligation of Christian worship for the whole people of God does not arise from church law, but from the fact that Christ's presence is to be expected among his gathered people wherever that may take place, in a cathedral, in a prayer room or in the forest. To what end is Christ present among his people? So that his "story continues." Christian worship is the way for the Risen Christ to make his story continue among his people. What matters finally is not the readiness of the worshiper;

on a mountain in Galilee there were some who doubted his presence, but all knelt to worship him (Mt 28:16-17), and so Christ was present.

McClendon summarizes his bold Baptist vision with these striking words:

> If *membership* in the church is intentional, then the church becomes a live circuit for the power of the Holy Spirit. That is the power of unity that the ecumenical movement seeks to realize in the churches. If *leadership* in the church is a gift among gifts granted in the fullness of Christ, then ordination . . . and hierarchy . . . are not essentials of leadership, and may concretely resist the realization of that fullness. If *the church itself* is a sign of the rule of God, the foretaste of humanity reconciled to God, then to come to church is to come "to Mount Zion, the city of the living God, the heavenly Jerusalem, the myriad of angels, to the full concourse and assembly of the firstborn who are enrolled in heaven" (Heb 12:22-23). (p. 371)

# 14

# Lesslie Newbigin

## MISSIONARY ECCLESIOLOGY

### Ecclesiology as Mission

The new conciliar understanding of mission is based on the idea that the essential nature of the church is missionary, rather than mission being *a task* given to the church. This is the reformulation of Roman Catholic missiology of Vatican II with its accent on the "missionary nature of the church."[1] It is also the most recent emphasis of World Council of Churches (WCC) documents, such as Faith and Order of Santiago de Compostela, with its underscoring of the intimate relationship between *koinonia*, common confession of the apostolic faith and common witness in mission and evangelism.[2] Two theologians have been in the forefront to wake up the church and theology to the challenge of mission, the late South African David Bosch[3] and Bishop Lesslie Newbigin.[4]

Newbigin, an Anglican churchman and theologian from England, who has worked over three decades in India (1936-1959 and 1965-1974) and also as an ecumenical officer in the WCC, has seen perhaps more clearly than anybody else that the challenge of mission does not relate only to the areas outside the West but is an urgent task also in the former center of Christendom.[5] The last two decades before his death in 1998, he devoted his life to critical analysis of

---

[1]*Ad Gentes* [The Missionary Document of Vatican Council II], p. 2.

[2]*Towards Koinonia in Faith, Life and Witness* (The Dublin Paper), Fifth World Conference on Faith and Order (Geneva, Switzerland: WCC Publications, 1993), 18.2.1.

[3]David Bosch, *Transforming Mission: Paradigm Shifts in Theology of Mission* (Maryknoll, N.Y.: Orbis, 1991).

[4]Lesslie Newbigin, "The Logic of Mission," in *New Directions in Mission and Evangelization*, ed. James A. Scherer and Stephen B. Bevans (Maryknoll, N.Y.: Orbis, 1992), pp. 16-25.

[5]A fine recent dissertation on Newbigin's basic ideas concerning the mission to (post)modern Western culture, unfortunately written in Finnish and so not accessible for an international audience, is Jukka Keskitalo, *Kristillinen usko ja moderni kulttuuri: Lesslie Newbiginin käsitys kirkon missiosta modernissa länsimaisessa kulttuurissa* (Suomalaisen Teologisen Kirjallisuusseuran Julkaisuja 218; Helsinki: STKJ, 1999).

the nature and task of the church amidst the post-Enlightenment culture of the West. A whole movement, mainly in England, by the name Gospel and Culture has arisen as a result of this reflection. Newbigin's main ecclesiological ideas were presented quite early in his career when he published a small but significant book, *The Household of God: Lectures on the Nature of the Church*.[6] We turn next to the main ideas of this book; then we will analyze his later writings on the mission of the church.

## A Pilgrim People

If one were to characterize Newbigin's overall ecclesiological approach with a few catchwords, they could be *missionary, ecumenical* and *dynamic*. For Newbigin the church is a pilgrim people of God, called to visible unity under one God to spread the knowledge of Christ to all people.

The missionary motif, so prevalent in Newbigin's later writings, was already present in his earlier outline of ecclesiology. According to Newbigin, the missionary contact of the church with dominant non-Christian religious cultures outside the West raised questions not only about the relations of the church to the world, but also about the nature of the church itself. Those churches who had the luxury of living amidst the once "Christian" culture of Europe and America, tended to become "loosely compacted fellowships within a wider semi-Christian" culture.[7] On the other hand, the national churches of the West often failed to make a distinction between the "world" and the church. A missionary church outside the West can no longer take either of these attitudes. It lives between two seemingly opposing challenges. Even though it lives over against often hostile non-Christian cultures, it cannot divest itself of responsibility for those who have responded to its call. For Newbigin, this tension comes to focus in Christ's promise, "'I, if I be lifted up, will draw all men unto myself,' and its goal is 'to sum up all things in Christ.'"[8]

In Newbigin's missionary ecclesiology, the church is the pilgrim people of God. "It is on the move—hastening to the ends of the earth to beseech all men to be reconciled to God, and hastening to the end of time to meet its Lord who

---

[6]Lesslie Newbigin, *The Household of God: Lectures on the Nature of the Church* (London: SCM Press, 1953). A classic analysis of Newbigin's early ecclesiology is Antonio Bruggeman, *The Ecclesiology of Lesslie Newbigin* (Excerpta ex Dissertatione ad Lauream in Facultate Theologica Pontificiae Universitatis Gregorianae, Roma, 1965).

[7]Newbigin, *Household of God*, p. 6.

[8]Ibid., pp. 8-9 (quote on p. 9). Hereafter in this chapter, most page references to *The Household of God* will be given in parenthetical references.

will gather all into one" (p. 18). Nothing would be more foreign to this conception than a static view of the church.[9] In other words, the church is eschatological. This crucial idea was written into the very constitution of the Church of South India whose bishop Newbigin was; that church "confesses its own partial and tentative character by acknowledging that the final aim is 'the union in the Universal Church of all who acknowledged the Name of Christ.'"[10]

The eschatological nature of the church also comes to the fore in the future hope that not only all Christians but all creation will be participating in God's new creation:

> In the final consummation of God's loving purposes we and all creation will be caught up into the perfect rapture of that mutual love which is the life of God himself. What is given to us now can only be a foretaste, for none of us can be made whole till we are made whole together. The very meaning of the word salvation is that it is a making whole, a healing of that which sunders us from God, from one another, and from the created world. The idea of a salvation that is a completed experience for each of us privately, apart from the consummation of all things, is a monstrous contradiction in terms. (p. 147)

Consequently, the church is also ecumenical. When the church ceases to be both missionary and striving for unity, it contradicts its own nature. On its way to the end, the church cannot but acknowledge its goal, which is the unity of all people from all over the world under one God. Newbigin has been an ardent defender of Christian unity and also a helpful critic of the WCC. The heart of ecumenism for Newbigin lies in the fact that the churches have "covenanted with one another in constituting" the WCC and "intend to stay together."[11] Mere intention of being united is not enough for him, nor is unity in terms of a federation of churches. Nothing short of visible unity under one God is acceptable to Newbigin. Other conceptions of unity are too easily content with the current divisions.

For the Catholic Church the goal of visible unity is a special dilemma because of the fact that in their theology there is no place for any other sorts of union except for "returning" to the mother church. If Catholics believe, Newbigin argues, as they in fact do, that their church is the church of Christ, then the other "churches" are less than churches in the legitimate sense of the word (pp. 14-17

---

[9]See further ibid., pp. 150-51 especially.

[10]Ibid., p. 18; for the relationship between eschatology and mission, see pp. 153-59 especially.

[11]From the declaration of the founding assembly at Amsterdam in 1948, quoted in Newbigin, *Household of God*, p. 11.

especially). Of course, we have to take into consideration the fact that Newbigin was writing prior to Vatican II. Even so the basic dilemma still exists, especially in view of the fact that another ancient church, the Eastern Orthodox Church (whose ecclesiality the Roman Church is ready to affirm), has the same kind of understanding of its own ecclesiality; the Eastern Church regards itself as the church of Christ on earth. Both for Catholics and Orthodox ecclesiologies the lack of an episcopacy in most Protestant churches should be an obstacle to affirming their ecclesiality. On the other hand, if they fail to acknowledge that, for example, the WCC-related Protestant churches are churches, how then could the ecumenical vision take any steps toward fulfillment?

Even though the church of God is eschatological, it is also a visible congregation on earth. For Newbigin, the whole core of biblical history is the story of the calling of a visible community to be God's people. What the Lord left behind was a visible community (p. 20). The idea of an invisible church, at least in its popular use, misunderstands the biblical concept. Being a visible community, it has boundaries, but it is not exclusive. It is not "segregation but a congregation," constituted by divine love (p. 23).

Newbigin directs his criticism, perhaps unexpectedly, toward Protestant Reformers for the virtual disappearance of the idea of the church as a visible unity. This was partly because their view of an overemphasis on the sacraments as conveyors of faith by the Catholic Church, caused the Reformers to focus so much on the Word, and thus gave rise to overintellectualizing. This lack of emphasis on the visible community comes out in the Protestant idea of ecumenism; too many are content with the current state of affairs in which there is an endless division of the one church (pp. 51-55).

Both Word and sacraments are constitutive of the church. True, it is the saving presence of Christ that constitutes the church, as Luther especially insisted, but that takes place in the preaching and celebration of the sacraments. There is mutual relationship. The Word is preached and the sacraments are administered in and by the church as well as to the church, and Christ, the head of the body, acts in them and through them (p. 57).

## Three Ecclesiological Streams

Undoubtedly the most famous idea of Newbigin's ecclesiology is the division of Christianity into three dominant streams. The background to this division lies in the answer to the question, Where is the church of Christ on earth—that visible community of God? By what signs or works can a body rightly claim today to be the church of Christ? The first answer is that the church is to be found where there is the preaching of the gospel and the right administration of the sacraments. This is the approach of the Protestant Reformation. The second is that the church is where we are incorporated into the true church by sacramental participation in the historically continuous church. This is for Newbigin the essence of the Catholic view. And then there is the third one in which the defining thing is the living experience of the Spirit, rather than either the Word or the sacraments. Newbigin calls this, for want of a better term, the Pentecostal approach.[12]

Having stated these options one can easily notice that they are not necessarily exclusive of each other. Protestantism, especially in its Lutheran form, of course assigns a crucial role to the sacraments even though the preaching is the focus. But the main emphasis is upon faith, and faith comes by hearing. Besides the sacraments, the Reformers also, of course, acknowledged the important role of the Holy Spirit. But still they were reserved about "enthusiasm"; one may just recall Luther's cautious, almost hostile attitude toward the *Schwärmerei* of his own time.

Catholicism, conversely, honors preaching and acknowledges the necessity of faith, but it finds the center of church life on the altar, in the sacraments, rather than in the pulpit. It has also always claimed the possession of the Spirit, but gives primary place to the continuous sacramental order of the church.

The third type of ecclesiology, although it gives to preaching an honored place and has not eschewed the celebration of the sacraments, usually judges the value of each of them and all Christian actions in light of the experience of the Spirit. Power in the Spirit, rather than right understanding of the guarantee of continuity, is emphasized in Pentecostal spirituality.

While each of these approaches may find legitimate grounding in the Scripture, none of them alone is a sufficient way of viewing the church of Christ on earth. And while the first two streams have definite differences, in a sense they also share a lot of common ground and in this way stand over against the third one. What Catholicism and Protestantism share is an immense stress on the continuity, even though this is more important in the former. The rise of the ecumenical movement especially has turned the eyes of both Catholics and Protestants to the form of ecclesiology represented by their younger counterpart (p. 94).

---

[12]Brief definitions can be found in ibid., pp. 24-25; chapters two, three and four are devoted to a closer look at each of these models.

## The Community of the Holy Spirit

For Pentecostalism, the third stream, the Christian life is a matter of the experienced power and presence of the Holy Spirit today. Neither orthodoxy of doctrine nor impeccability of succession can take its place. If one asks Pentecostals, "Where is the church?" one must ask in fact, "Where is the Holy Spirit recognizably present with power?" (pp. 94-95). Pentecostals are not content with looking primarily at the continuity nor at the preaching or sacraments if the experience of the Spirit is missing. This is the contribution that the third stream of Christendom brings to the impasse of the Catholic-Protestant debate which has characterized the ecumenical movement. In fact, Newbigin contends that this dilemma, which he calls the separation of life and message, seems to be a false one. In the Lord of the church there is no such separation. He is himself the message. He is the Word made flesh. In him word and deed, message and being are one. In other words, the church is not merely the witness of Christ as Protestantism claims, it is also the body of Christ as the Catholics say. And conversely, the church is also a witness and not only the body. Distortions follow whenever there is a one-sided emphasis on either of these. On the one hand, the narrow Protestant emphasis may lead to a Christian life in terms of precisely formulated doctrinal statements. On the other hand, the church may be defined as an apostolic succession. This is for Newbigin nothing less than defining the church by purely natural standards—in other words, without any reference to the presence or absence of the Spirit (pp. 102-4).

Newbigin illustrates this dilemma by referring to the Acts 19 story in which the apostle asked the converts of Apollos one question, "Did you receive the Holy Spirit when you believed?" and got a plain answer. The modern successors, however, would ask either "Did you believe exactly what we teach?" (Protestants) or "Were the hands that were laid on you our hands?" (Catholic); if the answer is satisfactory, then the converts would be assured of the reception of the Spirit. Thus, both of these older forms of Christianity tend to forget the critical role of the Spirit in the church (p. 104).

But Pentecostalism also has its own dangers. It can easily be changed into a type of nonhistorical mysticism in which the work of the Spirit is separated from the work of Christ as it is encountered in the Word and sacraments. Also, there is the danger of an overemphasis on the freedom of the Spirit at the expense of God-willed order in the church. Both are needed for the upbuilding of the body of Christ (pp. 114-20).

The ecumenical challenge requires that all of these streams meet. It is to their own detriment and to the frustration of the efforts for unity, Newbigin laments, that they have been divorced from each other for too long (pp. 120-22).

## The Mission of the Church to Western (Post-)Modern Culture

In his later writings, Newbigin focused on the relationship between ecclesiology, mission and contemporary Western culture. The context of this mission is in the tension of Western culture between two basic stories going back to antiquity through the medieval period, namely, the Greek rationality and the Jewish faith.[13] The Enlightenment was both a culmination and a radical transformation of this heritage with its concept of human knowledge as that of an outside observer, with its subject-object dualism, and the dichotomy between practice and theory.[14] These and other developments in the aftermath of the Enlightenment contributed to both secularism and atheism, and to the removal of the question of meaning from the purpose of scientific explanations. In the analysis of Newbigin, the Enlightenment experience was almost a religious experience for many.[15] One of the results of the Enlightenment, which also has profound ecclesiological implications, is the emergence of individualism and individuality. Yet another was the growing optimism as a result of rapidly developing industrialism and scientific resources.

Newbigin laments that Protestant theology especially too easily succumbed to the new challenges of this changed intellectual climate. One unfortunate reaction of the Christian church was apologetic, attempting to defend itself against the growing impact of science and secular philosophy. This apologetic approach has taken several forms, such as deism, classical liberalism, historical-critical study of the Bible and subjectivistic pietism. Basically, the defense has been a tactical retreat; but from the vantage of later history these retreats begin to look more like a rout.[16] As a result, Christian faith has become privatized and divorced from the center of culture.

Newbigin's own proposal for the church to accomplish its mission in con-

---

[13]Lesslie Newbigin, *The Other Side of 1984: Questions for the Churches* (Geneva, Switzerland: WCC Publications, 1983) is his first major attempt to analyze this in more detail.

[14]I am indebted to the careful, detailed analysis of Keskitalo, *Kristillinen usko ja moderni kulttuuri*.

[15]I am indebted to the analysis and conclusions offered by Matti Luoma, *Länsimaiden kaksi uskontoa: kristinusko ja rationalismi: Filosofinen tarkastelu* (Porvoo, Finland: WSOY, 1990), pp. 17-19.

[16]Lesslie Newbigin, *The Gospel in a Pluralistic* Society (Geneva, Switzerland: WCC Publications, 1989), p. 3.

temporary Western culture goes against the tendency to adapt to the culture.[17] The prerequisite for such an approach is a critical reevaluation of the self-understanding of the church and its theology. Rather than trying to explain Christian faith in light of modern scientific rationality, modern culture should be analyzed from a specifically Christian standpoint. The church is called to challenge the prevailing thought forms and its questionable philosophical foundation. Necessarily, this will bring the church in tension with culture.[18] By doing so, the church invites people to *metanoete*, repentance, a change of mind. But rather than aiming at a pietistic subjectivistic conversion, "conversion of the mind" is the ultimate goal.[19]

In fact, Newbigin goes so far as to issue a call for a specifically Christian view of reality. For him, Christian faith represents a distinctive form of rationality. He revives his early idea of the church as the pilgrim people of God. Only a dynamic church on the way could take up this bold challenge:

> The Christian community, the universal Church, embracing more and more fully all the cultural traditions of humankind, is called to be that community in which a tradition of rational discourse is developed which leads to a true understanding of reality, because it takes as its starting point and as its permanent criterion of truth the self-revelation of God in Jesus Christ.[20]

Newbigin finds both reactionary fundamentalism and Cartesian "infallible certainty" impossible ways of defining the nature of Christian truth that the church possesses; neither is it only subjectivistic but genuinely universal. Based on the Augustinian principle "we believe in order to understand,"[21] which may lead to certainty, albeit not an absolute one, the message of the church is "public" and open to be recommended to all men and women.

The missionary challenge of the church amidst the postmodern, post-Christian West is enormous. The church finds itself sharing the gospel with a culture that, on the one hand, is permeated by the heritage of the Enlightenment and modernity and, on the other hand, by postmodern nihilism and hopelessness. People living amidst this tension tend to react to the message of the church in two seemingly opposing ways. Those whose roots are still in the project of

---

[17]The basic exposition is offered in Lesslie Newbigin, *Foolishness to the Greeks: The Gospel and Western Culture* (Geneva, Switzerland: WCC Publications, 1986).

[18]See, e.g., Newbigin, *Other Side of 1984*, p. 53.

[19]E.g., Newbigin, *Gospel in a Pluralistic Society*, p. 110.

[20]Ibid., pp. 87-88.

[21]See, e.g., Lesslie Newbigin, *Truth to Tell: The Gospel as Public Truth* (Grand Rapids, Mich.: Eerdmans, 1991), pp. 36-37.

modernism are usually very skeptical, whereas genuinely postmodern persons may welcome the narrative truth of the gospel, although only as *a* story among others. To be credible, the church has to respond to both of these reactions. The nature of the witness of the church in such a context, rather than claiming to possess the truth, is "bearing the truth and witnessing to the truth." At the same time the church is also a seeker of the truth, even though it also has access to it in the gospel.[22]

The lasting contribution of Newbigin's debated ecclesiological proposal is to link the church with her mission: no church without mission, no mission without the church. At the same time he has constantly reminded us of the influence of cultures—including our own, most recently that of modernism and postmodernism—on Christian faith, which needs to both affirm and criticize the cultures. In this sense, Newbigin serves as an appropriate bridge person: his missionary ecclesiology prepares us to move to the third part of this book, which inquires into global, crosscultural and other contextual ecclesiologies.

---

[22]Newbigin, *Gospel in a Pluralistic Society,* p. 12.

# Concluding Reflections on
# Leading Ecclesiologists

The discussion of some leading theologians on the doctrine of the church testifies to both a rich variety and a surprising unanimity among thinkers coming from the whole spectrum of the Christian church. An emphasis prevalent in all these thinkers is the growing significance of the *koinonia*, communion ecclesiology. While Zizioulas has explicated most clearly this leading ecumenical theme in current ecclesiology, Küng, Pannenberg and Moltmann, as well as Free church ecclesiologists McClendon and Volf, also pay careful attention to the category of community.

All of these theologians highlight the importance of the *essence* of the church before one talks about the ministry and functions of the church. The church first *is* the church before it *does* the work of the church. Even the missionary ecclesiology of Newbigin agrees: while it is necessary for the well-being and calling of the church to be engaged in mission, foundational is the church's missionary *nature*. The church exists as mission; mission belongs to the *esse* of the community of God.

An explicit ecumenical orientation is similarly visible in all of these theologians. Their understanding of the conditions of ecclesiality may vary—and it does, for example between Zizioulas's Orthodox ecclesiology and Volf's Free church views—but none of the ecclesiologists studied here dares turn his back on the call of Christian unity. For Pannenberg, the goal of ecumenism is the unity of all people and peoples under one God. For Volf, the church as the anticipation of the new creation under one God points to the same goal. Whatever the precise definition of ecumenism, the ultimate goal is similar.

There are, understandably, major differences between theologians representing so many various traditions. Clearly, Zizioulas is at the one end of the spectrum in his Orthodox insistence on the necessity of sacraments and consequently the bishop as the condition for ecclesiality; Pannenberg supports the idea of sacraments but not necessarily episcopacy. Coming from a Free church–flavored mentality of Reformed theology, with sympathies toward Latin American liberationists and American congregationalism, Moltmann perhaps surprisingly joins with McClendon and Volf in their downplaying of the sacraments and office as the necessary condition for the ecclesiality; this is not to say that these theologians undermine sacraments and office as such, but that for the church to be church they are not absolutely necessary.

Out of this basic ecclesiological standpoint, consequently, Moltmann, Volf and McClendon most strongly champion the role of the whole people of God as constitutive not only for the ecclesiality of the church but also for the ministry of the church. Here Küng departs from mainline Catholic theology and in an unexpected way joins this company while not, of course, leaving behind his Catholic sacramental and episcopal heritage.

Many of the ecclesiologists discussed here have interacted not only with classical Western theologies but also with the emerging Third World voices and other contextual interpretations such as feminists and postmodernists. Moltmann has both trained and learned from many liberationists on several continents, Newbigin has spent a significant part of his life in Asia, and Volf is actively involved in crosscultural interaction in his native Croatia and elsewhere. The third part of this book turns to the consideration of these global and contextual voices and testimonies.

# Contextual Ecclesiologies

$A$fter considering theological thinking about the church among movements and individual theologians associated for the most part with classical Western theology, the final part of this book delves into what is often called contextual theologies (sometimes also the term *global* is used, especially of those theologies arising outside the West). The devotion of one third of the space to this discussion reflects the author's conviction that it is here that the future of Christian theology lies. The emergence and growing significance of several kinds of contextual theologies does not, of course, mean that the Western theological tradition loses its significance; even theologians from outside the West are still primarily being trained either by Westerners or, even in their own contexts, in topics mainly deriving from the West. What will change in the near future—and the reverberations can already be felt—is that theologizing can no longer be the privilege of one culture only. It is going to be a global, interrelated enterprise.

The ecclesiologies in the final part of the book fall into several categories, and judgment on whether the rubric *contextual* is the most appropriate way to describe them will be left to the readers. First of all, there are three chapters that inquire into ecclesiologies in a specific cultural-geographic environment: Africa, Asia and Latin America. But saying this makes a hopelessly general statement. The aim here is not to give any kind of comprehensive presentation of African, Asian or Latin American ecclesiologies; that would be a book of its own (and a book much needed!). The aim for these three chapters is much more humble: to illustrate from various cultural-geographical contexts what kind of alternative types of ecclesiologies do exist currently. The "non-church" movement in Japan, illustrating one type of contextual challenge to traditional ecclesiologies, is contextual even within its Asian context and is certainly a minority voice. The ecclesiology of the (mainly) Catholic base communities in Latin America is a more representative example of church life among Hispanics, but by no means any kind of "mainline" phenomenon. The same can be said of the third case study in this category, African Independent Churches. While those Christian communities are quite influential in many parts of that continent, they only represent one segment of African Christianity.

The second category of contextual ecclesiologies is that represented by feminist thinkers. The discussion in that chapter is purposefully limited, yet hopefully representative in that basically two leading feminist ecclesiologists are studied more carefully, namely Letty M. Russell and Elisabeth Schüssler Fiorenza. There could be others, such as Rosemary Radford Ruether or Mary Daly, to give two obvious examples, but since the aim here is not comprehensiveness, not all the voices have to be given equal listening. And after all, Russell's and Fiorenza's contributions specifically to ecclesiology have been theologically most pregnant.

The third category of contextual ecclesiologies here is a cocktail of independent voices with little or no relation to each other, and their inclusion is based on the desire of the author to give testimony to the surprising richness and variety of alternative testimonies to what the church is. The Shepherding movement's ecclesiology testifies to a rapidly growing phenomenon among Christian churches, namely independent communities that do not belong to any established constituencies, not even to the newest ones. These are churches that are often small communities, sometimes isolated from others, with little or no structure other than the structure of the basic community. They are often charismatically flavored and unbelievably creative in their approach to worship, leadership and ministry. To give any kind of up-to-date survey of ecclesiologies in the beginning of the third millennium and not give hearing to these communities would just reinforce the deep eclecticism of traditional theology. Very different yet having somewhat similar leanings is the idea of the Catholic priest and missionary Vincent J. Donovan of the "world church," which echoes (without making the connection explicit) some of the emphases of Dietrich Bonhoeffer's "secular" or "religionless" Christianity. While Donovan is the main Catholic voice for this church, which really finds its being "in the world," he is also echoing some of the mindset of Vatican II with its call for the church to live in the "modern world," and some of the ideas of leading theologians such as Rahner. Therefore, while Donovan is the main voice in that chapter, the idea is wider. The same can be said of the last contextual case study, the church from the post-Christian era, which can also legitimately be called a postmodern ecclesiology (if there is any). Though the main dialogue partner here is Barry A. Harvey's *Another City*, the main goal here is not to analyze his ecclesiology, but to discern what kind of orientations may characterize thinking about the church after the coming of postmodernism. Again, one could select individual thinkers from a whole array of theologians, but for the sake of clarity and brevity this one has been chosen. It seems appropriate to finish a study on *Christian* theology of the church by looking at one postmodern proposition that searches for a church for the *post-Christian* era.

Since it is not the purpose of this book as a whole, let alone the aim of the third part, to refer to all available ecclesiologies, the choice of representatives has been selective. Many respected candidates have not made their way into this particular presentation, for example, African American ecclesiologies or the emerging ecclesiologies of many minorities such as Native Americans. Their exclusion in no way indicates any lack of significance; choices have been made for practical reasons, in order to not unduly expand an introductory survey.

# 15

# The Non-Church Movement in Asia

## Mukyokai

Known in Japanese as Mukyokai, a very distinctive ecclesiological movement founded by Kanzo Uchimura emerged in the beginning of the twentieth century. Uchimura did not have any intention to begin an indigenous church in Japan, but rather just to investigate the nature of true *ekklesia*. On the one hand, Uchimura wanted to affirm the central tenets of the Protestant Reformation—biblical revelation, justification by faith and especially the priesthood of all believers; on the other hand, the Mukyokai movement also criticized the Reformation churches for an incomplete and less than satisfactory work of reform.[1]

Kanzo Uchimura[2] (1861-1930) shared in his personality both his genuine Asian heritage and an extended exposure to the Western culture and form of Christianity. His roots as a member of the Samurai class were in Confucian ethics, and his conversion to Christianity as a young college student set him on his path with tension and creativity. His less-than-happy experiences with some Western missionaries also contributed to his growing criticism of the Western type of church life. Uchimura was also heavily involved with social movement and social criticism. He was a prophet and evangelist whose life and work are considered by many to be the most original single contribution as yet made by Japan to world Christianity.[3] Emil Brunner character-

---

[1]Hiroyasu Iwabuchi, "An Evaluation of the Non-Church Movement in Japan: Its Distinctives, Strategy and Significance Today" (D.Miss. diss., Fuller Theological Seminary, School of World Mission, 1976).

[2]*The Complete Works of Kanzo Uchimura* (Tokyo: Iwanami Shoten) are published in English (1932) in wenty-one volumes.

[3]Richard H. Drummond, "The Non-Church Movement in Japan," *Journal of Ecumenical Studies* 2 (1965): 448.

ized it as standing unique in all Christianity.[4]

After forming a Bible study group, a fellowship of believers, Uchimura sharpened his critical look at the existing institutional churches. He was in the search for a "true *ekklesia*."[5] His severe criticism toward the institutional church, however, has to be put in the right perspective. What lay at the basis of his rejection of the institutional church and also represented his goal was his positive, affirmative attitude toward the true church.[6]

## *The Invisible Church*

Uchimura's approach to ecclesiology is practical and Bible centered. He felt his vocation was Bible teaching, and he eschewed theology for its abstract nature and metaphysical connotations. Characteristic of his ecclesiology is a sharp dualism and tension:

> Uchimura's position lies in a sharp, two-dimensional distinction between the Word of God and the word of man, between the flock of believers in Christ and the institutional Church, between faith in Christ and the rites of the Church, between spiritual life and physical organization. And since in each case the former of the two is expressive of the truth of the Gospel, the latter is regarded as relative.[7]

Whereas for Lesslie Newbigin the most salient feature of the church is its visibility, the opposite is true for the initiator of the non-church movement in Japan. "Faith in Christ is what brings the Church into existence, therefore the Church should be just as invisible as is faith. The Church as the essential 'ecclesia' cannot be seen by human eyes, since it is the gathering of a spiritual body."[8] The church exists among the people who gather and have fellowship in the name of Christ.

Uchimura saw both Christ and the church as completely spiritual beings. Men and women can be in the church only if they are in the Spirit. Uchimura identified the church with the kingdom of God and contended that Paul's view of the church, if examined closely, points to that which is completely separated from the earth. The church is where the Holy Spirit is; "it is the invisible

---

[4]Emil Brunner, "A Unique Christian Mission: The Mukyokai ('Non-Church') Movement in Japan," in *Religion and Culture: Essays in Honor of Paul Tillich* (New York: Harper, 1959), p. 287.
[5]A useful historical survey is Akio Dohi, "The Historical Development of the Non-Church Movement in Japan," *Journal of Ecumenical* Studies 2 (1965): 452-68. See also Iwabuchi, "An Evaluation of the Non-Church Movement in Japan," pp. 12-13.
[6]See further Dohi, "Historical Development of the Non-Church Movement," 454.
[7]Ibid., pp. 453-54.
[8]Iwabuchi, "Evaluation of the Non-Church Movement," p. 20.

spiritual fellowship of those who have received the Holy Spirit."[9]

The leading principle of Mukyokai is opposition to the institutional church, which Uchimura thought had deviated from the centrality of the gospel. W. Norman, who has extensively studied the ecclesiology of Mukyokai in Japan, is correct when he states that it is a Japanese expression of an abiding element in Christian history of "spiritual dissent."[10] In fact, Uchimura, at one point in his spiritual life, had contacts with Quakers, especially in America, and he is known to have expressed his admiration of the Society of Friends. The Baptist Raymond Jennings offers an interesting comment when he states that he found Uchimura "not too far from what I had long considered a more pure type of Baptist thinking than was prevalent in many Churches."[11]

The church is primarily life, not institution. For him, the institutional nature of the church tends to quench the life. In the church, all have direct fellowship with God. No human mediator is needed to facilitate this direct relationship with the Lord. For Uchimura that which is usually called the church is not the church. What Christ called his church is a household of faith whose only rule is love.

Even though Uchimura emphasized the invisible nature of the church, he also recognized the visible and concrete community on earth. But "the visible and concrete community" refers not to the institutionalized church but to the church as a gathered community.

What about the sacraments? While Mukyokai in general rejects them, Uchimura basically acknowledged their validity. He did not regard them as a means of grace, however. Mukyokai also refrains from calling them ordinances. Rather, the sacraments are an expression of the fellowship of believers with Christ. The church may enjoy the sacraments but is not dependent on them. It is only through the Word of God that faith comes and is sustained. So for him the sacraments are relativized, and he does not see them as constituting the order and marks of the church, which is perceived in conformity with faith in the gospel. However, Uchimura did not limit the sacramental to the sacraments of the church.[12]

---

[9]Drummond, "Non-Church Movement," p. 450; W. Norman, "Kanzo Uchimura—The Church," in *Contemporary Religions in Japan,* December 1964, pp. 355-57.

[10] Norman, "Kanzo Uchimura," p. 347.

[11]Raymond P. Jennings, *Jesus, Japan and Kanzo Uchimura* (Tokyo: Kyo Bun Kwan, 1968), p. iii.

[12]Drummond, "Non-Church Movement," p. 450.

## Subjective Mediation of the Church

How does the church emerge? What makes the church a church? These are the foundational questions with regard to the ecclesiality of the church. Let us take a more focused look at the foundational ecclesiology of Mukyokai with the help of one of the followers of Uchimura, Masao Sekine. He is one of the most famous second-generation Mukyokai leaders, also trained in classical theology. In fact, Sekine, over against his forebears, believes that if the non-church movement keeps on ignoring formal theological study and reflection, it is in danger of being marginalized as one of the many sects in Japanese culture.

The theological background to Sekine's idea of the church is that the "subjective self" of the human being is vanquished in the presence of the personal God. Following that, the self takes on a new subjectivity in faith and an objectivity before God. This self completely rejects the institutional church because the church identifies itself with the Bible and tradition. In Sekine's opinion, Scripture does not warrant an objective existence for the institutional church apart from the mediation of subjective faith. The church is

> not something that exists objectively as a place identical (with specific external forms or institutions) and to which then the man of faith comes to have a relationship. Where men of faith gather together, there first does the Church come into existence on earth. That is to say, men of faith subjectively come to constitute the Church; the Church is not something independently existing as a place apart from the mediation of subjectivity.[13]

There is therefore a subjective, individualized foundation for the church and its ecclesiality.

According to Sekine, the Protestant Reformation in fact started with a subjective apperception of the church, but then it came to define the church as the place for preaching and administration of the sacraments, and so separated the church from the subjectivity of faith in favor of objective existence.[14]

Out of this emerges a highly unique conception of Christian unity and divisions. In the institutional churches, the Reformation churches included, the subjective and objective churches were placed side by side and were not subjectively unified. Therefore, the subjective self proceeded further in the direction of sectarian divisions. In contrast, Mukyokai does not adhere to the

---

[13]Masao Sekine, quoted in Dohi, "Historical Development of the Non-Church Movement," p. 463.

[14]Dohi, "Historical Development of the Non-Church Movement," p. 464.

"church of identification," the church that identifies itself with the Bible and tradition. Therefore, he thinks that that kind of church cannot be sectarian.[15]

## A Gathered Church

For Uchimura, the main metaphor to describe the church is the body of Christ. "The organic gathering in the spiritual 'koinonia' is the centrality of the true Church."[16] Since the spiritual is primary, the concept of the church is highly dynamic. Uchimura also expresses this with a paradoxical idea that the church is to be forever constructed while being forever destroyed.[17]

The idea of a noninstitutional church becomes understandable when we realize that Uchimura understood salvation mainly in terms of union with Christ. Personal union with Christ is a natural consequence of experiencing the resurrection of Christ.[18] It is against this background that the root of Uchimura's criticism toward the institutional church comes to the fore. Akio Dohi expresses it pointedly:[19]

> It is the approach by which man lays hold of Christ in a kind of solitary independence and thus comes to trust and depend upon God. From this faith-experience issues the life of the man of independent autonomy. Uchimura's position is that without this approach there can be no Christian corporate or community relationship.

The term *independence*, however, has to be rightly understood, since it can be easily mixed with a purely Western connotation. The Japanese word used here for *autonomy* does not mean absolute autonomy; it sometimes can be translated by the English word *identity* and means the freedom to make responsible and ultimate decisions. Thus, for Uchimura it is an affirmation of the fact that the church is being built up, so to speak, from "below to above," from individuals to the community, not vice versa.

But Uchimura's conception of the church is more complicated than just an idea of a gathering of believers. Yes, the church is invisible. But there is also another side to it. The gathered church, a fellowship of believers quite different from that which is in heaven or invisible, must exist in manifestation within

---

[15]Ibid., p. 464.
[16]Iwabuchi, "Evaluation of the Non-Church Movement," p. 28.
[17]Norman, "Kanzo Uchimura," pp. 358, 360.
[18]He does not specify what kind of union is meant, but he seems to mean a sort of mystical union with the believer and Christ.
[19]Dohi, "Historical Development of the Non-Church Movement," p. 455.

history as the body of those who make Christ their head, just as the gospel of Christ is a revelation within history. Life in the Spirit is not that which hinders such a manifestation; rather, as he says, it is specifically "that which takes form and becomes manifest."[20]

## The Gospel and the Church

Uchimura's developing ecclesiology and his struggles are manifested in his extensive dialogue and debate with Toraji Tsukamoto, one of his ablest followers. It was also Tsukamoto's conviction that the pure gospel of salvation by faith alone was preserved by the Mukyokai alone, and he forthrightly criticized the standpoint of both Roman Catholicism and Protestantism, which he felt put this in jeopardy. In Tsukamoto's understanding, both of these traditions put the church in the primary place, implying that if one does not belong to the church, he or she does not have an access to the gospel either. We may leave aside the question whether Tsukamoto's assessment is accurate and just look at how this insight fit in his own thinking and in relation to his celebrated teacher. Indicative of his approach is the title of the first issue of *Seisho Chishiki* magazine from January 1930: "Non-Church Magazine—There is Salvation outside the Church."[21]

Even though Uchimura and Tsukamoto are felt to be in tension with each other, I think that they were still unanimous about their basic orientation to the church. For Uchimura, the relationship between the gospel and the church is perhaps more complicated, as we saw above, but especially during the later years of his life Uchimura also came to separate the gospel and the church. He regarded the church as secondary in significance, but he did not make an issue of it. Tsukamoto, however, believed that if the pure gospel is proclaimed, it is necessary to come into direct confrontation with the church, which—while giving nominal allegiance to the gospel—in fact forces the authority of the church on men and women as the primary issue of religion. Accordingly, the idea of non-church was a matter of life and death to the follower of Uchimura.[22] He even goes so far as to say, "If what I believe is wrong, and what the Church believes is right, and it is not possible to be

---

[20]Uchimura, *Complete Works*, 10:227; see also Dohi, "Historical Development of the Non-Church Movement," 454.

[21]I am indebted to Dohi, "Historical Development of the Non-Church Movement," p. 458, for this information.

[22]Ibid., p. 458.

saved by faith alone, then my salvation is but cause for despair and my reason for believing in Christ is lost."[23] Uchimura, however, even in his severe
criticism was not ready to abandon the church, but said, "It is time to become
their friends and to lead them."[24]

## *Lay Movement*

Uchimura often stressed the priesthood of all believers, which he saw as one
of the most celebrated treasures of the Reformation. He preferred to speak of
the "ministerhood" of all believers. Recognizing the diversity of spiritual gifts,
Mukyokai insists that all believers are able to perform all the ministerial duties. The main task of ordinary believers is to witness in their daily life.
Uchimura considered this testimonial ministry of all believers as prophetic
and conducive to the renewal of the church.[25]

Mukyokai is critical of professional clergy for two reasons. First, there is always the danger that ministers regard themselves as a higher rank before God
than laypeople. Second, often the professional ministers do not carry out the
mission in a genuine Christian spirit. Uchimura also came to the conclusion that
the ministerial institution known in the institutionalized churches produces a
peculiar sort of domain that does not correspond to the spirit of the Protestant
Reformation. Consequently, Uchimura also downplayed formal theological education. What was decisive was a deep personal calling from God.[26]

Finally, Uchimura came to the conclusion that the proper way to carry out
the ministry was to do so while holding a secular job. This also means that
ministers of the church do not expect financial remuneration, but rather refuse
it even if it would be available. The reason is obvious: financial independence
is closely related to independence of faith. Establishing a financial foundation
for themselves, the ministers obtain an autonomous faith and ministry. Financial independence also makes it possible for a minister to speak the Word of
God boldly without fearing the criticism of the people.

As a solely lay movement, Mukyokai is different from the lay involvement
of the institutional churches. The institutional churches encourage the lay people toward a particular goal, such as evangelism or deaconal work, while the
main duties are performed by the paid clergy. In Mukyokai there is no distinc-

---

[23]Ibid.
[24]Ibid., p. 459.
[25]Iwabuchi, "Evaluation of the Non-Church Movement," pp. 29, 31-32.
[26]Ibid., pp. 39-40.

tion between ministers and believers. Laypeople conduct even ministerial duties such as weddings and funerals. Mobilizing laity is not a method or
strategy but the very essence of the church.[27]

## The Church in the World

Uchimura's tension-filled ecclesiology comes to focus in his view of the relationship between the world and church. On the one hand, the church always
confronts the world since the values of the church are different from those of
both the Asian and Western societies. In this regard, he was strongly influenced by the spirit of pietism, However, for Uchimura this confrontation with
the world did not mean a withdrawal from the world into isolation, but rather
an involvement with the secular world. Mukyokai has attempted to follow the
Lord of the church in the midst of the upheaval of society. Church renewal
could never mean divorce from the world but rather action in the world.[28]

Uchimura was critical of a separatist mentality in Christianity. He was especially critical with regard to a "Japanese westernized Christian" who often
finds himself or herself on the margins of the culture and society. Mukyokai
also rejects the dichotomy between the sacred and secular. That dichotomy derives from non-Christian religions, such as the Buddhist concept of "The Land
of Happiness" which leads to an escapist view. Perhaps because of this active
involvement with society, especially earlier on, the movement attracted Japanese in positions of social importance.

Evangelism is the central task of the church. Its main concern is to proclaim
the gospel to all people of all classes. Evangelism focuses on the preaching and
spreading of the gospel of Christ, and has nothing to do with the extension of
the institutional church or its influence. Evangelism takes place in the ordinary
life rather than through specifically designed evangelistic meetings. Evangelism for Uchimura takes place not only by preaching, but also by deed. Therefore, social responsibility and social involvement have been emphasized in the
movement. In fact, the church is to act as a prophet against social injustice.

---

[27]Ibid., pp. 41-42.
[28]Ibid., p. 30.

# 16

# Base Ecclesial Communities in Latin America

## The Church for the Poor

Since the time of Vatican II, liberation theologians of the Roman Catholic Church—followed by many in the Protestant churches as well—have come to see Christ as identified with the poor and oppressed, and have focused on the self-understanding of the church "from underneath."[1] The 1971 Synod took up the topic of "Justice in the World," and produced a notable declaration on the integral relationship between action for justice and evangelization: "Action on behalf of justice and participation in the transformation of the world fully appear to us as a *constitutive dimension of the preaching of the Gospel*, or, in other words, of the church's mission for the redemption of the human race and its liberation from every oppressive situation."[2] This is the first time, to my knowledge, that an official Catholic document describes social justice as a "constitutive" dimension of the preaching of the gospel. Christian love of neighbor and justice cannot be separated, for love implies a demand for justice.[3] The church, therefore, is called both to denounce injustice and to examine its own lifestyle.[4]

The Latin American church has been a pioneer in this Catholic reorientation toward an emphasis on social justice. CELAM, The Second Conference of Latin American Bishops at Medellín, Colombia (1968), meeting in the presence of Pope Paul VI, placed three interrelated themes on its agenda: efforts toward justice and peace, the need for adaptation in evangelization and faith, and the reform of the church and its structures. This regional conference was actually

---

[1]For an overview, see, e.g., M. D. Chenu, "Vatican II and the Church of the Poor," in *The Poor and the Church*, ed. Norbert Greinacher and Alois Müller, *Concilium* 104 (New York: Seabury, 1977), pp. 56-61.

[2]"Declaration from the Roman Bishops of Synod of 1971," in *Mission Trends*, vol. 2, ed. G. Anderson et al. (Grand Rapids, Mich.: Eerdmans, 1975), p. 255; hereafter *DRBS (1971)*; the page number refers to Anderson (emphases mine).

[3]Ibid., p. 256.

[4]Ibid., pp. 257-58.

a turning point in the identity and mission of the church of that continent with its clear articulation of the people's cry for justice and liberation, its espousal of the cause of the poor and its recognition of base Christian communities as primary centers for Christian community and evangelization.[5] To bring about justice, however, it is not enough to change political structures; people need to be authentically converted to the "kingdom of justice, love and peace."[6] What CELAM, the Latin American Catholic Bishops' Conference, was for Latin America, Manila (1979) was for Asia. Its point of departure was "the Asian context" and included three dialogues: with local culture, with Asian religious traditions and with the life of the people, especially the poor. The Asian bishops acknowledged that, with the local church as the focus of evangelization and with dialogue as its essential mode, they would help Asian Christians to work for salvation and solidarity with the poor and oppressed, as well as attempt a true dialogue with the ancient religions of the area.[7]

## *Ecclesiologenesis:* A New Ecclesiology

Modern society has produced a wild atomization of existence and a general anonymity of persons lost in the cogs of the mechanisms of the macro-organizations and bureaucracies. . . . Slowly, but with ever-increasing intensity, we have witnessed the creation of communities in which persons actually know and recognize one another, where they can be themselves in their individuality, where they can "have their say," where they can be welcomed by name. And so, we see, groups and little communities have sprung up everywhere. This phenomenon exists in the church, as well: grassroots Christian communities, as they are known, or basic church communities.[8]

It seems clear that there are two major reasons for the emergence and rapid growth of the CCBs (the base ecclesial communities, or basic Christian communities) in the Latin American Roman Catholic Church.[9] On the one hand,

---

[5]*The Church in the Present-Day Transformation of Latin America in the Light of the Council: Second General Conference of Latin American Bishops, Medellín, August 26-September 6, 1968*, vol. 2, *Conclusions* (Washington, D.C.: National Conference of Catholic Bishops, 1968), especially chaps. 1, 14, 15 [hereafter *CELAM II*].

[6]Ibid., p. 33.

[7]*Report of the Catholic Bishops' International Conference on Mission in Manila, 1979*, p. 19.

[8]Leonardo Boff, *Ecclesiogenesis: The Base Communities Reinvent the Church* (Maryknoll, N.Y.: Orbis, 1986), p. 1.

[9]For a detailed history and emergence of base ecclesial communities, see Guillermo Cook, *The Expectation of the Poor: Latin American Basic Ecclesial Communities in Protestant Perspective* (Maryknoll, N.Y.: Orbis, 1985), pp. 11-85.

these communities are an expression and reaction to the desperate lack of community in the society in general and in the church—especially in the Roman Catholic Church with its tendency toward "an organizational form with a heavily hierarchical framework and a juridical understanding of relationships among Christians, thus producing mechanical, reified inequalities and inequities"[10]—and on the other hand, a cry for the liberation of the poor and other outcasts in the society. In other words, base communities champion freedom and liberation.

Ecclesiologically, however, it would be too simplified to say that these new Christian communities are only a sociological response to some felt needs in the society or church. Theologically, they also represent a new ecclesiological experience, a "renaissance of very church," and an action of the Spirit. Seen in this way, Leonardo Boff, the main ecclesiological architect of the movement, contends that these basic church communities "deserve to be contemplated, welcomed, and respected as salvific events."[11] In other words, the base communities theologians argue that these Christian communities present more than just renewal movements of the church or bear some legitimate ecclesial elements. They argue for the ecclesiality of the communities within the larger church, the Roman Catholic Church. For the base communities theologians, these communities represent a "new ecclesiology," new formulations in the theology of the church.[12] This is "ecclesiogenesis," "birthing the church," "starting the church again."[13]

Not only do the base communities argue for the ecclesiality of the church, but also for a *specific* type of ecclesiality, namely the birthing of the church community "from below," from the people of God. In this interpretation of the Gospels, Jesus' whole preaching could be seen as an effort to awaken the strength of the community aspects for the people. In the horizontal dimension, Jesus called human beings to mutual respect, generosity, a communion of believers and simplicity in relationships. Vertically, Jesus sought to open human beings to a sincere filial relationship with God, characterized by openness, love and trust. These very same features of relationships are to characterize the church of Jesus Christ. If so, then it means also that the church reclaims its apostolicity: "The church sprung from the people is the same as the church

---

[10]Boff, *Ecclesiogenesis*, p. 1.
[11]Ibid.
[12]Ibid., p. 2.
[13]Yves M.-J. Congar, "Os grupos informais na Igreja," *Communidades eclesiais de base: Utopia ou realidade?* ed. Alfonso Gregory (Petropolis, Brazil: Vozes, 1973), pp. 144-45.

sprung from the apostles."[14] This is the defining moment of the base communities' claim for the ecclesiality of their communities: whether you start from the people of God (the community of brothers and sisters) or from the institution (the hierarchy).

## *"Particularist" and "Universalist" Ecclesiologies in Tension*

The emergence of the basic ecclesial communities has intensified the debate concerning the ecclesiality of the church in Catholic theology. Following the lead of Boff[15] and other base communities theologians, Avery Dulles has named this a debate between two orientations, namely "particularist" and "universalist." According to Dulles, Vatican II ecclesiology includes two major tendencies, what he prefers to call "personalist" and "particularist" approaches, or "juridico-mystical" and "universalist" approaches.[16] The particularist approach starts from the local church, while the universalist starts from the global community. The latter tends to understand the meaning of *koinonia* as participation in the divine life, achieved through the objective means of grace (sacraments), while the former is inclined to understand *koinonia* as directly signifying a fellowship of love and intimacy achieved in a local community. The particularist view tends to see groups as being spontaneously formed under the impulse of the Holy Spirit and as constituting themselves. The base communities, naturally, represent the particularist orientation. Dulles admits that the particularists "are on solid ground when they argue that the Holy Spirit can inspire ecclesial initiatives that are not directly dependent on the hierarchy of the great Church."[17] On the other hand, Dulles argues that universalists would seem to be correct in insisting that the church was originally founded as a single society and only gradually came to be articulated as a plurality of particular churches.[18]

Another noted Catholic ecclesiologist, Susan K. Wood, takes a slightly dif-

---

[14]Boff, *Ecclesiogenesis*, p. 7.

[15]For the definition of the question, see especially ibid., pp. 7-9.

[16]Avery Dulles, "The Church as Communion," in *New Perspectives on Historical Theology: Essays in Memory of John Meyendorff*, ed. Bradley Nassif (Grand Rapids, Mich.: Eerdmans, 1996), p. 133.

Dulles notes that other terms are also used, such as ecclesiologies "from below" and "from above" (see Joseph Kkomonchak, "The Church Universal as the Communion of Local Churches," in *Where Does the Church Stand? Concilium* 146 [Edinburgh: T & T Clark, 1981], pp. 30-35).

[17]Dulles, "Church as Communion," pp. 133-35 (quote on p. 135).

[18]Ibid., p. 135.

ferent approach in her categorization of recent ecclesiologies. She speaks of "objective or structural" and "subjective or experiential" models. In the former, the church is conceptualized as a communion of particular churches and the Eucharist is the locus of communion. In the latter, "faith as a subjective experience constitutes the 'communing' within the model of church as communion."[19] Wood regards the base communities as a paradigm of the subjective, experience-focused model. In fact, Leonardo Boff claims that the community as the people of God exists antecedently to the church as organization.[20] In this view the risen Christ and the Spirit are immanently present in the community.[21] According to Boff, "these communities are characterized by the absence of alienating structures, by direct relationships, by reciprocity, by a deep communion, by mutual assistance, by communality of gospel ideals, by equality among members."[22]

Even if this characterization perhaps says more of the ideal than of the actual state of the base communities, it faithfully reflects the general orientation of this ecclesiological understanding. Wood is right when she concludes that in the base communities model the basis for communion is the faith of the church and the sharing of the gospel.[23] As far as Catholic theology is open to acknowledge the ecclesiality of the church along these lines, the base communities may be legitimately described as churches; if not, then they represent at their best "renewal" movements in the church, a sort of auxiliary in the service of the Mother Church.

This kind of fundamental ecclesiological question is not likely to be solved easily, but the debate itself has helped focus the development of the Catholic doctrine of the church and has extended its influence far beyond the Catholic contours. In a very legitimate sense, the ecclesiological question raised by the base communities also represents the fight of various Protestant Free churches for the acknowledgement of their ecclesiality. Even though, at least to my knowledge, there has been little if any comparison and correlation between these two debates, the defining questions are similar: Are there alternative ways of defining the ecclesiality of the church? Is it possible for Christian theology to sustain and champion complementary ways of acknowledging the

---

[19]Susan Wood, "Communion Ecclesiology: Source of Hope, Source of Controversy," *Pro Ecclesia* 2, no. 4 (1993): 427.
[20]Boff, *Ecclesiogenesis*, p. 26.
[21]Wood, "Communion Ecclesiology," p. 428.
[22]Boff, *Ecclesiogenesis*, p. 4.
[23]Wood, "Communion Ecclesiology," p. 429.

churchly nature of communities? And, especially with regard to the Roman Catholic Church, is it possible for a worldwide Christian church to affirm the ecclesiality of communities within itself?

It is instructive to see how the base communities specifically argue for and elaborate their distinctive understanding of the ecclesiality of the church "from below."

## An Ecclesiology "from Below"

On what basis do the base communities argue for the ecclesiality of their communities? According to the study of Fr. Alfonso Gregory, the communities themselves presented the following responses to support their claim: a foundation on the common Christian faith, a sense-of-the-people, the priority of strictly religious activities rather than social, and work at the grassroots "for a communication in faith, through humanization."[24] While these and similar arguments are not irrelevant for the question of ecclesiality, they might not convince theologically. Jose Marins, one of the most ardent champions of the ecclesiality of these communities, anchors the question of the ecclesiality in the mainstream of Catholic doctrine of the church, still building on the ecclesiology "from below":

> For us, the basic church community is the church itself, the universal sacrament of salvation, as it continues the mission of Christ—Prophet, Priest, and Pastor. This is what makes it a community of faith, worship, and love. Its mission is explicitly expressed on all levels—the universal, the diocesan, and the local, or basic.[25]

Leonardo Boff makes the important note that in the ecclesiology of Vatican II, the ecclesiality of the local church was definitively acknowledged (*Lumen Gentium*, #26). In these local churches, the essential constitutive elements of the church are present, namely the gospel, the Eucharist and the presence of the apostolic succession in the person of the bishop. On the basis of this, the Medellín Conference (1968) acknowledged the foundational, initial churchly nature of base communities:

> Thus the Christian base community is the *first and fundamental ecclesiastical nucleus*, which on its own level must make itself responsible for the richness and expansion of the faith, as well as of the cult which is its expression. This community becomes then the *initial cell* of the ecclesiastical structures and the focus of evan-

---

[24]Boff, *Ecclesiogenesis*, pp. 11-12.
[25]Ibid., p. 12.

gelization, and it currently serves as the most important source of human advancement and development. The essential element for the existence of Christian base communities are their leaders or directors. These can be priest, deacons, men or women religious, or laymen.[26]

This is a surprising Catholic statement: the church is not being thought of from the top down but from the bottom up, from the grassroots, from the "base." Even though the "leaders or directors" are mentioned as the essential element, there is an unheard of openness for defining them as either ordained or non-ordained, laymen or religious. This is an affirmation of the "Grassroots church."[27] Understandably, one pressing question for the base communities in Latin America is the desperate lack of ordained priests. Is it possible to affirm the ecclesiality without a consecrated minister? The base communities' theology of the church once again takes its point of departure from the ecclesiology "from below." If the church abides and is founded on the people of God as they continue to come together, convoked by the Word of God and the discipleship of Jesus Christ, then the existence of an ordained minister cannot be seen as a necessary prerequisite for the being of the church. On the contrary, the priest participates in the church in these communities.[28]

The ecclesiology "from below" of the base communities challenges the way traditional theology has understood the classical "marks of the church." Leonardo Boff calls the dominant Catholic way of looking at these attributes of the church a "dissymmetrical" one. In that understanding, oneness appears as monolithic uniformity: one and the same discourse, one and the same liturgy, one and the same ecclesiastical set of regulations and so on. Holiness is a characteristic of the church insofar as the faithful take part in the "ethos of the historico-religious bloc under the hegemony of the hierarchy." In this dissymmetrical mode of religious production, apostolicity is the property of only one class, the bishops, the successors of the apostles; catholicity is strictly tied to uniformity, and the quantitative aspect is stressed. The emphasis is on one and the same church present all over the world.[29] On the contrary, the base communities envision the oneness of the church as unity-in-diversity, composed of several *ecclesiae*; holiness in the sanctification of all the people of God;

---

[26]*CELAM II*, pp. 10-11, as quoted in Boff, *Ecclesiogenesis*, p. 15 (emphases Boff's).

[27]See further Leonardo Boff, "Theological Characteristics of a Grassroots Church," in *The Challenge of Basic Christian Communities*, ed. Sergio Torres and John Eagleson (Maryknoll, N.Y.: Orbis, 1981), pp. 124-44.

[28]Boff, *Ecclesiogenesis*, p. 13.

[29]Boff, "Theological Characteristics of a Grassroots Church," pp. 131-32 (quote on p. 131).

apostolicity as the life of the whole church as characterized by the lifestyle of the apostles; and catholicity as the wholeness of the gospel and church life. Rather than absolutizing any particular mode of being of the church, it relativizes the church: it means looking at the church in its "relation to" its reason for being and its finality. The opposite course would be to "absolutize," to regard it as the ultimate point of reference, as the total, overall horizon.[30]

## *"An Oppressed People Organizing for Liberation"*[31]

> The CCBs [Base Christian Communities] are one of the most fruitful and significant events in the present-day life of the Latin American church. Their growth throughout our continent has helped to raise the hopes of the poor and oppressed. They are a privileged meeting place for a people trying to familiarize itself with its situation of misery and exploitation, to fight against that situation, and to give an account of its faith in a liberating God.[32]

The base communities not only identify with the poor and the weakest in the society, they *are* a church of the poor, made up of poor people.[33] The "base" means the poor, the oppressed and the marginalized for whatever reason. It is from them that these Christian communities are arising. "From these poor, oppressed sectors the Spirit is bringing to birth a church rooted in the milieu of exploitation and the struggle for liberation."[34] The shared standpoint against social injustice is based on two convictions, shared by many other liberation movements: first, the main root of the oppression of common people is an elitist, exclusive, capitalist system;[35] and second, people resist and are liberated to the extent they unite and create a network of popular movements.[36] As such the base communities resist the widespread Christian ethos of reducing Christianity to the intimate sphere of private life. "Jesus preached and died in pub-

---

[30]José Miguez Bonino, "Fundamental Questions in Ecclesiology," in *The Challenge of Basic Christian Communities*, ed. Sergio Torres and John Eagleson (Maryknoll, N.Y.: Orbis, 1981), pp. 145-48 especially. See also Cook, *Expectation of the Poor*, p. 3.

[31]Chapter title in Boff, *Ecclesiogenesis*, p. 34.

[32]Gustavo Gutiérrez, "The Irruption of the Poor in Latin America and the Christian Communities of the Common People," in *The Challenge of Basic Christian Communities*, ed. Sergio Torres and John Eagleson (Maryknoll, N.Y.: Orbis, 1981), p. 115.

[33]See further ibid., pp. 107-22.

[34]Ibid., p. 116.

[35]See further Luis A. Gómez de Souza, "Structures and Mechanisms of Domination in Capitalism," in *The Challenge of Basic Christian Communities*, ed. Sergio Torres and John Eagleson (Maryknoll, N.Y.: Orbis, 1981), pp. 13-23.

[36]Boff, *Ecclesiogenesis*, p. 35.

lic, out in the world, and he is Lord not only of the little corners of our hearts, but of society and the cosmos as well."[37] The preaching of the gospel, good news to the poor, kindles in them the fire of hope and transforms their lives.[38] The gospel has a necessary political dimension.[39] To foster this, the base communities have developed, in collaboration with other liberation movements, the "hermeneutic of the grassroots communities," a style of Bible reading that does justice to the social and political aspects of the gospel.[40]

This focus on the social implications of the gospel not only does not mean minimizing spirituality, but rather means prioritizing spirituality. In the understanding of the base communities, the social flows from the religious.[41] The focus of the base communities is, of course, not to make their members rich, nor to produce goods, but rather to create priceless values and types of human relations and coexistence that are in keeping with the Christian dignity of the human being.[42] In this, the base communities continue the mission of Jesus, the Messiah of the poor. To fail in preaching the good news to the poor, Alvaro Barreiro argues, is to betray the church's mission.[43]

In the Latin American context the liberating work of the base communities has not limited its focus to the poor, but also speaks against the oppression of women.[44] Several base communities theologians openly question the denial of ordination of women in the Roman Catholic Church.[45] They argue that limiting the ministry only to male members of the church is yet another way of oppression. That kind of exclusivism is also against the teaching and attitude of Jesus, who welcomed all regardless of their sex, status or class. The main purpose of base communities is, therefore, to live out that kind of open and inclusive community life that does not erect any kind of social, political, religious or other boundaries but affirms the value of all people, especially the rejected and oppressed.

---

[37]Ibid., p. 38.

[38]Alvaro Barreiro, *Basic Ecclesial Communities: The Evangelization of the Poor* (Maryknoll, N.Y.: Orbis, 1977), p. 1.

[39]See further Cook, *Expectation of the Poor*, pp. 73-76.

[40]See further ibid., pp. 108-26.

[41]Boff, *Ecclesiogenesis*, pp. 41-42.

[42]Barreiro, *Basic Ecclesial Communities*, p. 42.

[43]Ibid., p. 50.

[44]See further Cora Ferro, "The Latin American Woman: The Praxis and Theology of Liberation," in *The Challenge of Basic Christian Communities*, ed. Sergio Torres and John Eagleson (Maryknoll, N.Y.: Orbis, 1981), pp. 24-37.

[45]Boff, *Ecclesiogenesis*, pp. 76-97.

# 17

# The Feminist Church

## No Walking Away from the Church

I have always found it difficult to walk away from the church, but I have also found it difficult to walk with it. . . . The alienation is shared with many other women and men whose pain and anger at the contradictions of church life lead them to challenge the very idea of talking about a feminist interpretation of the church. It is also increased by knowledge of the disdain and anger of those theologians and church officials who consider women like me to be the problem rather than the church itself.[1]

The question is often asked of me: "Why don't you leave the church if you don't agree with the church's opinion and teaching?" In the past years, I have encountered this challenge again and again from right-wing Catholics and feminists alike. However, to seriously entertain this question already concedes the power of naming to the reactionary forces insofar as it recognizes their ownership of biblical religions.[2]

These quotations from two leading American feminist ecclesiologists reveal the anguish and dilemma many women—and men—share concerning the way the church reacts to women. Letty Russell's comment brings to surface the built-in tension that feminist and other liberationists share about the locus of the Christian message: "It is impossible for me and for many other alienated women and men to walk away from the church, however, for it has been the bearer of the story of Jesus Christ and the good news of God's love."[3]

Living as we are now in an age of "hermeneutics of suspicion" we find

---

[1]Letty M. Russell, *Church in the Round: Feminist Interpretation of the Church* (Louisville: Westminster John Knox, 1993), p. 11.

[2]Elisabeth Schüssler Fiorenza, *Discipleship of Equals: Critical Feminists Ekklesia-logy of Liberation* (New York: Crossroad, 1993), p. 3.

[3]Russell, *Church in the Round*, p. 11.

many conventional ways of talking about religion threatening. Mary Daly insists that the personification of God as Father is the foremost symbol of patriarchy. She also claims that the image of the Father-God makes the mechanism for the oppression of women appear correct, and from this grows male-dominance.[4] There is no denying the fact that most images of God are modeled after the ruling class of society.[5] Even though, generally speaking, it might be an overstatement that the symbol of divine fatherhood has been the source of misuse of power in terms of violence, rape and war, it is true that language not only reflects reality but also constructs it.[6]

The questions posed by feminist theologians go beyond the debate of whether to address God as Father or Mother or something else. This questioning involves the whole Trinity: How does Jesus' maleness relate to the other half of humankind? And is the Spirit masculine or feminine?

## "She Who Is"

Even though Christian theology has been slow to change the traditional masculine language, the problem is not totally new.[7] Gregory of Nazianzus ridiculed his opponents who thought God was male because God is called Father, or that deity is feminine because of the gender of the word, or the Spirit neuter because it does not get personal names. Gregory insisted that God's fatherhood has nothing to do with marriage, pregnancy, midwifery or sexuality.[8] It has also been noted that we do not often think God as male, even though we call God *him*. It is just a conventional way of using language. The liberationist Jose Comblin rightly notes that over against many other religions, the Christian God is not sexist: none of the divine Persons has a gender. But still in their action in humanity and the world, each Person is manifested under names borrowed from the genders.[9]

Even though Augustine's influence in the West was decisive in eliminating all feminine references from theology because of his unfortunate view of women as not fully the image of God,[10] his writings also display God's im-

---

[4]Mary Daly, *Beyond God the Father* (Boston: Beacon, 1973).

[5]Rosemary Ruether, *Sexism and God-Talk* (Boston: Beacon, 1983).

[6]See further Ted Peters, *God—the World's Future: Systematic Theology for a Postmodern Era* (Minneapolis: Fortress, 1992), pp. 109-20

[7]For a historical overview, see Schüssler Fiorenza, *Discipleship of Equals*, pp. 151-79.

[8]Peters, *God—the World's Future*, p. 109.

[9]Comblin, *The Holy Spirit and Liberation* (Maryknoll, N.Y.: Orbis, 1987), p. 50.

[10]Ibid., p. 39.

manence in a warm, loving spirituality. In Augustine's theology, the Holy
Spirit points to a distinctively feminine aspect of God and with that the feminine qualities of cherishing love, hence the preservative, receptive aspect of
God. Thus, Augustine likens the Holy Spirit to a mother hen.[11] Martin Luther
uses the same imagery.[12]

Sallie McFague has tried to escape the problem of sexist talk about God with
the help of metaphorical talk. Attempting to avoid literalism, so "rampant in
our time," she suggests piling up metaphors to relativize the Father symbol and
give room for complementary symbols, such as God as mother, lover or
friend.[13] Elizabeth Johnson's approach shares many similarities with Mc-
Fague's. Johnson argues in her book *She Who Is: The Mystery of God in Feminist
Theology*[14] that we need to envision and speak of the mystery of God with female images and metaphors in order to free women from a subordination imposed by the patriarchal imaging of God. Her own preference is "She Who Is."[15]

Jürgen Moltmann places the question of sexism in relation to the Spirit of
God in a wider perspective, namely that of community. Actually, theologically
it is not enough just to criticize traditional theologies for neglecting feminine
terminology and attempt to replace the masculine with another limited, exclusive usage. Moltmann insists that according to biblical ideas, what makes us
*imago Dei* (image of God) is not the soul apart from the body. The image of God
consists of men and women in their wholeness, in their full, sexually specific
community with one another. God is not known in the inner chamber of the
heart, or at a solitary place, but in the true community of women and men. As
a result, the experience of God and God's Spirit is "the social experience of the
self and the personal experience of sociality."[16]

Therefore, Moltmann asks questions like this: What fellowship do women
and men arrive at in fellowship with Christ and in their experience of the Spirit who desires to give life to all flesh? How do women and men experience one

[11]Bernard Reynolds, *Toward a Process Pneumatology* (Toronto: Associated University Press,
1990), p. 125.
[12]See further Veli-Matti Kärkkäinen, *Pneumatology: The Holy Spirit in Ecumenical, International
and Historical Perspective* (Grand Rapids, Mich.: Baker, 2002), p. 82.
[13]For details, see Sallie McFague, *Models of God: Theology for an Ecological Nuclear Age* (Philadelphia: Fortress, 1987). For a critique, see Peters, *God—the World's Future*, pp. 119-20.
[14]Elizabeth Johnson, *She Who Is: The Mystery of God in Feminist Theology* (New York: Crossroad,
1992).
[15]Ibid., pp. 127-41.
[16]Jürgen Moltmann, *The Spirit of Life: A Universal Affirmation* (Minneapolis: Fortress, 1992), p.
94.

another in the community of Christ's people, and in the fellowship of the life-engendering Mother Spirit? These are not just questions of church politics, but first of all questions of faith:

> According to the promise in Joel 2:28-30 "It shall come to pass in the last days, says the Lord, that I will pour out my spirit on all flesh; and your sons and your daughters shall prophesy" (cf. Acts 2:17ff.). The eschatological hope for the experience of the Spirit is shared by women and men equally. Men and women will "prophesy" and proclaim the gospel. According to the prophecy in Joel 2, through the shared experience of the Spirit the privileges of men compared with women, of the old compared with the young, and of masters compared with "menservants and maidservants" will be abolished. In the kingdom of the Spirit, everyone will experience his and her own endowment and all will experience the new fellowship together.[17]

## *The Church Around the Table*

One of the most innovative approaches to feminist ecclesiology is Letty Russell's *Church in the Round,* which utilizes the symbolism of the table to create new images of the church. As is well known, in many cultures the table symbolizes hospitality and sharing. Much in the home happens around the kitchen table, and some of the most precious memories go back to table fellowship. It also speaks of God's hospitality and inclusive attitude. The "church around the table" is a "discipleship of equals," the title of Fiorenza's feminist ecclesiology. One could also express the core of feminist ecclesiology by describing the church as "connective"; there is a living, dynamic connection between men and women and between God and human beings. "If the table is spread by God and hosted by Christ, it must be a table with many connections."[18]

A feminist church attempts to reach to the margins and searches for liberation from all forms of dehumanization, be it sexual, racial or any other form of exploitation. This means that men can also be feminists if they are willing to advocate for women. The search for freedom and equality is continuing the ministry of Christ, who welcomed people of all ages and both sexes into God's reign.[19]

> Those of us who "fall in faith" with this man and his story of God's welcome experience cognitive dissonance, a contradiction between ideas and actual experi-

---

[17]Ibid., pp. 239-41.
[18]Russell, *Church in the Round,* p. 18.
[19]Ibid., pp. 22-23.

ence, when we turn from reading the Gospels to looking at the way this message has been interpreted in the church through the ages. . . . We find ourselves seeking out communities of faith and struggle that speak of life in the midst of all forms of death-dealing oppression.[20]

This "critical principle" of feminist analysis borrows from liberation theologies of various sorts;[21] it is what the liberationist Gustavo Gutiérrez has called "theology from the underside of history."[22] Feminist ecclesiologists join this liberation tradition in moving from the questions of those at the center of society to those considered less than human because they are powerless and unimportant. They also read the Bible "from the margin"[23] or do what Russell calls "talking back to tradition."[24]

## *"Leadership in the Round"*[25]

Leadership in the church both mirrors its ethos and shapes it. It is clear that those churches that consider ordination essential to the being of the church often tend to restrict ordination to the sacramental or pastoral role and limit priesthood to celibate men as in the Roman Catholic Church. The feminist understanding, however, considers ministry in the life of the church to be the recognition of gifting from God and thus open to both men and women. Ministries are *"gifts* of God rather than *givens* of God." Feminist ecclesiology is also critical of the dualistic division of the church into "upper-class" clergy and "lower-class" laity.[26] Therefore, the core issue of ministry is not necessarily an insistence on the right of ordination for women but rather a revision of the whole concept of ordination.[27] For example, leadership is not the idea behind ministry. It is specifically a reference to service of others.

In patriarchal styles of leadership, so characteristic of most churches, au-

---

[20]Ibid., p. 23.
[21]Schüssler Fiorenza, *Discipleship of Equals*, pp. 53-79; she calls feminist theology a "critical theology of liberation."
[22]Gustavo Gutiérrez, *The Power of the Poor in History: Selected Writings* (Maryknoll, N.Y.: Orbis, 1983), p. 183.
[23]See for example Phyllis Trible, *Texts of Terror* (Philadelphia: Fortress, 1984), pp. 8-29, for a feminist reading of the story of Sarah and Hagar.
[24]Russell, *Church in the Round*, especially pp. 35-41. For a feminist Bible reading, especially from a postmodern perspective, see Elisabeth Schüssler Fiorenza, *But She Said: Feminist Practices of Biblical Interpretation* (Boston: Beacon, 1992).
[25]Chapter title in Russell, *Church in the Round*, p. 46.
[26]Ibid., pp. 47-54 especially (quote on p. 50; emphases in the text).
[27]See further Schüssler Fiorenza, *Discipleship of Equals*, pp. 23-38, where she asks critically, "Should Women Aim for Ordination to the Lowest Rung of the Hierarchical Ladder?"

thority is exercised by standing above in the place of power.[28] Feminist styles of leadership would draw their model of behavior from a partnership paradigm that is oriented toward community formation.[29] In feminist styles of leadership, authority is exercised by standing with others and seeking to share power and authority. Power is seen as something to be multiplied and shared rather than accumulated at the top. In this search for a new approach to leadership in the church, feminist ecclesiologists are again drawing from the example of Jesus who literally turned the tables.[30]

Churches are structured with a clear indication of leadership. But with regard to structure, Russell suggests two directions: missionary structures and liberation structures. She has participated in the World Council of Churches' search for missionary structures for local churches.[31] Structures that enhance the participation of local churches in God's mission may take several forms such as the "family type," which was seen as a residential congregation of not more than a hundred persons, small enough so that people of all ages, races, classes and lifestyles could learn to become a family.[32]

For Russell and many other feminist ecclesiologies the question of church structures, and by implication of leadership models, also carries theological significance. Basically they are ready to call "churches" all Christian communities that struggle in faith and faithfulness to work for the liberation of all God's people. With liberationists such as Leonardo Boff, these feminists "assume that these groups *are* church when they gather as church and ask about how they are seeking to show this faithfulness in their structures and mission. What makes them distinctive is not their traditional church life but their willingness to be connected to the struggle of particular groups for freedom and full humanity."[33]

Letty Russell claims that in North America, feminist Christian communities are the most widespread form of alternative Christian community. These largely ecumenical Christian groups have emerged out of attempts to bring feminist perspectives to mainline Christian churches.[34] They have many simi-

---

[28]See further Schüssler Fiorenza, *Discipleship of Equals*, pp. 211-33, for the comparison between patriarchal structures and the discipleship of equals; see also pp. 237-48.

[29]Ibid., pp. 269-74.

[30]Russell, *Church in the Round*, pp. 54-63, 67-74.

[31]See further *The Church for Others and the Church for the World*, Department of Studies in Evangelism (Geneva, Switzerland: WCC Publications, 1967).

[32]See further Letty Russell, "Forms of the Confessing Churches Today," *Journal of Presbyterian History* (Spring 1983): 99-109.

[33]Russell, *Church in the Round*, p. 94.

[34]Ibid., pp. 104-5.

larities with the base communities of the Roman Catholic Church in Latin America and beyond and are sometimes called "Women church."[35]

Not all feminist theologians are convinced that just working with existing churches and helping them become more like Women church would be enough. The most vocal critic of more moderate feminist theology, as represented by Russell and Schüssler Fiorenza, has been Rosemary Radford Ruether. Her idea of *Women-Church* is much more radical than the ideas on which this chapter has focused. She calls women, not just a few individuals but whole communities, to separate themselves for a while from men to avoid patriarchy. This ideology of separatism would not be an end in itself but rather a stage in a process, "a stage that is absolutely necessary, . . . a stage toward a further end in formation of a critical culture and community of women and men in exodus from patriarchy."[36] This kind of a period of withdrawal from men and of communication with each other is essential for the formation of the feminist community, "because women, more than any other marginalized group, have lacked a critical culture of their own," Ruether contends.[37] The approach of Ruether, in other words, is not content with changing structures of the church, but seeks to form a new community—for a certain period—with its own structures, leadership and ethos. While Ruether's voice is widely heard, any response in the form of practical action has been quite meager, and so it seems like the approach of Russell and Schüssler Fiorenza and like-minded women seems to be the majority feminist voice in ecclesiology.

## "Justice and the Church"[38]

Letty Russell has worked for years for the healing of AIDS communities and individuals affected by that disease.[39] She notes that the church today is often unable to deal with the crisis of AIDS simply because its understanding of who is saved is so narrow that there is not room for the AIDS patients. "Salvation has been sexualized, privatized, futurized, and restricted to a chosen few."[40]

---

[35]For the question of authority in feminist ecclesiology, see further Letty Russell, *Household of Freedom: Authority in Feminist Perspective* (Philadelphia: Westminster Press, 1987).

[36]Rosemary Radford Ruether, *Women-Church: Theology and Practice of Feminist Liturgical Communities* (San Francisco: Harper & Row, 1985), p. 60.

[37]Ibid., p. 59.

[38]Chapter title in Russell, *Church in the Round*, p. 112.

[39]See further Russell, ed., *The Church with AIDS: Renewal in the Midst of Crisis* (Louisville: Westminster John Knox, 1990).

[40]Russell, *Church in the Round*, p. 114.

Personal morality, especially conformity to conventional sexual norms, is emphasized as the condition for sexuality, while structural sins are often overlooked in the church. Feminist readers of the Bible remind us that the biblical notion of salvation entails various perspectives such as liberation, wholeness, peace and blessing of all life. Aligning with liberation theologies, feminist theologies recognize salvation as holistic shalom, social and physical wholeness and harmony. Salvation is understood relationally, between human beings and in relation to God.[41] Only that kind of holistic approach can equip the church to fulfill its task in promoting justice, peace and wholeness.

Very early in Christian theology there was a tendency to reduce and narrow the broader understanding of shalom in the light of the Hellenistic separation of the body and soul. In liberation and feminist theologies there are two overlapping motifs of shalom, namely liberation and blessing, as "God's intention for full humanity of women together with men . . . for the mending of all creation."[42] The larger meaning of salvation as shalom includes not only blessing and liberation, but also justice and righteousness.

If it is God's action that justifies and puts things right, how is it, Russell asks, that the church has come to lay claim to itself as the place of salvation, declaring that there is no salvation outside the church? Feminists would rather modify that to "No salvation outside the poor." The "preferential option for the church" has to be replaced by the preferential option for the poor and other outcasts. Not only is the church the place of salvation because Christ promises to be present there, but so also are the poor the place of salvation, since Christ promises to be present amidst them. God's option for the poor is a sign of God's desire to mend the whole of creation, especially those parts that are broken.[43] White, male-dominated mainline churches in the United States and elsewhere have had a difficult time joining in solidarity with the poor and marginalized. They have also contributed to the unhealthy separation between social and personal sin.

### Women, the Earth and the Church

Many feminist writers have noted that how we structure life in the church is also reflected in how we treat other communities, the community of creation included. In other words, there is interrelation between the community of

---

[41]Ibid., pp. 114-19.
[42]Ibid., pp. 116-17.
[43]Ibid., pp. 119-23.

God's people and God's creation. Another reason for a careful analysis of church structures derives from the impending natural crisis we are facing now. Elizabeth Johnson's *Women, Earth, and Creator Spirit*[44] is a groundbreaking study in that it combines the concerns of two complementary approaches, namely that of feminist and ecological theologies. The thesis of the book is that "the exploitation of the earth, which has reached crisis proportion in our day, is intimately linked to the marginalization of women, and that both of these predicaments are intrinsically related to forgetting the Creator Spirit who pervades the world in the dance of life."[45]

In a careful survey of the current ecocrisis in the first part of the book, Johnson claims that the only legitimate way to address the problem is that of "ecofeminism." An analysis of the ecological crisis does not get to the heart of the matter unless it sees the connection between the exploitation of the earth and sexist exploitation.[46]

Johnson is weary of the prevailing "hierarchical" dualism in Christian theology that leads to abuse of both nature, the other sex and one's own body.[47] It has also affected the Christian understanding of God; often God has been depicted in hierarchical terms, and this leads to hierarchical conceptions of the church.[48] The feminine, nature, the body, sexuality and women are separated. Now it is the task of the ecofeminist theology to seek a new wholeness, a new community of equals.[49] Ecofeminist theology emphasizes unity between nature, women and men, and with our bodies, and so looks favorably toward "kinship models."[50]

Feminist approaches to theology in general and ecclesiology in particular draw resources from the wells of pneumatology. An ecofeminist "theology of the Creator Spirit overcomes the dualism of spirit and matter with all of its ramifications, and leads to the realization of the sacredness of the earth."[51] It leads away from a one-sided anthropocentric or androcentric model and toward a life-centered, biocentric model.

---

[44]Elizabeth Johnson, *Women, Earth, and Creator Spirit* (Mahwah, N.Y.: Paulist, 1993).

[45]Ibid., p. 2.

[46]Ibid., p. 10.

[47]For the dangers of dualistic anthropology and its influence on the church life, see also Schüssler Fiorenza, *Discipleship of Equals*, pp. 97-98.

[48]Cf. Jürgen Moltmann, *The Spirit of Life: A Universal Affirmation* (Minneapolis: Fortress, 1992), pp. 239-40.

[49]Johnson, *Women, Earth, and Creator Spirit*, p. 25.

[50]Ibid., p. 39.

[51]Ibid., p. 60.

Feminist theology in general and ecclesiology in particular currently represent various kinds of orientations toward liberating women to the status of an equal human being with men. As our survey has indicated, there are those who champion a more radical action, even to the temporary isolation of women from men's communities, and those who favor working toward restructuring and shaping existing communities. Ecologically oriented feminists are not only content with looking at interpersonal relations in light of man-woman equality but also see it important to extend the reform to how we treat nature; in their view, how human beings treat each other is indicative of the way creation is treated.

# 18

# African Independent
# Churches' Ecclesiology

## African Reformation[1]

According to the recent estimation of Walter J. Hollenweger, the two main catalysts for the rapid growth of Christianity in the south hemisphere are African Independent Churches (AICs) and various groups related to Pentecostal/Charismatic movements.[2] Certainly in Africa the AICs and other independent churches have numerically far outstripped their mother churches.[3] For example, The Zion Christian Church of Bishop Lekhanyane, with millions of adherents, has spread all over South Africa. In Zimbabwe the Independent churches are claiming fifty percent or more of the Christians in rural areas. Already in the beginning of the 1980s, David Barret reported that the AICs claim thirty-one million adherents throughout the African continent; the current number is, of course, significantly larger.[4] This is what the African theologians have called the new "centers of universality."[5]

The acronym AIC stands for several interrelated titles: African Indigenous Churches, African Initiated Churches or African Independent Churches. The

---

[1]A new title by one of the leading AIC researchers, Allan H. Anderson, *African Reformation: African Initiated Christianity in the Twentieth Century* (Trenton, N.J.: Africa World Press, 2000).
[2]W. J. Hollenweger, "Foreword," in *African Initiatives in Christianity: The Growth, Gifts and Diversities of Indigenous African Churches—A Challenge to the Ecumenical Movement*, ed. John M. Pobere and Gabriel Ositelu II (Geneva, Switzerland: WCC Publications, 1998).
[3]A recent good introduction to various facets of AICs is offered by Cephas N. Omenyo, "Essential Aspects of African Ecclesiology: The Case of the African Independent Churches," *Pneuma* 22, no. 2 (2000): 231-48. See also Zablon J. Nthanmburi, "Ecclesiology of African Independent Churches," in *The Church in African Christianity: Innovative Essays in Ecclesiology*, ed. J. N. K. Mugambi and Laurenti Magesa (Nairobi: Initiatives, 1990); J. S. Pobee, "African Instituted (Independent) Churches," in *Dictionary of the Ecumenical Movement*, ed. N. Lossky et al. (Geneva, Switzerland: WCC Publications, 1991), pp. 10-12.
[4]David B. Barrett, *Schism and Renewal in Africa* (New York: Oxford University Press, 1982), p. 815.
[5]See further Kwame Bediako, *Christianity in Africa* (Maryknoll, N.Y.: Orbis, 1995), p. 111.

last name is gaining more and more following in recent theological literature. Bengt Sundkler's *Bantu Prophets in South Africa*, published in 1948, was one of the first monographs to deal systematically with what we know today as the African Independent Churches. In the introduction to the second edition he points out that the official term is "Native Separatist Churches."[6]

Daneel prefers the term "African Independent Churches" because it does not necessarily imply a value judgment. It is not in itself a pejorative term. But Daneel goes on to say that the term presupposes a demarcation of the field that excludes "protest movements" within the "historical" or "established" churches and such movements as Black Theology.[7] In fact, the AICs, as genuine expressions of African culture and religious context, both protest against the Western "missionary mentality" of the past and creatively employ local cultural elements.

What might be theologically and ecumenically the most significant feature in the AICs ecclesiologies is the fact that they have "testified to the existence of some generalized trends in the African response to the Christian faith in African terms."[8] In other words, the AICs have the potential of embodying a type of Christian spirituality and faith that does not merely contextualize some superficial elements of a Western interpretation of Christianity but rather represents a legitimate version of Christian faith, a non-Western religion, that has taken root in the distinctive heritage of that continent. Being rooted in African

---

[6]B. G. M. Sundkler, *Bantu Prophets in South Africa* (Oxford: Oxford University Press, 1961), p. 18. Stephen Hayes gives the following historical sketch: "Sundkler finds this unsatisfactory, partly because the term 'native' was offensive to blacks in South Africa at that time and also because he thought that it might suggest that white secessionists were not 'separatist.' He therefore proposed to speak of 'Bantu Independent Churches.' Later writers have generally preferred to speak of 'African Independent Churches,' partly because 'Bantu' soon became even more offensive than 'native' to blacks in South Africa, as it became closely linked to the apartheid ideology of the South African government. There was another reason for rejecting the term 'Bantu.' Until it was adopted by the apartheid ideologists, it was mainly used as a *linguistic* rather than as a *racial* category. The 'Bantu' languages were those in which the word for 'people' was similar to the Nguni word 'abantu.' The independent churches Sundkler described were indeed to be found among people who spoke Bantu languages, but similar movements were also to be found among people from other linguistic groupings and indeed throughout the African continent. 'African' therefore seemed preferable and was used partly in a racial and partly in a continental sense" ("African Independent Churches: Judgement Through Terminology," *Missionalia* 20, no. 2 [August 1992]:139). See also P. Makhubu, *Who Are the Independent Churches?* (Johannesburg: Skotaville, 1998), p. 1.

[7]M. L. Daneel, *Old and New in Southern Shona Independent Churches*, vol. 1, *Background and Rise of the Major Movements* (The Hague: Mouton, 1971), pp. 31-32.

[8]Bediako, *Christianity in Africa*, p. 66; I am indebted to Omenyo, "Essential Aspects of African Ecclesiology," p. 234, for this quotation.

soil, the theological mode of the AICs is different from their Western counter-parts; theirs is the oral and narrative style so prevalent also elsewhere outside the West.[9]

Allan H. Anderson has provided a typology for these churches that is based on their distinctive ecclesiological features:[10] (1) "Ethiopian" and "African" churches that do not claim to be prophetic or to have special manifestations of the Holy Spirit were called "Ethiopian" or "Ethiopian-type" churches in Southern Africa and "African" churches in Nigeria. These churches are gener-ally earlier in origin than the other two types, and arose primarily as a political and administrative reaction to European mission-founded churches. (2) "Prophet-healing" and "spiritual" churches have their historical and theolog-ical roots in the Pentecostal movement, although they have moved away from this movement in several respects over the years, and may not be regarded as "Pentecostal" without further qualification. (3) "New Pentecostal" churches must be distinguished from the "prophet-healing" AICs. The term "New Pen-tecostal" will be used for those churches of more recent origin (mostly after 1980) that also emphasize the power and the gifts of the Holy Spirit. A signif-icant number of their members come from both the European mission-found-ed churches and from the prophet-healing churches, and this is sometimes a source of tension. The difference between these churches and churches of Western Pentecostal origin is mainly in church government, which is entirely black and has more of a local, autonomous nature with no organizational links with Pentecostal denominations outside Africa. These churches tend to op-pose some traditional African practices as well as those of older AICs.

## African Koinonia

Cephas M. Omenyo of Ghana has recently argued that the category of *koinonia*, the catchword for much of ecumenical ecclesiology since the 1980s, best de-scribes the ecclesiology of the AICs. He argues that the concept of communion is very fundamental in understanding the ecclesiology of the AICs mainly be-cause the sense of community is the *sine qua non* (necessary condition) in under-standing African societies.[11] This sense of community reflects the deeply rooted African conviction that it is only in the community that people in general and

---

[9]See further Allan H. Anderson, "Pluriformity and Contextuality in African Initiated Churches" (September 1997) <http://artsweb.bham.ac.uk/aanderson/index.htm >.
[10]Anderson, "Pluriformity and Contextuality," pp. 3-7.
[11]Omenyo, "Essential Aspects of African Ecclesiology," pp. 235-36.

Christians in particular can find the meaning to their life.[12] Communal living is the way to promote and maintain the well-being of the individual and of society in general. Omenyo cites Kofi Asare Opoku, another African theologian:

> If I gain my humanity by entering into a relationship with other members of the family, both living and dead, then it follows that my humanity comes to me as a gift. This does not mean to say that it is not mine, that my being is part of the group, so that I have no individual value and destiny. It means rather that it is not something that I can acquire, or develop, by my own isolated power. I can only exercise or fulfill my humanity as long as I remain in touch with others, *for it is they who empower me.*[13]

Perhaps no one else has put it as succinctly as John Mbiti, in his delightful maxim, "I am because we are, and since we are, therefore I am."[14] Some have therefore proposed that maybe the clan, rather than any Western-type structure, might be the appropriate model for ecclesiological being in the African context.[15]

In the midst of dramatic societal and cultural changes, the AICs have the potential of providing a close community for their members. The AIC-type churches appeal to Africans apparently because those churches live out the lifestyle of community more so than imported Western-type churches.[16] "The supportive nature of the AIC members as a family, provides a model of a caring Christian community that comes close to both the African communal cohesiveness and the model of the early Christian community in Acts of the Apostles 2:42, which enhances community life."[17]

Omenyo observes that in their theology the AICs do not necessarily attribute their *koinonia* to efforts merely to replicate patterns of African communal living, but rather to the activity and presence of the Spirit.[18] If this is so, an important theological principle follows, namely that in a very real sense the AIC spirituality may represent an authentic African ethos. The work of the

---

[12]See further Daniel J. Antwi, "Sense of Community: An African Perspective of the Church as *Koinonia*," *Trinity Journal of Church and Theology* 6 (1996): 10.

[13]Omenyo, "Essential Aspects of African Ecclesiology," p. 236.

[14]John S. Mbiti, *African Religions and Philosophy*, 2nd ed. (London: Heinemann, 1989), p. 106.

[15]See further John Mary Waliggo, "The African Clan as the True Model of the African Church," in *The Church in African Christianity: Innovative Essays in Ecclesiology*, ed. J. N. K. Mugambi and Laurenti Magesa (Nairobi: Initiatives, 1990).

[16]See further Kwame Bediako, *Christianity in Africa: The Renewal of a Non-Western Religion* (Edinburgh: Edinburgh University Press, 1995), p. 67.

[17]Omenyo, "Essential Aspects of African Ecclesiology," p. 238.

[18]Ibid., p. 239.

Spirit is just affirming what people embedded in that culture are deeply feeling in their innermost beings.

Naturally, the worship of the AICs is very communal; it is also spontaneous and engaging, employing the rich musical and artistic heritage of African cultures. The services are enriched by dancing, clapping of hands, rhythmic instruments, African music and traditional chants. Participation by all, not only the clergy, is encouraged and enhanced.

## A Spirited Church

Of the many distinctive features of the AICs, perhaps the most visible is the strong emphasis on the Holy Spirit and pneumatology. M. L. Daneel from the Dutch Reformed Church in South Africa has offered us a contemporary picture of the distinctive understanding of the Holy Spirit among the Christians in the African Instituted Churches.[19] In this dynamic pneumatological ecclesiology that has arisen out of a painful struggle with the more traditional theology of the Western missionary churches, the Holy Spirit is depicted in four major roles.

First, the Spirit is the Savior of humankind. The Apostle Johane Maranke va-Postori of the AIC of Zimbabwe saw in a vision two books received from God that he could only understand through the inspiration of the Holy Spirit and not through education received at the European mission station. The content of these books was eternal life. In his vision Johane saw himself as a Moses figure, leading his followers from many countries through hostile terrain and fires to a safe place. The new laws and customs of the church are justified by attributing them directly to the inspiration and command of the Holy Spirit. The black race of Africa—the neglected, the poor and the oppressed—is now the exalted and the elected, called by the Spirit to spread the message of salvation.

Second, the Spirit is healer and protector. Healing and protection against evil forces manifest the power of the Spirit. Speaking in tongues became the prelude to all prophetic diagnostic sessions during which the Holy Spirit would reveal to the prophet the cause of the patient's illness. All symbols used during healing rituals, such as holy water, paper, staffs and holy cords, symbolized the power of the Holy Spirit over all destructive forces. "Jordan" bap-

---

[19]My exposition in this section is based on M. L. Daneel, "African Independent Church Pneumatology and the Salvation of All Creation," in *All Together in One Place: Theological Papers from the Brighton Conference on World Evangelization*, ed. H. D. Hunter and P. D. Hocken (Sheffield, U.K.: Sheffield Academic Press, 1993), pp. 96-126. For other contributions, see also Allan H. Anderson, *Moya: The Holy Spirit from an African Perspective* (Pretoria: University of South Africa Press, 1994).

tisms increasingly became purifying, healing and exorcising sessions.

Third, in the prophetic movements of the AIC the activity of the Holy Spirit has never been restricted to spiritual matters or healing alone; he is also the Spirit of justice and liberation. The late bishop Samuel Mutendi of Zion Christian Church in Zimbabwe entered the political arena by opposing the colonial administration on education, land and religious issues. The spiritual mobilization of the community to take action was effected through sermons, prayer and a role model, often accompanied with prophecies. The Holy Spirit was depicted as the "guardian of the land" and the Spirit was directing the liberation fighters.

The fourth role of the Holy Spirit in AIC theology and spirituality is earth-keeping. In the post-Independence period in Zimbabwe, starting in 1980, the AICs increasingly turned their attention to various development projects, for example, the development of several church nurseries for exotic fruit and indigenous trees at or near prophetic church headquarters. The Holy Spirit's function as healer and life-giver encompassed everything relating to human well-being, including also the healing and protecting of crops. The practice of prophets diagnosing the illness of Mother Earth is one distinctive way AIC Christians live out their Charismatic life. Significantly enough, the this-world dimension of the Spirit's work is connected to a strong evangelistic orientation, and the cosmic dimension of the Spirit's work is not set over against the Spirit's role in personal salvation.

## The "Pentecostalization" of African Churches

There is no way to give any kind of survey of African theologies in general and ecclesiologies in particular without reference to the largest segment of the African churches and spirituality, namely the Pentecostal/Charismatic movements. Even those churches that do not identify themselves formally with Pentecostal/Charismatic movements often reflect spirituality that has been associated with those movements.[20] In brief, this term refers to those Christian

---

[20] Allan H. Anderson, "Gospel and Culture in Pentecostal Mission in the Third World" (paper presented at the 11th Meeting of the European-Pentecostal Charismatic Association at Missionsakademi of the University of Hamburg, Germany, July 13-17, 1999). Anderson's main argument can be found in *Pentecostals After a Century: Global Perspectives on a Movement in Transition,* ed. Allan H. Anderson and Walter J. Hollenweger (Sheffield, U.K.: Sheffield Academic Press, 1999). See also Allan H. Anderson, *Bazalwane: African Pentecostals in South Africa* (Pretoria: University of South Africa Press, 1992); Allan H. Anderson, *Zion and Pentecost: The Spirituality and Experience of Pentecostal and Zionist/Apostolic Churches in South Africa* (Pretoria: University of South Africa Press, 2000).

churches in Africa that emphasize—and some would suggest to the exclusion
of all else—the working of the Holy Spirit in the church; it includes the many
Zionist and Apostolic churches in Southern Africa as well as African Pentecostal churches originating in the northern hemisphere.[21] The common historical,
liturgical and theological roots that these different church groups have in the
American Holiness movement and in the Pentecostal and Christian Zionist
movements means that they still have much in common, despite significant
and sometimes striking differences.[22]

One of the differences between Western churches and the AICs grows out
of the distinctive worldview prevalent among various African-based cultures.
On the basis of their alternative worldview, the Africans see spiritual and
physical beings as real entities that interact with each other in time and space.
Those African Christians reject both the secularist worldview as well as missionaries' Western conceptions of reality and spirit. "Orthodoxy" has left
Christians helpless in real life and so an alternative pneumatology has been
needed that relates to the whole range of needs that includes the spiritual but
is not limited to abstract other-worldly spiritual needs.[23] African religions in
general, Christianity included, serve existential needs and relate to everyday
issues more so than their Western counterparts. Religion is expected to make
life worth living, to maintain and protect it against illness, enemies and
death.[24] As Turner rightly observes, "it is the independents who help us to see
the overriding African concern for spiritual power from a mighty God to overcome all enemies and evils that threaten human life and vitality, hence their
extensive ministry of mental and physical healing. This is rather different from
the Western preoccupation with atonement for sin and forgiveness of guilt."[25]

A major attraction for Pentecostalism in African context has been its emphasis on healing. In these cultures, the religious specialist or "person of God"
has power to heal the sick and ward off evil spirits and sorcery. This holistic
function, which does not separate the "physical from the "spiritual," is restored in Pentecostalism, and indigenous peoples see it as a "powerful" religion to meet human needs. For some Pentecostals, faith in God's power to heal

---

[21]See further Allan H. Anderson, "Challenges and Prospects for Research into African Initiated Churches in Southern Africa," *Missionalia* 23, no. 3 (1995): 283-94.
[22]Allan H. Anderson, *MOYA: The Holy Spirit in an African Context* (Pretoria: University of
South Africa Press, 1991): 26-29; Anderson, *Bazalwane*, pp. 20-32.
[23]Derek B. Mutungu, "A Response to M. L. Daneel" in *All Together in One Place*, pp. 127-31.
[24]See further Omenyo, "Essential Aspects of African Ecclesiology," pp. 243-47.
[25]H. W. Turner, *Religious Innovation in Africa* (Boston: G. K. Hall, 1979), p. 210.

directly through prayer resulted in a rejection of other methods of healing.[26]

Allan H. Anderson of South Africa (now teaching at the University of Birmingham, England) has argued that Pentecostalism has been capable of incorporating into its spirituality various kinds of local customs, beliefs and rituals. African Pentecostalism is in constant interaction with the African spirit world. Anderson contends that in Africa the Pentecostal and Pentecostal-like movements manifested in thousands of indigenous churches have radically changed the face of Christianity simply because they have proclaimed a holistic gospel of salvation that includes deliverance from all types of oppression such as sickness, sorcery, evil spirits and poverty. This has met the needs of Africans more fundamentally than the rather "spiritualized" and intellectualized gospel that was mostly the legacy of European and North American missionaries:

> All the widely differing Pentecostal movements have important common features: they proclaim and celebrate a salvation (or "healing") that encompasses all of life's experiences and afflictions, and they offer an empowerment that provides a sense of dignity and a coping mechanism for life, and all this drives their messengers forward into a unique mission.[27]

---

[26] Anderson, "The Pentecostal Gospel, Religion and Culture in African Perspective" (May 29, 2000) <http://artsweb.bham.ac.uk/aanderson/index.htm >.
[27] Anderson, "Gospel and Culture," p. 11.

# 19

# The Shepherding Movement's Renewal Ecclesiology

## A Grassroots Experiment in Ecclesiology

When the Charismatic movement exploded in the older churches in the 1960s and soon began to also create new independent churches and fellowships, it emphasized—like its older "cousin" the Pentecostal movement—enthusiastic spirituality rather than theology. Even the church structures and ministry patterns tended to change from one group to another; flexibility and creativity, rather than critical analysis, were characteristic. Against this background it might come as a surprise that some analysts of the movement have characterized the Charismatic Renewal "ecclesiocentric."[1]

One of the most creative, and also most controversial, ecclesiological developments of the Pentecostal/Charismatic Renewal at the grass roots level has been the emergence of the "Shepherding movement." This movement has sometimes been called the Discipleship/Shepherding movement or just the Discipleship movement. The term "Shepherding movement" is concise and more descriptive of the movement's emphasis on personal pastoral care.[2] From its beginning, the movement tended to create divided opinions, and in the early history of the Charismatic Renewal, it had the potential for dividing the movement.[3] The movement was also closely connected with the so-called house church movement, which also generated controversy, especially with

---

[1]Rodney Clapp, *A Peculiar People* (Downers Grove, Ill.: InterVarsity Press, 1996); David Moore, "The Shepherding Movement: A Case Study in Charismatic Ecclesiology," *Pneuma: The Journal of the Society for Pentecostal Studies* 22, no. 2 (2000): 249.

[2]Still another self-designation of the movement is the "Covenant movement" (Moore, "Shepherding Movement," p. 249, n. 3).

[3]See further Kilian McDonnell, "Seven Documents on the Discipleship Questions," in *Presence, Power, Praise: Documents on the Charismatic Renewal*, 3 vols., ed. Kilian McDonnell (Collegeville, Minn.: Liturgical Press, 1980), 2:116.

regard to its ecclesiology.[4] The following example illustrates the harsh criticism that has been directed against the movement:

> There is no doubt that a great need exists within the Church for "scripturally based" discipleship and authority. Such must be founded on the concept of authority as servanthood, ministered in love and humility by those mature in the faith. Shepherding-Discipleship as the movement it became, however, is nothing less than spiritual child-abuse. Through intimidation by the instilling of fear and unfounded guilt, it bludgeons babes in Christ into obedience to the wills of the "shepherds" in authority. And not only babes, but many "mature" Christians have fallen prey to this evil due to the misuse of Scripture to establish "coverings" over every member.[5]

For academic theology, it is too easy to simply ignore experiments at the grassroots level for the simple reason that most often these kinds of popular movements lack needed theological clarity and precision. This is, in fact, the case with regard to the Shepherding movement. This fact, however, is nothing more than a cheap excuse for theologians not to engage with phenomena like this and start asking theological questions, such as: What was the driving need and agenda for the emergence of the movement? Or, what is there in the movement that made it so appealing to so many people? Theologians should also ask questions like What is it that is missing in the more traditional ecclesiologies that makes Christians hungry for experiments like this? In other words, the Shepherding movement's Charismatic ecclesiology offers theologians of the church a contemporary, controversial and challenging contextual case study.

Fortunately, we currently also have available a recent academic study on the ecclesiology of the movement; David Moore, himself an active participant in the movement, has recently finished his dissertation on the topic and published his research in the form of a monograph.[6] Moore argues that the story of the Shepherding movement "provides a unique case study in renewal ecclesiology," an ecclesiology that was central to the Shepherding movement's

---

[4]See further Kirk Hadaway, Stuart A. Wright and Francis M. DuBose, *Home Cell Groups and House Churches* (Nashville: Broadman, 1987).

[5]Anonymous, "Shepherding Discipleship" (August 2001) <www.cephasministry.com/shepherding_movement_z.html >.

[6]S. David Moore, *The Shepherding Movement: History, Controversy, Ecclesiology* (Sheffield, U.K.: Sheffield Academic Press, 2001). For an up-to-date, concise summary, see Moore, "Shepherding Movement," pp. 249-70. My discussion of the Shepherding movement here is heavily indebted to Moore's analysis.

self-understanding.[7] At the same time, the movement also offers an interesting ecumenical case study since the leaders come from various church contexts, including both traditional and recent ones.

## In Search of a Spiritual Authority

"The Shepherding movement" is a term applied to the teachings and persons originally coming from the Shepherd's Church in Fort Lauderdale, Florida. The main leaders in the movement have been the leaders of the Fort Lauderdale congregation, including Bob Mumford, Charles Simpson, Derek Prince, Don Basham, Ern Baxter and John Poole. The official name of their organization is Christian Growth Ministries, and its major publication is *New Wine* magazine.

The leading idea of the Shepherding movement is "discipleship" or "shepherding," and it emphasizes the need for personal, one-on-one pastoral care. The leaders of the movement soon developed a distinctive teaching about submission, spiritual authority, discipleship, pastoral care, covenant relationship and Christian community. This very same ethos brought the movement under heavy criticism and debate, since many experienced this teaching as a form of domination by leaders and misuse of power and authority. S. David Moore notes this:

> The controversy over these issues was so furious that the movement's distinct and focused ecclesial character has been overlooked. As is often the case with renewal groups, the movement has largely been defined by its critics and disillusioned former members who have focused on its faults and excesses. Until recently no serious and dispassionate study has been undertaken to understand this unique expression of the Charismatic Renewal.[8]

A chief biblical text for the movement is the reference to pastor-teachers in Ephesians 4:11, which designates them as "called and equipped to give oversight and care to God's people." Discipling is seen as a comprehensive word that denotes a God-given authority. All shepherds understand that they are to give account of their stewardship to the chief shepherd. Just as Jesus regarded few of the professional religious leaders of his day as true shepherds, so the leaders of the Discipleship movement often find unacceptable the ministry of those who are exercising ecclesiastical authority over people in our day. This criticism recalls that of Christian sectarian leaders in past history, such as Montanus, the

---

[7]Moore, "Shepherding Movement," p. 252.
[8]Ibid., p. 251.

Spiritual Franciscans, the Anabaptists and the radical pietists. The criteria for effective discipling also include the avoidance of selfish preoccupation with power and personal status, in line with the admonition in 1 Peter 5:1-6. In addition, there is the responsibility of shepherds to equip the saints for ministry. This involves instructing and admonishing each member in public and in private.[9]

The concept of discipling is related to the goal of encouraging and measuring growth in Christian discipleship through the behavioral change that results from a consistent application of biblical principles to personal and corporate Christian living. According to Mumford, the shepherd is to nurture discipleship through a three-part program, including baptism by water, discipleship by a man "commissioned by God," and acknowledging the abiding presence of Christ with the shepherd (or disciple maker) and his disciples. Mumford advocates avoiding spiritual independence that would lead to religious anarchy in favor of embracing the yoke of Christ as a symbol of discipleship.[10]

## *The Concept of Shepherding*

The term "Shepherding movement" indicates its purpose. The main agenda of its theology and practice was to revive the biblical concept of a pastor in the form of a shepherd. The task of the pastors and other church leaders was to be instruments of authority and care, which was characteristic of the New Testament church and which was to be re-claimed by this new movement. Jesus' relationship to his disciples while on earth serves as a paradigm for this concept. According to the leaders of the movement, discipleship was "a very fundamental and vital ongoing relationship which brings maturity to the believer." The Christian life is much more than just the adoption of knowledge or new behavioral patterns; Christianity means a new relationship. The disciple-shepherd relationship best described the essence of this.[11] The search for this kind of one-to-one personal relationship is the key to understanding the ethos and driving force of the movement's ecclesiology:

> Nothing more distinguished the movement than its teaching on shepherding care. Every believer was to have a personal definite, committed relationship with a shepherd affirmed by a verbal, and occasionally written, covenant agreement.

---

[9]See further J. S. O'Malley, "Shepherding Movement—Discipleship Movement" (August 2001) <http://mb-soft.com/believe/txc/shepherd.htm>.

[10]Ibid.

[11]Mumford, *Life Changers Newsletter* (November 1975), p. 2; Moore, "Shepherding Movement," p. 261.

The need for "personal pastoral care" was the cornerstone of the movement's ec-clesiological practice.[12]

According to the movement's teaching, submission to a shepherd provided spiritual "covering" by being in right relationship to God's delegated author-ity in the church. The shepherd assumed responsibility for the well-being of his sheep. "This responsibility included not just their spiritual well-being, but their full development emotionally, educationally, financially, vocationally, and socially."[13]A person joined one of the movement's churches through es-tablishing a relationship with a shepherd/pastor. There were many younger people who wanted and needed the discipline the shepherding relationship brought into their lives.

In a typical Discipleship community, household fellowships gathered in closed weekly meetings. Often the leading shepherds in a community were di-rectly trained by one of the above-named leaders. The members were often obliged to submit to covenantal norms, such as tithing, obedience to the au-thority of the community (which also may have authority in the area of male/female relationships) and the requirement of holding a job for all but married women.[14]

## Renewal Ecclesiology

According to S. D. Moore, the main architects of the Shepherding movement, in line with all other contextualizers of the gospel, read carefully the signs of their times and concluded that society was coming apart in all dimensions. Bob Mumford and others were greatly concerned over the marginalization and immaturity of the church. Out of this concern and on the basis of biblical teaching, a distinctive restorationist ecclesiology emerged. The principle of restorationism is understandable in the Shepherding movement in view of the "back to roots" mentality that has shaped the whole ethos of Pentecostalism and the Charismatic movements. The restorationist movements throughout church history, from Montanism to Donatism to Anabaptism to various Reviv-alist movements, have envisioned a "return" to a future church life fully in tune with the glorious apostolic beginnings.[15] Thus, the pioneers of the Shep-

---

[12]Moore, "Shepherding Movement," p. 262.

[13]Ibid.

[14]O'Malley, "Shepherding Movement—Discipleship Movement."

[15]Cf. the title of Bob Mumford, Decline/Dark Ages/Restoration of the Church, part 1 (Oklahoma City, Okla.: September, 1977, audiocassette).

herding movement firmly believed that they had been chosen to lead the church back to the New Testament church order and practice. The leaders read the church history exactly the same way most restorationist Christians have done: after the Spirit-filled apostolic church, there was a decline, perhaps even apostasy all through the Middle Ages; then Reformation brought a partial light, to be complemented by this "Latter Day" renewal that was to usher in the final revival and even eschatological consummation.[16]

The leading idea behind the movement's ecclesiology is the kingdom of God.[17] Standing as the movement does in the restorationist tradition, it firmly believed that the time had come for God to restore the idea of the kingdom. According to their shared vision, the leaders were convinced that this reclaimed emphasis on the kingdom of God was to take the Charismatic Renewal beyond the emphasis on Spirit baptism and spiritual gifts to a deeper appropriation of God's purposes in which God established "his love and authority in the individual believer, and then through that believer to the nations of the world (Matt 28:19)."[18] In line with New Testament scholarship, they argued that the kingdom of God spoke of the reign and rule of God. The message of the kingdom naturally raised the issue of authority. Christ's earthly ministry expressed the breaking in of the power of God into the human situation. Following his victory, Christ gave his followers the gifts to build up his church, the offices of apostle, prophet, evangelist, shepherd and teacher. According to Mumford,

> The message of God's Rule and the impact of the whole New Testament speaks to us about God's reign over His Church through those whom He delegates (see Ephesians 4:11-13) to implement that authority. When we speak of authority, it means God's order, not authoritarianism. Submission, authority, and discipleship, as I understand and teach them, are the uncomplicated and basic ingredients necessary for the practical outworking of the Lordship of Christ in the life of every believer.[19]

On the basis of Psalm 110, they believed that Christ would establish God's rule to reign through his people on earth. The church, therefore, was the key to the establishment of God's kingdom. It was the task of human leadership in the church to be an instrument of God's rule. By submitting to delegated au-

---

[16]Moore, "Shepherding Movement," pp. 254-55.

[17]For the centrality of the kingdom to the Shepherding movement, see further Charles Simpson, *A New Way to Live* (Greensburg, Penn.: Manna Christian Outreach, 1975).

[18]Bob Mumford, *Life Changers Newsletter,* November 1975, p. 2; Moore, "Shepherding Movement," p. 257.

[19]Mumford, *Life Changers Newsletter,* November 1975, p. 3, quoted in Moore, "Shepherding Movement," p. 258.

thority, believers were submitting to Christ. S. D. Moore argues that it is "plain that this concept drove their emerging ecclesiology."[20]

## The Church as the Gathered People of God

The Shepherding movement's renewal ecclesiology drew heavily both from the tradition of Free church ecclesiology and the Pentecostal and Charismatic ecclesiologies. They also acknowledged their indebtedness to Anabaptism in terms of being a persecuted community for their distinctive ecclesiological views, and also to Methodism, Puritanism and, surprisingly, even Monasticism.[21]

Its emphasis on power, renewal and gifts of the Spirit situated the movement firmly in the mainstream of the Pentecostal/Charismatic phenomenon. Its accent on the church as the gathered people of God, following Christ's example and nurturing the community of believers, made it a contemporary successor to the Free church ethos. What made its teaching so distinctive was the stress on authority, submission and delegation.

In line with the Free church doctrine of the church, the Shepherding movement acknowledged the invisible, universal church, but came to stress the visible and local nature of the church.[22] As such the church was to be a visible "alternate society which sets forth unequivocal norms for behavior and community life [that will] produce the kind and quality of people capable of influencing society."[23]

Whatever else the Shepherding movement was, it was a highly creative, unique mixture of ecclesiological influences and experiments. S. D. Moore summarizes:

> Certainly, the Shepherding movement was a curious mix ecclesiologically. On the one hand they were clearly in the Free church tradition, defining the church as visible, local, covenant communities of disciples. Their restorationism made them strongly anti-institutional in their rhetoric and they consistently refused to call themselves a denomination. Through all the years . . . [they] maintained that their church network was a voluntary association based solely on personal relationships. Yet, growth and controversy forced them to organize and they became functionally and increasingly hierarchical institutionally.[24]

---

[20]Moore, "Shepherding Movement," pp. 258-59.

[21]Ibid., p. 269.

[22]Mumford, "The Vision of the Local Church," New Wine, July/August 1975, pp. 4-8.

[23]Mumford, "Discipleship Position Paper"(1976), p. 5, as cited in Moore, "Shepherding Movement," p. 260.

[24]Moore, "Shepherding Movement," pp. 267-68.

Here the observation of Howard Snyder concerning the ethos of most renewal movements is once again verified, namely that they are "typically naïve
concerning institutional and sociological realities and blind to the institutional
dimensions of their own movement."[25]

## The Challenge and Legacy of the Shepherding Movement

The actual life of the Shepherding movement never lived up to its high ideal,
and its dissolution soon became inevitable. Many factors led to it; the movement's naive idealism did not stand the test of time. Its vulnerability to trium-
phalism limited its openness to critique. The whole ethos of being persecuted
for its commitment to restore biblical church vision made the movement
defensive, which hindered its ability to continue developing this emerging
ecclesiology and enter into a constructive self-criticism. The lack of formal
church structures left the movement under the powers of strong leaders and
changing circumstances. The leadership could not be challenged, and consequently was in practice exempt from criticism.[26]

Yet, S. D. Moore contends that the Shepherding movement has been unnec-
essarily vilified by its critics, and its specific contribution to ecumenical thinking about the church has been totally dismissed. Regardless of its many
extremes, even dangerous ones, with regard to the abuse of spiritual authority,
the underlying agenda was legitimate: how to provide ecclesiological structures and practices that would give an opportunity for holistic care and discipling. There is no doubt that a great need exists within the church for
scripturally based discipleship and authority. But, as one of the critics of the
movement has argued, the response to this need "must be founded on the concept of authority as servanthood, ministered in love and humility by those mature in the faith."[27] Especially in Western cultures toward the end of the second
millennium this need has been tremendous, but the prevailing culture made it
almost impossible to find a balance. Beginning from the tumultuous years of

---

[25]H. Snyder, *Signs of the Spirit* (Grand Rapids, Mich.: Zondervan, 1989), p. 273, quoted in
Moore, "Shepherding Movement," p. 268.

[26]See further Moore, "Shepherding Movement," p. 266.

[27]Anonymous, "Shepherding Discipleship." For a balanced critique and acknowledgment of
the contribution of the Shepherding movement, see "The Discipleship and Submission
Movement," the report of the Committee to Study the Discipleship and Submission Movement. The report was adopted by the Assemblies of God General Presbytery, August 17,
1976.

the 1960s, those who had violently thrown away all authoritarian structures were the very people who needed community and support. However, negative experiences of traditional Christian church structures and authority patterns had made them almost allergic to any kind of submission to any authority. Resolving this impossible equation was the ambitious vision of the movement. It never could accomplish its task, and it left many Christians wondering whether all talk of spiritual authority belongs to Christendom's past. Still, this open question begs for fresh experiments in the postmodern world in which most church members long for community support while also wanting to affirm their total freedom.

The desire of the movement to find a countercultural community, in the anticipation of and in line with the coming kingdom, has been shared by many renewal communities and ecclesiological experiments. In any contexts the church encounters the temptation to succumb uncritically to the prevailing culture. The Shepherding movement, in the spirit of contextualization, took notice of a pressing need in the surrounding culture and confronted it with an idea that challenged the very same culture. It is yet to be seen what shape will be taken by the next ecclesiological experiment that dares to attempt the same.

# 20

# "A World Church"

## Rediscovering Christianity

Reading a book by the title *Rediscovering Christianity*[1] as a student of theology made a lasting impression on me and challenged my thinking about Christianity and Christian mission vis-à-vis other religions. The author, Catholic missionary to Africa Vincent J. Donovan, argued that the "core of Christianity" should be free from Western or other cultural baggage and should present to the people the bold claims of Christ. He heavily criticized earlier approaches to mission that tried to win a hearing for the gospel by wrapping it in a package of education, medicine and money. Notwithstanding good intentions and genuine love, this kind of missionary approach led people to misunderstand the real message of the Bible and confuse it with higher living standards, more solid education or convenient homes. Living and working amidst a proud African tribe, the Masai, Donovan refused to bring with him any material gifts; rather, he sat down with the tribe leaders and other people, introduced them to the bare message of the Bible and let them decide whether they wanted to accept it or not.

The similar kind of reformatory voice is heard in Donovan's radical ecclesiological work, *The Church in the Midst of Creation*.[2] Having done missionary work mainly in Africa and returned to his home country, the United States, he engaged in pastoral ministry among secular Western people. Out of this crosscultural experience grew a cry for a new, more inclusive and relevant ecclesiology that would take the church and its sacraments out of its narrow Christian ghetto and place them boldly in the midst of creation and the world. By reflecting on the opposing experiences of a vital church in the

---

[1]Vincent J. Donovan, *Rediscovering Christianity* (Maryknoll, N.Y.: Orbis, 1987).
[2]Vincent J. Donovan, *The Church in the Midst of Creation* (Maryknoll, N.Y.: Orbis, 1990).

mission field and a stagnating church back home, the latter still possessing some signs of vitality such as committed lay people and renewed interest in the Bible, he began to dream of a world church, the "planetary church," a church for all people and for all creation. To attain this, the church and its theologians have to come to grips with the dramatically changing horizons of the postmodern world.

The new emerging church, the church in the midst of creation, is the third church after the rise of the early church from its Jewish soil and the later Western church that has dominated the first two millennia of Christianity. According to Donovan, no other Catholic theologian has seen so clearly the need and potential of the new emerging world church as the late Karl Rahner. Rahner saw in the Second Vatican Council not only the first self-realization of the world church but also the beginning of a new age, a new epoch in the history of the church. In fact, for Rahner, such a radical break with the past has happened only once before in church history and in Christianity, and that was in the very earliest days of the church when it changed from Jewish Christianity to Gentile Christianity.[3] Rahner calls the second stage Hellenistic European Christianity, a time when the church was predominantly of European origin and under European influence. The third, emerging period is the period in which the sphere of the church's life is the entire world.[4]

## On the Threshold of a New Era

Donovan analyzes in great detail the historical unfolding of various patterns of the church and ecclesiology as the church has been more or less captive to the general cultural history of the times. By utilizing the scheme of Pitirim Sorokin, the Russian-born philosopher, historian and sociologist, Donovan takes account of these changes and their influence on the makeup and ethos of the Christian church. In Sorokin's analysis, history repeats itself in constantly recurring triple cycles.[5] The first cycle he calls "ideational," a period of a unified spiritual system of thought and action, based on a single principle or idea. This time is marked by a negative attitude or indifference to the sensory world. The second is "idealistic," a time of integrated thought in which reality is seen as

---

[3]Ibid., pp. 18-26, chronicles in detail the often painful transition from Jewish to predominantly Gentile church.

[4]Karl Rahner, "Toward a Fundamental Theological Interpretation of Vatican II," *Theological Studies* 40, no. 47 (1979): 717-21

[5]Pitirim Sorokin, *The Crisis of Our Age* (New York: E. P. Dutton, 1941).

partly sensory, partly suprasensory. There is an attempt for synthesis of all thought and life. The third cycle Sorokin calls the "sensate" cycle, in which true reality is perceived as sensory. Reality is empirical, secular, this-worldly. The Roman Empire best symbolizes this cycle.

According to Sorokin, the first cycle took place from the eighth to the sixth century B.C. throughout the known world, in Brahman India, in Buddhist and Taoist cultures, in Greek and Egyptian societies, in Babylonian and Hindu-Chinese worlds. The second cycle lasted until the first century A.D. The first four centuries of the Christian era were in the sensate cycle, beginning to give way again to the ideational cycle. Then the dominant idea was, of course, God; God's influence was felt everywhere from law to family to the arts. In the late Medieval period, the idealistic age returned with Aquinas and others and the attempt again for a synthesis of ideas and sensations. The Reformation paved the way and the Enlightenment ushered in the return of the sensate age: the sensory, empirical, secular, this-worldly approach culminating in the rise of scientific-technological mastery. According to Sorokin (writing in the 1940s), we are now again on the threshold of a new era, in the transition period from the sensate to another ideational culture.[6]

So, what will be the shape of the Christian church amidst these radical changes? How can it communicate and live out its message in a world church that is no longer tied to a particular culture, not any more Western than non-Western. "The final, pluralistic form which that proclamation takes will depend primarily on the peoples of the cultures to whom it is proclaimed. But that pluralistic proclamation of the gospel cannot take place until, first of all and *now*, a serious effort is made to take the present versions of the Christian religion and return or reduce them to the "final fundamental substance of the Christian message.'"[7] According to Donovan, the final and fundamental substance of the Christian message and the whole of ecclesiastical faith will have to be reformulated along the cultural lines of actual history. Here he is echoing the earlier call of Rahner to strip away from Christianity all the cultural accretions that have attached themselves to it over the ages, all "the baggage."[8] This could be, in Sorokin's words, "the beginning of a creative tomorrow."[9]

---

[6]Donovan, *Church in the Midst of Creation*, pp. 7-31.
[7]Ibid., p. 30 (emphasis his; the last phrase comes from Rahner, "Toward a Fundamental Theological Interpretation," p. 275).
[8]Donovan, *Church in the Midst of Creation*, p. 30.
[9]Sorokin, *Crisis of Our Age*, p. 13.

## The Industrial Captivity of the Church

Building on the analyses of Sorokin, Rahner and others,[10] Donovan outlines in critical terms a portrait of the Western church during the last three centuries or so.[11] Historically, this development that he criticizes began much earlier than the industrial revolution of the seventeenth century in that the Christian church wanted to maintain uniformity in its faith, liturgy, structure and even church life. While Donovan acknowledges the need for a basic unity—which has ample biblical attestation—uniformity finally leads to stagnation and an inability to become a global church, a church for the whole world. When the liturgy and sacraments, the training of the priests, the organization of the church and the development of dogma are put into a neat box—until recently a European box—Christianity loses its dynamic and is reduced to just another religion among others.

Along with the drive for uniformity, the need for specialization arose at the cost of generalization. Industrialization was built on the ideas of specialization, effectiveness and calculation, and so the church amidst that culture was also dominated by the same sensate ethos. Even though the principle of standardization so poorly fits the dynamics of church life, it was imposed. Furthermore, the focus turned from local communities to central headquarters, since they are more easily managed and pressed into a uniform mold. Finally, this imitation of the ethos of industrialization led to synchronization, concentration and maximization. What can be counted and managed is what matters: the number attending church services, the amount of offerings, the size of buildings and so on.

How poorly this matches the image of the "Mediterranean Christ"[12] is easily seen. People of this age of effectiveness and maximization see him as a person from another world. On the other hand, the "European, Gentile Christ" does not correspond to the Christ of the Bible. But that is not Donovan's main concern. He does not want to stop at finding the Jesus of the Bible or even the "historical Jesus," since that would leave Christ to the age that has already been left behind centuries ago.

---

[10]Donovan also dialogues with another secular thinker who has analyzed the development of cultural history, Alvin Toffler, author of The Third Wave (New York: Bantam, 1980). Even though Toffler's categorization differs from that of Sorokin, the outcome is surprisingly similar.

[11]Donovan, Church in the Midst of Creation, pp. 35-47. Hereafter in this chapter, most page references to The Church in the Midst of Creation will be given in parenthetical references.

[12]Donovan, Church in the Midst of Creation, p. 48-60. In his analysis of Christology and its relation to ecclesiology, Donovan builds critically on the work of Edward Schillebeeckx especially.

### A World Church and a "Planetary Christ"

> We have to admit that after all this extensive and scientific scholarship, after near-
> ly two thousand years of Christianity, the Christ that is worshiped in our church-
> es, the Christ that is the basis for our church and all its faith life and activity, is no
> more than a Mediterranean Christ. That is as far as Christ has grown. European
> and American theologians see nothing wrong with that, nothing wrong with the
> fact that we have not even begun to think of, or search for, the meaning of a plan-
> etary Christ, a world Christ. We continue to let all our efforts revolve around a
> Mediterranean Christ. We of the West have monopolized Christ. (pp. 56-57)

Yet, Donovan contends, the Spirit of Christ is still active all around the
world. "The Spirit is still being poured out on non-Christians, as much to our
astonishment as it was to our Jewish forebears in the time of Peter and Corne-
lius. Revelation is still going on in the midst of traditional religions, Hinduism,
Buddhism, in the knowledge behind the scientific revolution, in the universe—in all creation" (p. 57).

What Rahner meant when he identified the post-Vatican II age as the third
stage of the church, the epoch of the world church, was that until the time of
Vatican II, the church had not made its presence felt in the great non-Christian
religions of the world. Neither was there dialogue with other world religions:
Islam, Buddhism, Hinduism or others. Christian missionaries boldly disregarded the contribution of local religions as if they were blank pages, not no-
ticing the fact that in those cultures people are more deeply embedded in
religions than in the West. To remove the influence of religions, one almost had
to destroy the culture itself.

Revelation is what God wants human beings to know and to do, and faith
is the authentic response to that revelation from the midst of human lives. Religion, then, is what we make of the revelation. There are two choices here. On
the one hand, if people respond to revelation authentically, it leads to inclusiv-
ity, "whether it be the humble worship of the one God of Africa, or the beautiful reverence for life of the American Indian and the Hindus, or the admirable
and total submission to God of the Muslim, or the joy and hope of Christian
peoples" (p. 85). But people can also take the revelation into a totally other direction and make it their own exclusive religion. All religions tend to do so and
have done so.

Revelation and religion can never be considered identical even though they
are related. "Religion stabilizes us and reassures us. Revelation destabilizes
and disturbs us. Revelation calls into question everything solid and taken for

granted. Religion so often tries to use God as a means to human ends. It makes God a projection of self rather than the God of biblical revelation. Religion is filled with answers to every question. The God of the Bible is a divine questioner, not an answerer."[13]

The emerging planetary church, in opposition to the stable church of the Industrial Revolution with all ready-made answers, is a questioning church, the church on the way. It is critical of developments in ecclesiology and church life that are foreign to revelation, such as honorary titles, privileged positions, respect for possession and so on. It is also critical of a church that only reaches its own. The church that only cares for its own people represents religion while the church of revelation reaches far beyond its own boundaries to the ends of the earth. A church that points to the presence of the Holy Spirit outside its walls is "revelation" while a church that fails to see the signs of the Spirit outside Christianity is "religion" (pp. 89-93).

## A Destandardized Church

For a Christian church to be universal, plurality and variety have to be allowed. Donovan argues that it is highly questionable whether, for example, a uniform doctrine should even be a goal for that kind of world church. In Donovan's reading of the New Testament, Jesus never called anyone to follow a doctrine or a sterile ethic. He spoke about the Father and concern for other human beings. The person of Jesus Christ, rather than a particular teaching about him, stands at the center of Christianity. If so, then the church has to become destandardized. Sacraments are meaningful but they can be celebrated in various ways. Forgiveness is a central message, but it can never be reduced to the sacrament of penance only. Conversion belongs to the core of Jesus' preaching, but it is much more than weekly devotional confession or spiritual mentoring.

In a destandardized church privileged positions are not delivered according to earthly standards. The oneness of the church does not mean adherence to one doctrinal formulation but tolerance of various, sometimes even conflicting reflections on the Christ-event. The holiness of the church can never be identified with moral codes or the lifestyle of the clergy or the canonized saints, but rather is a comprehensive discipleship of the whole people of God. The catholicity of the church cannot be guaranteed by a single form or structure of the church and ministry but rather by a cultural and religious inclusiv-

---

[13]Donovan, *Church in the Midst of Creation*, p. 88. Donovan follows the thought of the French theologian Jacques Ellul who eschewed defining Christianity as a religion.

ity of all kinds of people in the flock of Christ. The apostolicity of the church is not the same as a technically defined apostolic succession but rather faithfulness to the life and power of the church of the apostles of the New Testament (pp. 104-7).

In a decentralized church, as in the churches of the New Testament, the focus is on the local community worshiping one God and ministering to each other. This experience of community on a very local level does not, of course, militate against a profound sense and need of unity with others, whether Christian or non-Christian, outside that particular community. According to Donovan, an organization that is exclusive of outsiders is not a community at all (pp. 108-9).

## The Church in the Midst of Creation

According to Donovan two almost opposing worldviews are bitterly vying for attention and dominance: the religious view and the secular, scientific view. The former is still involved with the saving and redeeming of a fallen world, while the latter focuses on the creation of a new world. Too often, he laments, the energies of the church are spent in condemning sin and saving people from worldly temptations. What makes this situation so ironic to Donovan is that in fact the secular mindset is doing much of what the church was supposed to do, namely saving life on earth and caring for creation. "It is we who originally believed in the new creation, already begun on this planet earth with the resurrection" (p. 112).

It is time for the church to move away from a theology of salvation and redemption to a theology of creation. In Donovan's terminology, the holy way of salvation is indeed the same thing as the continuing process of creation, since the saving God is the creating God as well. The same earth that gives growth to the ingredients of daily bread also produces the bread of the Eucharist. "And as we handle it with faith we believe that, through human intention and human word, the bread has a long way to go, destined as it is to become the body of Christ. And so it is with the earth and with the world. They, too, have a long way to go—destined, through divine power and human intervention, to become the body of Christ" (p. 112).

Donovan warns the church of the danger of missing the messianic vision and giving it over to the scientific world. The scientific community, freed from the once-dominant fear of the metaphysical, has begun to take a more comprehensive look at metaphysical reality.

Even in the midst of creation and the radical transformation of the world, the church is called for the purpose of evangelization. Evangelization is, of course, not proselytism, or brain-washing, or propaganda. Donovan defines it as a dialogue between an authentic gospel and a true openness to conversion.[14] The task of the church is to bring to the dialogue a full, cosmic Christ, nothing less. It will be of no value if Christians bring a watered-down version of the gospel. But by doing so, even Christians have to be open to conversion, conversion to a fuller truth.

Evangelization of people of various cultures, and honest dialogue with the scientific community, will be helpful reminders to the church that the earth is indeed sacred. Donovan asks, "Should anyone be more zealously aware than a Christian of the urgency of the question of life and death of the planet earth itself?" (p. 116). While Christians should be reminded of the sacredness of creation, the scientific community needs to learn the lesson concerning the presence of the divine in the midst of the world of things.

Honest dialogue for the coming third church is opening up to the challenges of creation. It is also a search for a common language around the common ground which is creation. "Evangelization is a movement outward from the center toward the culture being evangelized." Donovan encourages the church to adopt the basic scientific concept of creation as a truth possessed by that culture as common language. Then the language of science, for example, with regard to the origins of the world, could also be the common language of the church and so facilitate dialogue and evangelization. Anyhow, according to both the scientific and biblical view, the process of creation is not over. It is continuing into the new creation (p. 120).

Science is convinced that a definitive and qualitative change has taken place at the present time in the continuing creation process, because its future direction is now in the hands of humankind itself, for the first time. This is both a startling new understanding of the biblical responsibility given to humankind (Gen 1) and a challenge for the church to wrestle with.

## Sacraments of the World

In the new planetary church, the sacraments also relate to the world, not primarily to the inner life of the church. Theological tradition has located the meaning of the sacraments in carefully defined doctrines and in the meanings

---

[14]Donovan, *Church in the Midst of Creation*, p. 115, referring to Raimundo Panikkar, *The Intra-Religious Dialogue* (New York: Paulist, 1978).

assigned to them by churchgoers. A host of rules have emerged as to who may administer, who may participate, how the rite should be administered and so on. But, ironically again, the meaning of the sacraments in relation to the world and creation has been neglected, almost lost. In Donovan's vision, their ultimate meaning would lie not within the sign, not within the individual receiving them, not even within the church, but rather outside, in the midst of human life. The everyday life, creation, politics, family life, play—these, rather than the altar or a temple, are the proper arena for the sacraments.

What the Christian church has done has been exactly the opposite. The church has been accustomed to going away from the world; sacraments have been understood as means of saving us from an impure world. Donovan echoes the "turn to the world" of Rahner to whom in a sacrament, "rather than entering a temple which walls off the holy from the godless world outside, man sets up in the open expanse of God's world a sign proclaiming that not in Jerusalem alone—but everywhere in spirit and truth, God is adored and experienced."[15]

Donovan calls the traditional way of receiving sacraments "a child-like manner," "a kind of self-centered way." He issues a call to maturity, to reach adulthood. Rather than expecting Christ to be physically present at the celebration, a mature recipient of the sacrament looks up to God to reveal Godself in the world, "in that primary locale of revelation—in creation, in the universe, in the world of created human beings that surround us" (p. 65). The liturgy of the sacraments is not conducted primarily in the church but in the world, amidst its innocent suffering, hatred, stupidity, but also in faithfulness, joy and peace. For Donovan, this is a liturgy, "a terrifying, sublime death and immolation liturgy celebrated by God." It reaches its ultimate meaning and culmination in the liturgy of the Son of God on the cross (p. 66).

On the basis of the biblical promise and exhortation, "until he comes," the Christian church has celebrated the Eucharist. Whatever brings the world closer to that goal is sacramental ministry. Seen from that perspective, the notion of sacramentality will be widened radically. The Gospels are filled with the meaning of sacrament and sacramentality, the feeding of thousands, quenching the thirst of a woman at the well and healing the sick. Everyday experiences, like those recorded by the Evangelists concerning the appearance of the Resurrected One, could be sacramental: a cheerful greeting in a garden, an encounter with a beloved friend, a walk down a country lane with doubting

---

[15]Karl Rahner, "How to Receive a Sacrament and Mean It," in *The Sacraments: Readings in Contemporary Sacramental Theology,* ed. Michael J. Taylor (New York: Alba House, 1981), p. 74.

men, dinner at a village inn and so on (pp. 68-69).

Baptism is the initiatory rite for membership in the world church, the community that is a sign of the unity of humankind. Rather than just being an "element," baptismal water stands for much more. Life is sustained by water, but life is also destroyed by flooding streams. Water gives life and kills people. The faith needed on the part of the baptismal candidate is not primarily a subjectivistic faith for personal salvation but faith that the grace of God everywhere present and active in our world will continue restoring and transforming our world. Therefore, everything that makes the Christian community a sign of unity, a bond of love, is baptismal. Every activity that builds up, sustains, heals that community is baptismal ministry (pp. 70-75).

The Eucharist, the sacrament that stands for the whole of Christianity and the church, points to the world and all creation:

> It speaks for all the Bible from the food of the tree of life in the primeval garden to the messianic banquet at the end time; from the blood of goats and heifers of the Old Covenant to the blood of the New Covenant. It is the presence of God in the world. It is the cross and resurrection of Christ. It is the forgiveness of sins and reconciliation. It is salvation and the new creation. It is inexhaustible. It is Shalom. It is the breakthrough in the spiritualization of the material world. It is the ultimate destination toward which all the religions of the world, with all their sacred symbols from the beginning of time, have been tending and striving. (pp. 76-77)

Therefore, the authentic ministers of the Eucharist are not gathered around an altar, but rather they are to be found in the world, in the midst of human life. Their authorization comes from baptism rather than from a bishop. The Eucharistic bread is an empty symbol if the hungry are not fed, but the action of feeding the hungry is Eucharistic ministry when it satisfies the hunger of needy people (pp. 78-82). This is an integral part of the ministry of the world church.

# 21

# The Post-Christian Church as "Another City"

## Ecclesiology for a Postmodern, Post-Christian Age

The term *postmodern* has a peculiar tone to it. On the one hand, all kinds of problems of current life are attributed to postmodernism, from the fragmentation of society and desperate isolationism to a loss of the meaning of life. On the other hand, Christian theologians and philosophers of almost every persuasion vision an unholy alliance between their faith and this conception that by definition defies any strict definition. Add to this confusion the fact that most people in the third millennium find themselves living in "the city," if not literally (although statistics are staggering), then at least under its pervasive hegemony:

> The irony is deep, pervasive, and seemingly all-encompassing. In virtually every corner of the globe human beings spin round and round, living out their lives as individuals paradoxically compelled in their "private" lives to make choices from a range of options that are enumerated and managed by institutions they cannot see and people they never meet face-to-face. . . . The groove of the City is decisive, making its inhabitants believe they can do what they want and get away with it. A peculiar mix of permissiveness and supervision thus characterizes the comings and goings of the global Cosmopolis, as people do exactly what it wants them to do, yet all the while saying to themselves that they are free.[1]

Barry A. Harvey's engaging book *Another City* is *An Ecclesiological Primer for a Post-Christian World* that attempts to chart waters for the Christian church amidst postmodernism after the era of Christendom—if there ever was such an age—has been definitively left behind. Harvey freely admits that the spell of postmodernism, that is, "a dreary sameness," lurks above the Christian

---

[1]Barry A. Harvey, *Another City: An Ecclesiological Primer for a Post-Christian World* (Harrisburg, Penn.: Trinity Press International, 1999), p. 2. Hereafter in this chapter, most page references to *Another City* will be given in parenthetical references.

church and makes a majority of those who continue to call themselves Christians "retain a vague notion of religious identity" while "their lives are distinctively secular, with the experience of God in worship and prayer not figuring very prominently in all that they do."[2] The irony of postmodern people lies in that they behave as though they had approved of what has happened to their traditional ways of life. "They need not accept the life. It is enough for them to have accepted life with it and in it" (p. 135). However, he also acknowledges that those who served as midwives to the birth of the postmodern "City" did not set out to deliver a monster. Rather, they were the rebellious children of Christendom who "sought to realize reason's sweet dream of an earthly paradise that would be fashioned solely by human abilities and resources."[3] Whatever postmodernism means, Harvey believes that it is "modernity without illusions"; in other words, modern hopes for an earthly kingdom of peace, happiness and joy have been buried. The "messiness" of our world will stay.[4]

Rather than attempting to reinstitute ancient Christianity, Harvey aims to help the church speak again in a self-consciously authoritative way and thus let it reclaim itself as a distinct people who enact a different story in the midst of the world, not only for its own sake and survival, but for the salvation of the world (pp. 20-21, 25). The church of the post-Christian age is to reclaim the vision of the early church that understood itself to be a definitive sign of the gathering of all the people of God into God's kingdom. "The very existence of the Christian community made this destiny known to a fallen word that did not know either what it was . . . or its ultimate destination" (p. 59).

## Altera Civitas, *"Another City"*

What are then the choices available for the Christian church in such a post-Christian, postmodern, post-everything age; what would be the *modus vivendi* (the mode of existence) for the churches after Christendom? The church no longer occupies the privileged position it held in the past. Indeed, its current social status more closely matches that of the early church than it does of any other time and place in history. The nostalgia for what once was has often taken one of two forms. Some Christians desire to go back to the institutional and

---

[2]Harvey, *Another City*, p. 3, cites here from Vigen Guroian, *Ethics After Christendom: Toward an Ecclesial Christian Ethic* (Grand Rapids, Mich.: Eerdmans, 1994), p. 89.

[3]Harvey, *Another City*, p. 7; for an analysis of the form and impossibility of the dream of modernism, see pp. 101-11 especially.

[4]Harvey, *Another City*, p. 6, quoting from Zygmund Bauman, *Postmodern Ethics* (Cambridge: Blackwell, 1993), p. 32.

cultural synthesis between Christianity and society. Others try to make themselves more adjusted to the current culture by resorting to a secularized notion
of the Christian message. Still others are tempted to embrace the dream of a
pure church of Donatism and later revivalist movements. "Like Noah's Ark,
which kept its occupants safe and secure from the dangers outside, a handful
of groups and individuals believe that the church must seal itself off, withdraw into a separate society where its citizens will be protected from the taint
of the world" (p. 13). [5]

Predictably, Harvey is not willing to embrace any of these options. As an alternative he submits an idea of the church as an *altera civitas*, another city. This
way of describing the people of God goes back to Scripture and the traditions
of both Judaism and Christianity. The imagery of a city was, of course, power-
fully employed by Augustine in his *City of God*. What makes this picture so appealing to Harvey is that already in the New Testament it is connected with
political concepts of city, citizen and commonwealth. It depicts the church as
an alternate community ready to challenge prevailing assumptions about the
way of life and beliefs (see Mt 5:14; Eph 2:12, 19; Phil 3:20; Heb 11:10, 16). In
fact, the life and convictions of the early church as a new and radical form of
social life are unintelligible apart from a politics (pp. 15-16, 64).

As an alternative city, the early church grounded its way of life and beliefs
in the Jewish soil of the Old Testament. Theirs was the ethos of Diaspora people, of nomadic Old Testament tribes wandering toward the Promised Land.
They lacked their own place since they were looking forward "to the city . . .
whose architect and builder is God" (Heb 11:10). Harvey reminds us of the fact
that Christians could have taken refuge under a provision in Roman law that
allowed for the establishment of a *cultus privates* (private cult) dedicated for an
otherworldly personal salvation, but did not do so. Instead, they challenged
the power of Rome and proclaimed allegiance to the one and only king, the
Christ. By confronting Rome on its own terms, the early church specifically po-
sitioned itself as the other city of Roman society (pp. 18-19, 21-22), in Václav
Havel's words, "a parallel *polis* [city], a distinct community that coexisted with
the dominant structures of the empire." [6]

The early church, contrary to the mindset of the contemporary church, did

---

[5]Harvey, *Another City,* pp. 12-14. Harvey refers the reader to R. A. Markus, *Saeculum: History
and Society in the Theology of St. Augustine* (Cambridge: Cambridge University Press, 1970),
pp. 112, 122, 178.
[6]Václav Havel, "The Power of the Powerless," in *Living in Truth,* ed. Jan Vladislav (London:
Faber & Faber, 1987), p. 13.

not restrict relationships to what modern thought labels the "private" sphere. Rather, the relationships were formed in connection with everyday business, building houses and roads, tending gardens and sowing crops, and so on. These activities, again in distinction from their contemporary counterparts, were not assigned to the realm of the "secular" by the early Christians. The distinction between the "spiritual" and "secular" was virtually unknown in the ancient world, and more certainly in first-century Palestinian Judaism (pp. 59-60).

Since the early church as an alternative city did not have a permanent place, nor did it set its hopes on an earthly kingdom, it defined itself as an eschatological fellowship. They were the people of the age to come, now living between two ages and two overlapping social orders. This eschatological ecclesiology—or, as Harvey also calls it, ecclesial eschatology—of early Christianity did not originate with Jesus, nor on the day of Pentecost, but was rooted in Israel's faith. Therefore, Harvey devotes a considerable section in his book to tracing the Jewish roots of his ecclesiology.[7] Jesus, the *Autobasileia* (the Very Ruler) of God as the bearer of the kingdom in his person, did not renounce this Jewish conception of the kingdom but refashioned it to fit the eschatological program of God.

## The Presence of the Kingdom in Jesus and the Reformulation of the Jewish Hopes

Contrary to what is often said, Harvey argues that the differences between Jesus and the synagogue were not the result of Jesus stripping away the "extraneous" political and social dimensions of the Jewish tradition. Yes, the church did definitively relativize the demands of Torah and Temple; but the real difference had to do with the question whether the messianic rule of God in the person of Christ had really broken in, and what were the implications of this for the rest of the world, outside the covenant community. Harvey summarizes the points of contention between Israel and Christianity in these terms:

1. The coming of the kingdom was already at hand rather than having been relegated into a distant future.

2. The kingdom at hand continued to make its presence known through the

---

[7]Harvey, *Another City*, pp. 31-35. For details, see further the two subsections of chapter two, titled "The Rule of God in the People of Israel" and "Tremors of Eschatology in the History of Israel" (pp. 35-53).

community of Jesus' disciples after the resurrection. The Christian community as a new *politeia* ("city") of God repudiated the militaristic nationalism of many Jews of the time, since the followers of Christ were not to take up the sword. However, they were revolutionary, even more so than the Jews (pp. 57-62). This they did

> by a doubly revolutionary method: turning the other cheek, going the second mile, the deeply subversive wisdom of taking up the cross. The agenda which Jesus mapped out for his followers was the agenda to which he himself was obedient. This was how the kingdom would come, how the battle would be won.[8]

3. The fact that the kingdom had drawn near in and through the work of Jesus meant that people could now enter it by responding to the proclamation of redemption through repentance and faith. Its constituency was no more limited to the Chosen People but also included the Gentiles even though Jesus himself limited his ministry to "the lost sheep of Israel."

4. The cost that the drawing near of God's reign would exact from those who heeded Jesus' summons to repent and believe became evident on the cross. As impossible as it was for the followers of Christ to envision the way of the cross, that was the only path not only for the Master but also his slaves.

For the Christian church, it has been a struggle to learn to accept the Jewish rootage of the church and faith. For the most part, following George Lindbeck, Harvey contends that Christianity remains as Gentile in its self-understanding as ever.[9] The implications have been many, the most fatal being that Christian theology in general has relegated faith to the private sphere in the soul and divorced it from social, political and everyday life. Faith that is transferred to the spiritual and unseen world of the individual resembles second-century Gnosticism more than it does the messianic politics of Jesus. John Yoder even goes so far as to say that the way of life cultivated by the Jews of the Diaspora has been far closer to the messianic ethos of Jesus and his early followers than virtually anything we find in the subsequent history of Christendom.[10] We next turn to what the fateful "Constantinian shift," with the loss of Jewish roots, meant to the Christian church and ecclesiology.

---

[8]Harvey, *Another City*, pp. 13, 57, quoting N. T. Wright, *Jesus and the Victory of God* (Minneapolis: Fortress, 1997), p. 465.

[9]Harvey, *Another City*, (p. 13). 65; George Lindbeck, "The Church," in *Keeping the Faith*, ed. Geoffrey Wainwright (Philadelphia: Fortress, 1988), pp. 190, 193.

[10]See further John Yoder, *The Politics of Jesus: Vicit Agnus Noster*, 2nd ed. (Grand Rapids, Mich.: Eerdmans, 1994); Harvey, *Another City*, pp. 65-66.

## The Loss of the Missional Character of the Church

Christians constituted a distinct minority in the Roman Empire prior to the reign of Constantine. Under those circumstances, conversion was a public event, a social and political choice. What made things much more serious was the distinctive faith of the early Christian church. While they were anti-Roman in the sense that they pledged allegiance only to the One King, Christ, they still did not separate themselves from the world since the risen Christ was the ruler of all creation. In one sense they said no to the earthly kingdom, in another sense they affirmed it. Because the world had rejected the righteous will of God and his kingdom, it had already condemned itself, but even this rebellious world was a world redeemed and recreated in Christ, the true ruler. Against all opposition, the early church proclaimed boldly to the world that its future lies in the destiny of Christ and his kingdom. "This means that for those who believe in Christ and are united to Him, this very world—its time and matter, its life, and even death—have become the 'means' of communication with the Kingdom of God, the sacrament, i.e., the mode, of its coming and presence among men."[11]

The church and the world are therefore mutually and intimately related, but not along the traditional lines of "secular" and "holy." The relationship is more nuanced and complex. Both church and world are "secular" realities, in the original sense of the Latin term *saeculum* (literally: heaven) which refers to time, to the temporal period between fall and eschaton. The church's profession of Christ's lordship over earthly rulers authorizes it to speak to the world in God's name. But this changed dramatically after Christianity became established as the religion of the state. The change of status for Christians was sudden and unpredictable, from a harassed and persecuted counter-movement to the establishment of Rome.

What could Christians envision for the future other than an unprecedented opportunity to further and fulfill the coming of God's kingdom, now that even the emperor was favorable to God's cause? In its eagerness to perform this "holy service" for the world, Christians fell prey to a radically realized eschatology, thus also blurring the distinctions between the world and itself. In Harvey's words, the church began to "render to Caesar what belonged to God" (p. 73). The church soon embraced the privileged status and enjoyed earthly power in the form of the priest and king sharing the mandate of rulership, each ac-

---

[11]Harvey, *Another City*, pp. 67-69; the quotation comes from Alexander Schemann, *Church, World, Mission* (Crestwood, N.Y.: St. Vladimir's Seminary Press, 1979), pp. 29-30.

cording to his proper office. At its worst, during the Middle Ages, the hosts of the prince became "the police department of the Church."[12] The content and ethos of this dual rulership, understandably, derived more from the pagan world than from the gospel.

This radical shift totally altered and reshaped the missional character of the church. The carefully drawn distinction between the world and the church, the present age and the age to come, were to a large extent fused into one entity, the *corpus christianum*. This fusion led to the virtual loss of the church's missionary identity. It almost looked as though there was no more mission to be done in this new world under this providential, as it seemed, partnership between ecclesiastical and civil authorities. The tragedy was that "there was no further challenge to be issued to the rulers in the name of the ruling Christ."[13]

The decisive shift in the church's missionary consciousness, which oriented itself predominantly to earthly conquest of non-Christian territories, also brought with it another fateful change, namely a radical redefinition of the ideas of faith and grace. In the early church, Harvey reminds us, these notions were unintelligible apart from the community's diplomatic mission, which was to represent the rule of God to the earthly rulers. Rather, the focus came to be placed on the inward and private life of each individual (pp. 89, 90).

What is equally tragic is that despite the loss of political and moral power, most Christian communities continue to embrace some form of Constantianism, a mindset totally foreign to a postmodern, post-Christian world. The first two thousand years or so of its history have not yet convinced the Christian church of the need to retain its identity as another city. What is the place of the church in the third millennium, amidst the "risk culture" of a postmodern cacophony?

## The Spirituality of the Postmodern "Risk Culture"

Despite the prophecies of atheists and secular theologians of the 1960s, spirituality has not vanished from the modern and especially the postmodern world. Due to the emptiness of the postmodern subject, Harvey notes, "spirituality" has an important role to play. Of course, the goals and ethos of spiri-

---

[12]Harvey, *Another City*, p. 77, quoting from John Neville Figgis, *Studies of Political Thought from Gerson to Grotius, 1414-1625* (Cambridge: Cambridge University Press, 1956), p. 4.

[13]Harvey, *Another City*, p. 82, quoting from Oliver O'Donovan, *The Desire of the Nations: Rediscovering the Roots of Political Theology* (Cambridge: Cambridge University Press, 1996), p. 212.

tuality in this culture are very different from those of the early church or even the modern church. In fact, the concept of spirituality itself is a result of modernism. It was not until Descartes and others invented the idea of a secular domain of reality—in which the noble human project of building a paradise on earth would take place with human means—that "spirituality" as its counterpart was recognized.

Prior to the project of modernism, spirituality as a separate category did not even exist. The term *religio* derived its distinctive meaning in the Medieval period from monastic life and personal piety in distinction from the rest of life. The modern idea of religion derives from the Renaissance and Enlightenment when it came to mean a freestanding set of beliefs or propositions held by individuals about what is ultimately true and important in life, and "of most importance, which they can hold apart from their political loyalties." This notion of religion naturally enforces the separation of life into two distinct spheres, and this view fits very nicely within a postmodern risk culture. "The individual in the role of consumer is encouraged to pick and choose from a vast inventory of religious symbols and doctrines, to select those beliefs that best express his or her private sentiments" (pp. 128-29).

As with other areas of contemporary life, postmodern spirituality is characterized by the triumph of the therapeutic mindset. Such spirituality is totally individualistic; it does not require any form of communal direction or oversight, but may be enjoyed in the privacy of one's own life. Harvey calls this sort of piety a "kind of personalized 'diet plan' for the soul." This kind of spirituality is effectively delivered within the marketplace of desire. According to him, in many ways the spirituality that prevails in a risk culture more closely resembles ancient Gnosticism than early Christianity (pp. 129-30). This is a spirituality of the "post-Christian nation."[14]

The church of the third millennium finds itself amidst a culture that has become "nothing but a meeting place for individual wills, each with its own set of attitudes and preferences and who understand that world solely as an arena for the achievement of their own satisfaction, who interpret reality as a series of opportunities for their enjoyment and for whom the last enemy is boredom."[15] Understandably this kind of spirituality completely lacks the "spiritual force" needed to deal critically and creatively with the postmodern risk culture.

---

[14]See further Harold Bloom, *The American Religion: The Emergence of the Post-Christian Nation* (New York: Simon & Schuster, 1992), pp. 22, 32.

[15]Harvey, *Another City*, pp. 130-31, citing from Alasdair MacIntyre, *After Virtue: A Study in Moral Theory*, 2nd ed. (Notre Dame: University of Notre Dame Press, 1984), p. 25.

## A Call to "Holy Madness"

To the church of postmodernism Harvey issues a bold call to "holy madness." That is the critical stance toward the mindset that only accepts one way of thinking, the postmodern. All those who think and act otherwise are mad. To challenge this myth of postmodernism a community is needed, a *polis*, a church as another city, an alternate community. Christianity is "most especially a social event,"[16] and therefore the invitation of Jesus to holy madness is not a call to withdraw from the world but to constitute "a subversive presence within 'enemy territory.'" Those who understand the mode of life of an alternative city as an effort to withdraw from the world only offer a counsel of despair, for they are in fact asserting that no choices are available to deal critically with the postmodern mindset. "In short," Harvey concludes, "not only for its own sake, but for the world's sake, the church need not, indeed must not see itself on a continuum between sectarian withdrawal and secular servitude. It is rather summoned by its Lord to live as a parallel *polis* in the truth, that is, in the sacramental interval between Passion, Pentecost, and Parousia" (p. 138).

A life of holy madness can be fulfilled in a community of diaspora people of God, not unlike the people of the Old Covenant. Once again, this means for the church a return to its Jewish roots. In this diaspora mindset particular and universal are not set over against universal. God's election of Israel (particularity) served the principle of universality. Moreover, the truth can never be distilled into an abstract system of thought but is rather found in the concrete form of life (pp. 139-41).

The diaspora nature of the church is not an *ad hoc* strategy, solely out of necessity, any more than it was for the old people of God, but "the path of obedience, a safeguard of identity, protection against the 'lying dreams' of those who would trouble the exiles with unreal promises of restored national pride."[17] As such, the relationships fostered within the ecclesial household—over against the prevailing mindset of the culture—are not restricted to the "private sphere" but have to do with the activities that make up the business of everyday life: building houses, tending gardens, marrying, and so on.

Even though the church of the postmodern world is to look forward to the

---

[16]Harvey, *Another City*, p. 137, takes this phrase from John Milbank, *Theology and Social Theory: Beyond Secular Reason* (Oxford: Blackwell, 1990), p. 388.

[17]Harvey, *Another City*, p. 146, citing from John Yoder, "Withdrawal and Diaspora: The Two Faces of Liberation," in *Freedom and Discipleship: Liberation Theology in Anabaptist Perspective*, ed. Daniel S. Schipani (Maryknoll, N.Y.: Orbis, 1989), p. 82.

"city that is to come" (Heb 13:14), it does so by remembering its past liturgical-ly and sacramentally. The church's mandate as an outpost of heaven in this or any other age is finally not something other than its eucharistic worship—as Harvey contends in the Orthodox language "liturgy after liturgy" (pp. 150-65). This is the only way to fulfill the mission of the church, "to reveal to the world its *arche* [beginning, origins] and *telos* [goal] by offering to it the means and me-dia for living in love and therefore in truth" (p. 161).

# Epilogue

## ECCLESIOLOGICAL CHALLENGES FOR
## THE THIRD MILLENNIUM

W hat will be the future of theological thinking about the church? What will be the most significant challenges for ecclesiology? Is ecclesiology going to move to the center of Christian systematic theology? Questions such as these beg for answers at the turn of the third millennium.

Now that we have finished this long and winding road of Christian thinking about the church, it is time to look forward to future challenges of ecclesiology. Whatever we may dare to say about the future of Christian theology, one need not be a prophet to propose that the nature, purpose and distinctive features of Christian *community* will occupy theologians' agenda. The reason is simply this: in our fragmented world, with so many people looking for their roots and meaning, a community with purpose and hope for the future will be something to look for. The great ecclesiologist of the past generation, the Reformed Emil Brunner, in his influential *The Misunderstanding of the Church*,[1] forcefully argues that the church is nothing other than a fellowship of men and women, a fellowship of the Spirit, a *koinonia*. How well—or poorly—the Christian church is able to fulfill this basic task determines to a large extent how relevant the church is going to be for the third millennium. Alien forces of rampant individualism are also making gateways into postmodern religiosity.

Our survey showed that one's doctrine of the church is integrally related to one's denominational and theological background. The Roman Catholic ecclesiology looks different from, say, the Reformed or Free church ecclesiologies. Some of these differences we have noted at the end of each major part.

---

[1]Emil Brunner, *The Misunderstanding of the Church* (Philadelphia: Westminster Press, 1952).

Yet it also became evident that confessional boundaries do not limit the thinking about the church. Barth's version of the Reformed ecclesiology has tones surprisingly similar to those of the ecumenical Free church views of Volf and McClendon. Furthermore, the charismatically flavored version of Hans Küng's Roman Catholic doctrine of the church shares many emphases with Pentecostal-Charismatic pneumatological ecclesiology.

The rise and consolidation of the ecumenical movement is a healthy reminder to all ecclesiologies of the major challenge to the Christian church, namely, the common destiny of all people of God under one God. Related issues such as joint witness and testimony before the world will continue to be significant issues for the church which is, by its nature, missionary.

Furthermore, the "earthly church" is also integrally related to and dependent on sociological, historical and political conditions. Nothing would be more dangerous to our understanding of the church, Brunner warned, than to resort to the idea of a kind of "invisible" church, so prevalent in various strands of Christian spirituality and piety; it is not only foreign to the New Testament but also detrimental to our ecclesiology. The church, the fellowship of men and women, is rooted in the soil of human societies and cultures, yet goes beyond these. Our theological survey did not give much attention to those factors, not because there were deemed unimportant but because not everything can be accomplished in the confines of one study.

The future of Christian theology lies in global sensitivity: theologizing can no longer be the privilege of one culture, neither Western nor any other. Systematic theology is fast becoming a collection of various voices from all over the world, often a cacophony of dissonant sounds. What would a genuinely African ecclesiology look like? Or an Asian one? Or Latin American? Some scattered experiments are available, and we have listened to some occasional voices in the last part of the book. But there is much more to come. Undoubtedly these new developments—hopefully culturally more akin to their contexts and more creative in their responses than their predecessors—dare not ignore the rich Christian ecclesiological tradition developed mainly in the West. But neither will it suffice to add some cosmetic touches on the existing ecclesiologies. Classical Western theology may benefit in an unprecedented way from the encounter with these contextual and global voices. At its best, this dialogue may become an ecumenical exchange of gifts.

A plethora of other kinds of challenges and questions relate to some aspects of ecclesiology and need further attention as the church takes its first steps into the third millennium: How can a church and its structures fit both sexes, or minorities, or people with different mindsets? How can ministry patterns be created that would fuel, rather than extinguish, the flame of faith in the lives of ordinary Christians? What is the meaning of sacraments and the sacramental for people living amidst an unprecedented rise of (neo-)religiosity both in the West and elsewhere?

In light of the fact that Christian theology in the third millennium faces the challenge of how to relate to other faiths and theologies, ecclesiology can no longer accomplish its purposes in isolation from the rest of the world's religiosity. What is the distinctive nature of *Christian* community vis-à-vis other religious communities? How does the nature of the Christian church as *ekklesia*, a "called-out-people," relate to its lofty calling to be spread among the nations and become flesh in each particular cultural and religious setting? Now that it has become almost a commonplace to maintain that Christian systematic theology has to account for the claims and influences of religious thinking of other faiths, what will an ecclesiology of the next generation look like against that background? Few, if any, precedents yet exist specifically in ecclesiologies. Perhaps it will be left to the theologians coming from outside the West to be our guides and mentors in this enterprise.

# Names Index

Albrecht, Daniel E., 70-71
Althaus, Paul, 40, 42-43
Amant, C. Penrose St., 50, 54
Anderson, Allan H., 194, 196, 198-201
Anderson, Gerald, 175
Antwi, Daniel J., 197
Athanasius, 23
Augustine, 11, 19, 51, 185-86, 223
Avis, Paul D. L., 51
Badcock, Gary D., 62
Bainton, Roland, 50
Balthasar, Hans Urs von, 23-34
Barreiro, Alvaro, 183
Barrett, David, 8, 69, 194
Barth, Karl, 56-58, 117, 232
Basden, Paul, 50, 61, 64, 84
Basham, Don, 204
Bauckham, Richard, 127
Baxter, Ern, 204
Beasley-Murray, Paul, 65
Bediako, Kwame, 194, 197
Bennett, Dennis, 69
Best, Thomas, 81, 88
Bevans, Stephen B., 151
Bird, Thomas E., 17
Birkbeck, William J., 22
Bloom, Harold, 228
Boff, Leonardo, 59, 176-77, 179-82, 189
Bonhoeffer, Dietrich, 30, 164
Bonino, Jose Miguez, 182
Bosch, David, 151
Braaten, Carl E., 46, 87, 121
Bromiley, Geoffrey W., 56
Bruggeman, Antonio, 152
Brunner, Emil, 30, 167-68, 231-32

Buckley, James J., 56
Buren, Paul van, 145
Burgess, Stanley M., 68, 73
Calvin, John, 11, 50-56
Campenhaus, Hans von, 110
Carter, Craig A., 56
Chandler, Russel, 59
Chenu, Marie-Dominique, 175
Christenson, Larry, 69
Clapp, Rodney, 202
Comblin, José, 185
Congar, Yves M.-J., 17, 27, 34, 39, 62-63, 77, 94, 177
Cook, Guillermo, 176, 182-83
Cooke, Bernard J., 141
Cope, Brian E., 80
Cox, Harvey, 59
Cullman, Oscar, 81
Cummings, Owen F., 53-54
Cyprian of Carthage, 11, 29, 136
Cyril of Jerusalem, 10, 65
Daly, Mary, 164, 185
Daneel, M. L., 195, 198, 200
Dietrich, Donald J., 30, 164
Dockery, David S., 50, 61, 64, 84
Dohi, Akio, 168, 170-72
Donovan, Vincent J., 164, 165, 211-19, 227
Drummond, Richard H., 167
Duffy, Regis A., 29
Dulles, Avery, 14, 30, 94, 121, 178
Dunn, James D. G., 66, 80, 110
Eagleson, John, 181-83
Eastwood, Cyril, 65
Ebeling, Gerhard, 100
Ellul, Jacques, 216
Erickson, John H., 17, 23
Erickson, Millard, 144

Evdokimov, Paul, 19
Fahey, Michael A., 29, 34
Fatula, Mary Ann, 35
Faustus of Riez, 10
Feiner, Johannes, 12
Ferro, Cora, 183
Figgis, John Neville, 227
Fiorenza, Francis S., 29, 34, 164, 187-88, 190
Fischer, Balthasar, 65
Florovsky, Vladimir, 19
Frank, Sebastian, 61
Galvin, John P., 29, 34
Garijo-Guembe, Miguel M., 10, 43, 66
Garrett, James Leo, 64-67
Gassman, Gunther, 80
Geldbach, Erich, 81
Gelpi, Donald L., 35-36
Gerrish, Brian A., 53
Grebel, Conrad, 55
Gregory Nazianzen (of Nazianzus), 23, 185
Gregory of Nyssa, 10
Gregory, Alfonso, 177, 180
Grenz, Stanley J., 114, 118, 124
Gritsch, Eric W., 39, 45
Guroian, Vigen, 222
Gwyn, Douglas, 65
Haberman, Joshua, 129
Hadaway, Kirk, 203
Harnack, Adolf von, 10, 11, 143
Harper, Michael, 11-12, 30, 51, 65, 73, 77, 168, 190
Harvey, Barry A., 59, 165, 221-30
Havel, Václav, 223
Healy, Nicholas M., 57
Heller, Dagmar, 98
Hinze, Bradford E., 27
Hippolytus, 10
Hobbs, Herschel H., 65
Hocken, Peter D., 68, 73, 132, 198

Hodges, Melvin L., 73
Hofmann, Melchior, 64
Holl, Karl, 63
Hollenweger, Walter J., 68-
    70, 72, 194, 199
Holze, Heindrich, 86
Hooft, W. A. Visser't, 79
Humphreys, Fisher, 65
Hunter, H. D., 132, 198
Hut, Hans, 61
Ignatius of Antioch, 8, 23,
    34, 60, 135-36
Imbelli, Robert, 17
Irenaeus, 10, 23, 135
Iwabuchi, Hiroyasu, 167-68
Jennings, Raymond, 169
Jenson, Robert W., 39, 40,
    45-46, 87
Johann of Ragusa, 11
John XXIII, 34
John of Damascus, 10
John of Torquemada, 11
John Paul II, 37-38
Johnson, Elizabeth, 186,
    192
Johnson, Todd, 8
Kärkkäinen, Veli-Matti, 74,
    83, 114, 186
Kasemann, Ernst, 80
Kelly, J. N. D., 11
Keskitalo, Jukka, 151, 157
Khomiakov, Alexis, 20
Kinnamon, Michael, 80
Kiwiet, John J., 61
Küng, Hans, 13, 27, 43, 80,
    93-94, 103-12, 126, 160-61,
    232
Kuzmic, Peter, 73, 76, 139
Land, Stephen J., 72
Larentzakis, Grigorios, 19
Lawler, Michael, 87, 107
Lederle, Henry I., 69, 81
Lee, Paul D., 72-74
Legrand, Harvey, 31
Lekhanyane, Bishop, 194
Leo XIII, 27

Little, Franklin H., 63-64
Löhrer, Magnus, 12
Lombard, Peter, 11
Lossky, Nicholas, 80, 194
Lossky, Vladimir, 17, 19, 23-
    24, 95
Luoma, Matti, 157
Luther, Martin, 11, 19, 39-
    48, 50-51, 53-55, 62-63, 86,
    105, 119, 154-155, 186
MacIntyre, Alasdair, 228
Madigan, Patrick, 10, 43
Magesa, Laurenti, 194, 197
Makhubu, Paul, 195
Mannermaa, Tuomo, 46-47
Manz, Felix, 55
Marins, José, 180
Markus, R. A., 223
Mbiti, John, 197
McClendon, James Wm.,
    Jr., 13, 61-62, 93-94, 142-
    50, 160-61, 232
McClung, Grant, Jr., 69
McDonnell, Kilian, 30, 34,
    36, 76, 202
McFague, Sallie, 186
McGee, Gary, 68, 73
McGrath, Alister E., 46, 61,
    67
McNeill, John T., 50
Meeking, Basil, 89
Melanchthon, Philip, 11,
    123
Messori, Vittorio, 8, 60
Meyendorff, John, 18, 24,
    178
Meyer, Harding, 80-82
Milbank, John, 229
Möhler, J. Adams, 27
Moltmann, Jurgen, 13, 93-
    94, 104, 119, 126-33, 160-
    61, 186, 192
Moore, David, 202-9
Mugambi, J. N. Kanuya,
    194, 197
Müller, Alois, 175

Mumford, Bob, 204-7
Munro, Harry Clyde, 65
Mutendi, Samuel, 199
Mutungu, Derek B., 200
Nassif, Bradley, 178
Neill, Stephen, 66-67
Newbigin, Lesslie, 13, 75,
    93-94, 144-45, 151-61, 168
Nissiotis, Nikos A., 17
Norman, Williams, 169
Novak, Michael, 61
Nthanmburi, Zablon J., 194
Omenyo, Cephas N., 194-
    97, 200
Opoku, Kofi Asare, 197
Ositelu, Gabriel, 194
Ott, Ludwig, 12
Panikulam, George, 87
Pannenberg, Wolfhart, 10-
    13, 23, 42-43, 80, 93-94,
    113-25, 160-61
Parham, Charles F., 68
Patelos, Constantine G., 82
Paul VI, 34, 175
Pelikan, Jaroslav, 40, 141
Peters, Ted, 185-86
Peura, Simo, 86
Pitts, William L., 84
Pius X, 29
Pobee, John S., 194
Pobere, Cephas M., 194
Poole, John, 204
Prince, Derek, 204
Rahner, Karl, 28, 32-33, 37,
    94, 103, 108, 165, 212-15,
    219
Ratzinger, Joseph, 8, 60, 94,
    134
Raunio, Antti, 46
Reynolds, Bernard, 186
Rigal, Jean, 26
Riggs, John W., 52
Rosmini, Antonio, 26
Ruether, Rosemary
    Radford, 146, 164, 185,
    190

Ruthven, Jan, 70
Saarinen, Risto, 80, 82, 86, 99
Sachs, John R., 33-34
Sandidge, Jerry L., 34
Sartori, Luigi, 74
Scheeben, Matthias Joseph, 27, 109
Schemann, Alexander, 226
Scherer, James, A., 151
Schipani, Daniel S., 229
Schleiermacher, Friedrich E. D., 11-12, 114, 143
Schüssler Fiorenza, Elisabeth, 164, 184-85, 188-90, 192
Sekine, Masao, 170
Seymour, William J., 68
Shanahan, Thomas J., 87, 107
Simons, Menno, 67
Simpson, Charles, 204, 207
Smyth, John, 60, 65, 134-35
Snyder, Howard, 209

Sohm, Rudolph, 110
Sorokin, Pitirim, 212-14
Souza, Luis A. Gomez de, 182
Stott, John R., 89
Suenens, Leon Joseph, 34
Sullivan, Francis A., 76
Sundkler, Bengt, 195
Synan, Vinson, 70
Tappert, Theodore G., 39, 42
Taylor, Michael J., 219
Tillich, Paul, 144, 168
Toffler, Alvin, 214
Torrance, Thomas F., 56
Torres, Sergio, 181-83
Trible, Phyllis, 188
Troeltsch, Ernst, 63
Tsirpanlis, Constantine N., 17
Tsukamoto, Toraji, 172
Turner, Harold W., 200
Uchimura, Kanzo, 167-74
Vandervelde, George, 73, 87

Vischer, Lukas, 79-80
Vladislav, Jan, 223
Volf, Miroslav, 8, 12-13, 22, 59, 65, 73, 75-76, 93-95, 97-98, 101-2, 134-41, 160-61, 232
Wainwright, Geoffrey, 225
Waliggo, John Mary, 197
Wall, J. M., 129
Walton, Robert G., 65
Ware, Kallistos, 19-22
Weber, Otto, 136
Welker, Michael, 109
Wendel, François, 51
Williams, George H., 10, 64
Wood, Susan K., 87, 178-79
Wright, N. T., 225
Wright, Stuart A., 203
Yoder, John Howard, 67, 143, 146, 225, 229
Zizioulas, John, 13, 21, 30, 93-102, 134, 160-61
Zwingli, Ulrich, 50-51, 54-56

# Subject Index

African Independent Churches, 194-201
African spiritualities, 195-201
AIDS, 190-91
Anabaptism, 55, 57, 60-61, 64, 142, 145-46
Anglican Communion, 83
apostolic(ity), 182, 206-7
assembly, the church as, 64, 119-20, 136-37, 143-45, 171-72, 208-9
authority, ecclesiastical, 43, 54, 204-5, 207-8
Azusa Street Mission, 68
baptism
    spirit, 70-72
    water, 52, 55-56, 58, 63, 96, 106, 107, 119, 220
Baptist churches, 60-62, 64, 84, 89, 134, 142-50
base ecclesial communities, 175-83
believers' church ecclesiology, 56, 63-64
bishop, 21, 97, 135-36, 180
body of Christ, 31, 99, 108, 123
Brethren churches, 145
catholic(ity), 24, 182
charisms, 33-36, 70-71, 110-11, 131-32, 139-40, 208
Charismatic
    ecclesiology 24-25, 66, 74-76, 131-33, 139-40, 198-201, 202-4
    spirituality 70-72, 101
charismatic movements, 36, 69-70
Christ and church, 127-28, 136-37, 214-16

common witness, 87-90
communion ecclesiology, 10, 20, 30-32, 39-40, 74-75, 85-87, 95-102, 105, 119-21, 196-98, 231
comparative ecclesiology, 14
confession of faith, 137
contextualization, 9, 163-65, 200-201
covenant, 53-54
creation and church, 191-92, 211-12, 217-18
creeds, 10, 39-40
deification. *See* theosis
Disciples of Christ church, 65
discipleship, 204-5
discipline, 51-52, 67
doctrine, 142-43
earthkeeping and church, 132-33, 191-93, 199
Eastern Orthodoxy, 8, 17-25, 82, 88, 135-37
ecclesiality, 9, 59-60, 106-7, 135-36, 148, 177-82. *See also* marks of the church
ecclesiology
    history of, 9-11
    in systematic theology, 7-11
ecology. *See* earthkeeping and church
ecumenical movement, 7-8, 79-91
ecumenism, 36-38, 59-60, 79-91, 115-17, 137-38, 147-48, 153-54, 189-90. *See also* unity of the church
election, 57, 114, 123-25
enthusiasm, 71
equality in the church, 110, 128-29, 131-32, 187-90
eschatology, 52-53, 98, 100-102, 108-9, 116-17, 124, 126, 135, 138, 153

Eucharist, 20-22, 96-98, 101-2, 106, 120, 149, 180, 219-20
Eucharistic ecclesiology, 21, 31, 48
evangelical ecclesiology, 89
evangelization/ evangelism, 71, 87-91, 217-18
*ex opere operato*, 55
faith, ecclesial mediation of, 12, 62-63, 137-39, 170-71
faith and order, 88
Father, God as, 185-87
feminism, 134, 184-93
Free churches, 8, 16, 56, 58-67, 83-84, 134-36, 208
freedom, religious, 89, 108
gathered church. *See* assembly, the church as
global church, 8-9, 59-60, 232-33
glossolalia. *See* speaking in tongues
healing, 198-201
hierarchy, 24, 28, 100, 104, 110, 192
Holy Spirit, 10, 29-31, 40, 108-9, 156-57, 178-79, 153
    and Christ, 23-24, 27, 32-33, 57, 98-101, 121-22, 135-36
    *See also* pneumatology and ecclesiology
incarnation, the church as, 26-28
individualism, 11-12, 62-63, 144
infallibility of the Pope, 26-27
invisible and visible church, 40, 51-53, 57-58, 61-62, 154, 168-69
Japanese churches, 167-74
Jewish-Christian relations, 106, 145-47, 224-25

justice, 118, 182-83, 190-91,
    199
kingdom of God, 117-19,
    207-8, 224-25
koinonia. See communion
    ecclesiology
laity, 97, 140-41, 173-74,
    181. See also priesthood of
    all believers
leadership, 116-17, 188-90
liberation theologies, 59,
    188-89
liturgy. See worship
local church, 54, 97, 108,
    148, 180-81, 217
    and universal church,
        101-2, 111-12, 138-39
Lumen Gentium, 28-30, 34-
    37, 98
Lutheran Church, 39-49
marks of the church, 40-41,
    50-51, 181. See also
    ecclesiality
Mennonites, 61-62, 142-45
Methodist Church, 64
ministry, 100-101, 137, 148-
    49, 188-90
mission of the church, 57-58,
    64, 66-67, 157-59, 226-27
missionary (or missional)
    ecclesiology, 126-27, 151-
    59
Mukyokai, 167-74
neighbor love and church,
    46-49, 67
"offices of Christ," 130
oneness of the church. See
    unity
ordination, 31, 42-44, 97,
    188
    of women 183
patristic theologies, 10, 11,
    17-19, 23, 27-28, 95-96
Pentecost, 24, 45
Pentecostal-charismatic
    movements, 68-78, 127

Pentecostalism, 16, 68-78,
    89, 156-57, 199-202
people of God, 28, 106-8,
    124
pilgrim people, 28, 107,
    152-54
pneumatological
    ecclesiology, 22-25, 108-
    11, 121-23
pneumatology and
    ecclesiology, 17-18, 27, 32-
    36, 44-45, 56-57, 108-9,
    114, 191-93
political involvement, 118-
    19, 126, 130, 182-84
poor, the, 175-76, 182-83
Pope, the, 26-27, 116-17
postmodern(ism), 157-59,
    221-30
priest, 107-8
priesthood of all believers,
    29, 42-44, 65-66, 72, 107-8,
    140-41, 173-74
primitivism, 64
proselytism, 87-90
Reformation
    mainline (Protestant),
        9-11, 50, 154-55
    Radical, 55, 60-62, 65,
        142
Reformed Church, 50-58
renewal of the church, 69,
    103-5, 202-3, 206-8
Roman Catholic Church,
    26-38, 59-60, 82, 88-89,
    135-37, 154-55, 175-83,
    188
Quakers, 62-64
sacraments, 20-21, 31-32,
    40-41, 52, 55, 135-37,
    154, 169, 218-20,
    229-30
sanctification, 133, 181
sect, 63
Shepherding movement,
    202-10

simul justus et peccator,
    41-42
sobornost, 22
speaking in tongues, 68,
    132, 198
state and church, 64, 129
structures of the church,
    32-33, 75-76, 109-11,
    188-90
theosis, 18-19, 23-24
Trinity, the church as the
    image of, 17-20, 28-31, 79,
    95-96, 127-29, 134-35, 185
union with Christ, 46-49,
    53-55, 108
unity of humankind,
    115-17
unity of the church, 20, 22,
    24, 41, 79-81, 111-12,
    216-17
    various ecclesiastical
        views, 36-38, 81-84,
        138-39, 153-54
    visible unity (contra
        invisible), 84-85
    See also ecumenism
universal church. See local
    church
Ut Unum Sint, 36-38
Vatican Council I, 26-27
Vatican Council II, 8, 34,
    103-4, 106, 115, 151, 212,
    215
visible church. See invisible
    and visible church
Word and church, 40-41,
    154
Word and Spirit, 44-45
world and church, 174, 211-
    20, 223-24, 226
World Council of
    Churches, 8, 79, 127, 151,
    153, 189
worship, 21, 41, 70-71, 149,
    198, 200